Harvard
Business
Review
Sales
Management
Handbook

The Harvard Business Review Handbooks Series

HBR Handbooks provide ambitious professionals with the frameworks, advice, and tools they need to excel in their careers. With step-by-step guidance, time-honed best practices, real-life stories, and concise explanations of research published in *Harvard Business Review*, each comprehensive volume helps you to stand out from the pack—whatever your role.

Books in this series include:

Harvard Business Review Entrepreneur's Handbook

Harvard Business Review Family Business Handbook

Harvard Business Review Leader's Handbook

Harvard Business Review Manager's Handbook

Harvard Business Review Project Management Handbook

Harvard Business Review Sales Management Handbook

Harvard Business Review

Sales Management Handbook

How to Lead High-Performing Sales Teams

PRABHAKANT SINHA | ARUN SHASTRI | SALLY LORIMER

Harvard Business Review Press

Boston, Massachusetts

Library of Congress Cataloging-in-Publication Data

Names: Sinha, Prabhakant, author. | Shastri, Arun, author. |
   Lorimer, Sally E., author. | Harvard Business Review Press, issuing body.
Title: The harvard business review sales management handbook :
   how to lead high-performing sales teams / Prabhakant Sinha,
   Arun Shastri, Sally Lorimer.
Description: Boston, Massachusetts : Harvard Business Review Press,
   [2024] | Series: Harvard business review handbook | Includes index.
Identifiers: LCCN 2024010080 (print) | LCCN 2024010081 (ebook) |
   ISBN 9781647826802 (paperback) | ISBN 9781647826819 (epub)
Subjects: LCSH: Sales management. | Teams in the workplace—
   Management. | Success in business/
Classification: LCC HF5438.4 .S5246 2024 (print) | LCC HF5438.4 (ebook) |
   DDC 658.8/1—dc23/eng/20240308
LC record available at https://lccn.loc.gov/2024010080
LC ebook record available at https://lccn.loc.gov/2024010081

ISBN: 978-1-64782-680-2
eISBN: 978-1-64782-681-9

Contents

SECTION TWO

Talent Management

SECTION THREE

The Digital Transformation of Sales Management

Introduction

Sales Management in the Digital World

Salespeople are entrusted with a company's most valuable asset: its relationships with its customers. To buyers, the salesperson is the company. And as a sales manager, or any leader of a sales organization, you are also the face of the company, to both your sales team and customers. You connect the business to those it serves, bridging the gap between strategy and execution. Effective sales management directly supports revenue generation, customer satisfaction, and overall business success.

At the same time, your sales force—the extraordinary human capital that you are charged with leading—is expensive. For many companies, the team's costs are the largest part of selling, general, and administrative expenses. By our estimates, investment in US nonretail sales forces exceeds a trillion dollars per year, including personnel, travel, support, and technology.

The high impact and high cost of sales forces bring high expectations and constant scrutiny. Companies are always looking for ways to elevate the impact of their salespeople while reducing costs. Fortunately, as we will unpack in this book, every organization can do both.

Leading a high-performing sales team is fulfilling, complex (due to many moving parts), and dynamic (due to constant change). You must manage people who each have their own personality and needs. You are responsible for key talent processes such as hiring, coaching, and performance management. You must balance the goals of multiple stakeholders—customers, salespeople, other sales leaders, and other departments in your organization, including marketing, finance, and compliance. There are never-ending demands; the important and the urgent vie unrelentingly for your attention. And when change occurs in your sales organization, whether large or small, you are at the center of making it work.

The key driver of change in sales organizations today is *digital*, a term we use broadly to mean the use of technology, data, and analytics to design and support business processes and decisions. Digital has already led customers to become increasingly knowledgeable and self-reliant and to have higher expectations. Concurrently, sales organizations are leveraging evolving technologies, including artificial intelligence (AI), to streamline processes and enable more-informed decision-making. And companies are engaging customers through digital channels and more-immersive digital experiences.

Sales forces remain important for B2B organizations to bring solutions and innovations to their customers, even as the power of digital channels grows. Leading a sales force is at the confluence of art and science, of strategy and tactics, of people and processes.

The sales system

The sales organization is part of a system of five groups of decisions, processes, and resources that connect company strategy to customers. (See figure I-1.)

The five sets of sales decisions, processes, and resources are as follows.

- **Customer strategy** links business goals to priorities for who to sell to, what value to offer, and how to connect with customers to create mutual value.

FIGURE I-1

Sales system

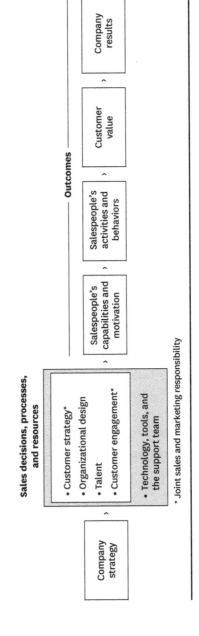

Sales decisions, processes, and resources

- Customer strategy*
- Organizational design
- Talent
- Customer engagement*

- Technology, tools, and the support team

* Joint sales and marketing responsibility

Company strategy

> Salespeople's capabilities and motivation

> Salespeople's activities and behaviors

> Customer value

> Company results

————— Outcomes —————

- **Organizational design** includes the sales channels, roles, and structures for providing effective and efficient customer coverage.

- **Talent** is about designing and operating processes to hire, develop, manage, and motivate salespeople and managers.

- **Customer engagement** involves designing and operating processes and systems for executing sales, marketing, and support activities with channel partners and customers.

- **Technology, tools, and the support team** enable the decisions and processes in the first four groups. Often, these resources are part of a sales or commercial operations function.

It is up to the leadership team to design and oversee all of these. Done effectively, your salespeople will have the needed capabilities and motivation and will engage in the right activities and behaviors to drive value for customers and, ultimately, the company.

The specific challenges you face depend on your role.

Sales leadership roles

These jobs range from head of sales to frontline manager, and the number of jobs in between varies with the size of your sales force. (See table I-1.)

Sales heads: Driving results through team and system management

With titles such as VP of sales, chief sales officer, sales director, and chief growth officer, a sales head leads one or more teams, including managers and salespeople. This role is accountable for aligning the sales vision and strategy with business goals and for driving outcomes by designing, operating, and constantly improving the decisions, processes, and resources that make up the sales system. Sales heads must also adapt the system continuously in response to change, both internal (e.g., a product launch or a revised marketing strategy) and external (e.g., a competitor's move or an economic shift). The goal is to keep all components—the team's size and structure,

TABLE I-1

Sales organization roles and responsibilities

	SALES LEADERS		
	Sales heads	**Sales managers**	**Salespeople**
Results	Drive performance of the sales force	Drive performance of a sales region or a team of salespeople	Drive performance of a sales territory
Customers	Be accountable for customer strategy	Localize customer strategy, engage customers through and with salespeople	Manage and engage customers, ensure customer success
Sales team members	Hire, develop, manage, motivate, and retain sales team members	Hire, develop, manage, motivate, and retain salespeople	
Sales systems and processes	Be accountable for design, enhancement, and innovation	Manage and execute, provide input for improvement	Operate, provide input for improvement
Change	Set vision and strategy, select leadership team, inspire change	Design and implement	Provide input and implement

the talent, and the customer engagement processes—aligned with each other and with the business strategy.

Sales heads work with and through their sales managers.

Sales managers: Achieving results by linking sales strategy to execution

Referred to in this book simply as "sales managers," frontline sales managers directly manage a team of salespeople. These managers have people management responsibilities, such as hiring, coaching, motivating, and managing performance. They also engage with customers, especially when it comes to key decision-makers and large opportunities. Sales managers are responsible for aligning, steering, and improving the business in their region by connecting salespeople, buyers, and the company.

These roles also collaborate with functions across the organization to ensure overall business success. They work with marketing to align priorities and actions. They work with customer support to ensure smooth post-sale customer experiences. And they collaborate with functions that aren't customer-facing, such as HR for recruiting, development, and performance management; IT for digital support; and finance and legal for contracts pricing and compliance.

How digital is changing sales management

For you, as a sales leader at any level, digital is the X factor—and you must constantly be solving for an ever-evolving X. Every day, you will grapple with questions around it: What does digital mean for you, and how do you leverage it? How will digital affect what your customers need and how they engage with your company? What digital sales channels will you use and for which customers and tasks? How will you and your salespeople use real-time data, analytics, and AI to make your work more impactful and responsive to the market? How will digital continue to change your business?

With the world becoming more information-powered, customers are growing more knowledgeable and more able to learn on their own. This knowledge makes them more demanding and assertive. They decide when and how to engage with salespeople and when to use digital self-service channels. And they expect interactions with salespeople to be tailored to their constantly changing needs, coordinated with other channels, and helpful in driving the success of their business.

Digital also has the potential to power everything sales leaders do, from how you hire, develop, and manage people, to how you and your team engage with customers, to the speed at which you must respond to changing needs and strategies. Making this new paradigm work is an exciting and ongoing part of your job.

You face an onslaught of new challenges as the digital world transforms how you and your salespeople work and the products they sell. AI, for example, is emerging as a valuable digital assistant for salespeople. Leaders are likewise embracing digital tools to help them identify opportunities and manage their teams and customers. Your job as a leader will continue to evolve as digital does.

The impact of digitalization extends beyond tools and technologies. It also affects the competencies required of salespeople and the structural design of sales organizations. And it enables the multichannel collaboration required to create a compelling customer experience.

As digital comes to sales, you must work with your team to ensure that you and your team embrace digital. You must drive consensus around a vision, help find the right change leaders, marshal the needed resources, and break down organizational barriers. Your role in enabling change is a dual one. First, you contribute to the design of the change by sharing on-the-ground perspectives about customer and sales force needs while catalyzing salespeople to do the same. Second, your words and actions guide and direct your team through change, impacting their willingness to embrace new systems, programs, and processes.

Why this book?

We wrote the *HBR Sales Management Handbook* to help you navigate the complex and ever-shifting world of sales management—a world that balances the digitally accelerated future and the time-honored fundamentals of building relationships, delivering value, and earning trust. The book shares easy-to-use decision frameworks and dozens of examples and lessons learned from organizations at the leading edge of the journey. Any reader—whether they are a new sales manager, an experienced sales executive, or a director of sales operations—will come away with tangible ideas they can put to work right away to lead high-performing teams.

The three authors are leaders at ZS, a management consulting and technology firm focused on leveraging leading-edge sales and marketing analytics to help clients improve outcomes. Founded in 1983 by two marketing professors, Andris Zoltners and Prabha Sinha, by 2024 ZS had grown to encompass more than fourteen thousand employees in thirty-nine offices worldwide. It has delivered services and solutions to more than four thousand clients in industries that include life sciences (pharmaceuticals, biotech, medical technology, health plans), financial services, high tech and telecommunications, industrials and business services, private equity, and travel and hospitality. With deep roots in data, analytics, and commercial strategy, ZS has helped sales organizations improve their efficiency and effectiveness and drive long-term growth. In this book Prabha is joined by two ZS colleagues, Arun Shastri, a leader in the AI practice who develops and implements strategies for sales organizations across industries, and Sally Lorimer, a coauthor of several books and more than seventy articles for *Harvard Business Review* and hbr.org on sales management.

The authors' personal consulting experience, along with ideas shared by numerous clients and other ZS leaders, is the foundation of the broad and practical perspective we share in the book. In addition, the research-driven roots of our founders provide an anchor for discovering cause and effect and generalizable patterns for improving our ideas. Those ideas are further shaped by our experiences selling services to our clients and observing how our teams deal with the salespeople who sell to ZS when we buy computer hardware, cloud technologies, travel services, and other products and services.

How to navigate this book

As an in-depth manual, this handbook is dense and rich with ideas, frameworks, checklists, and questions to ponder. You will likely get the most out of the chapters if you take some time between them to think about what you have learned and what it means for you and your organization. Also, each chapter stands on its own independently—take a look at the table of contents and feel free to skip ahead to any topics that speak to your interest or an acute challenge you're facing. An exception is if you are new to sales management or are currently a salesperson looking to move up. In that case, you will benefit most from reading the book cover to cover over a number of sittings.

This handbook is two books in one. The first half covers sales management fundamentals. The second half focuses on digital, delving into its reshaping of sales management—and how to manage that change in your organization.

We cover the fundamentals and digital impact separately to ensure every reader gets the most value from the book. Those new to sales management get a solid foundation in the basics before tackling the topic of digital impact. Seasoned leaders can dive right into aspects of digital change, while using the fundamentals chapters as a reference and a refresher. The book provides a logical progression from traditional concepts to the latest insights and trends that are reshaping and affecting the fundamentals of sales and sales management.

Sections 1 and 2: Sales management fundamentals

The chapters in these sections are directed at sales managers. We purposely keep the pervasive force of digital in the background to highlight key manager responsibilities with customers and salespeople. Most of the ideas covered are relevant no matter how much a company is affected by and leveraging digital.

Section 1, "Linking Sales Leadership to Execution and Results," sets the stage by sharing insights about the critical roles that salespeople and managers play in connecting customers and the company. The chapters and key questions are:

1. **Why we still need salespeople in a digital world.** What is the role of salespeople in meeting the needs of customers and the company as digital transforms the business landscape?

2. **The sales manager: The force behind the sales force.** How are the sales manager's responsibilities divided across customers, people, the business, and change management?

3. **Driving salespeople's success with customers.** How can managers use a market-sensing and agile cadence for customer planning and execution to empower salespeople's success?

Section 2, "Talent Management," is a guide and a reference for people management responsibilities. The chapters and key questions are:

4. **Personalizing talent management.** How can sales managers develop and use insights about each of their salespeople to manage them better?

5. **Hiring and onboarding for speed and impact.** How can managers ensure that they hire the right salespeople and help them get off to a strong start?

6. **Empowering salespeople with continuous learning and development.** What is the right blend of training, coaching, and work-based learning for building sellers' competencies?

7. **Managing performance to drive results.** How can managers energize stars and core performers, develop those with the potential to become stars or core performers, and prevent disengagement?

8. **Motivating sales teams with incentives and goals.** How can leaders collaborate with the sales operations team to design incentive plans and set motivating goals for directing salespeople's efforts?

9. **Managing retention and turnover.** How can managers hold on to their best salespeople and assure success despite inevitable turnover?

There is another use of the first half of this book, one that can benefit any sales manager. Most hospitals have checklists that surgeons use before engaging with patients. Two items on these checklists remind them to (1) wash their hands and (2) check the patient's name. All surgeons know they are supposed to do these things. But without a checklist to remind them, they may get distracted and omit these steps. A 2009 study published in the *New England Journal of Medicine* found that in a diverse range of hospitals worldwide, the use of such checklists cut patient death rates almost in half while significantly reducing inpatient complications. Subsequent research further supported the importance of checklists for reducing errors and improving patient outcomes. Checklists help overcome attention gaps, not knowledge gaps. In most chapters in sections 1 and 2, we include checklists that you will want to use, or adapt to use, with your team.

Sections 3 and 4: Digital

The chapters in these sections focus on the ever-increasing impact of digital on sales management, and on what leaders can do to help their organizations adapt. Leaders at any level will benefit as they work to keep their teams relevant and thriving.

Section 3, "The Digital Transformation of Sales Management," focuses on how digital is making sales management more market-sensing and agile. The chapters and key questions are:

10. **Leveraging the growing power of digital in sales management.** How is digital affecting customer strategy and engagement, organizational design, talent management, and more?

11. **Making faster and better decisions with analytics and AI.** How can sales organizations use data and analytics to complement managerial judgment for improved decision-making?

12. **Designing the sales organization for the digital age.** How can the structure of sales organizations (including channels and roles) keep up with the ever-changing needs of customers?

13. **Unlocking five digital-age sales competencies.** How is digital driving the profile of what it takes to succeed in sales, and how can managers bring new competencies to their teams?

14. **Synchronizing sales channels for maximum impact.** How can leaders enable collaboration across channels and find the right blend of in-person, virtual, and digital communication for meeting customer needs?

15. **Accelerating and streamlining selling with a digital customer hub.** How can companies bring together digital assets and expertise to support more-effective customer engagement?

16. **Amplifying the power of salespeople with digital assistants.** How can AI-based insights and recommendations increase salespeople's effectiveness?

17. **Boosting talent management with digital.** How can digital capabilities make talent management for sales teams more marketing-sensing, agile, efficient, and effective?

18. **Managing a recurring revenue business.** As recurring revenue business models become increasingly common, what does it mean for sales management?

Finally, section 4, "Driving Improvement and Implementing Change," brings management and digital impact together by exploring the dynamic nature of sales leadership and how you can bring continuous improvement to your team and navigate perpetual change. The chapters and key questions are:

19. **Continuously improving your business.** How can sales leaders prioritize, adapt, improve, and innovate to drive the long-term success of the business?

20. **Navigating sales force change.** How can sales leaders help the organization design, prepare for, implement, and sustain successful change?

Because of the immense variety of salespeople and customers, a manager's job is fast-moving and fulfilling. There are no repetitive days or weeks. You'll need to think creatively to address many of the situations you will face. You will interact with and influence your salespeople, your key customers, and colleagues inside your company daily. Your actions will have an impact on people and results. Your success will be visible.

As a sales leader, your job is vast in scope and dynamic in nature. The *HBR Sales Management Handbook* is not a list of silver bullets, nor is it an encyclopedia covering every aspect of sales leadership. Instead, this book is a collection of selected, time-tested yet also forward-looking ideas to help you win by helping your team and customers win. The topics balance the need to build and lead a team for company and customer success now, with the need to adapt as digital disruption changes sales and brings new opportunities for the future. This journey starts with you and your critical role in linking company strategy to execution.

Linking Sales Leadership to Execution and Results

1.

Why We Still Need Salespeople in a Digital World

With the growth of e-commerce and the buzz about digital and virtual, one can imagine a world where digital channels, self-service, and inside salespeople replace field salespeople. And without field salespeople, the thinking goes, there is no need for their managers. This all begs the question—do we still need salespeople (and managers of salespeople)?

It's true that the role of salespeople has been greatly reduced in some businesses. From 2005 to 2017, US pharmaceutical companies slashed one-third of their sales forces, while the use of digital information sources (email, podcasts, mobile apps, websites) grew. From 2014 to 2020, industrial supply distributor W.W. Grainger cut more than 40 percent of its branch locations and more than seven hundred outside sales jobs in the United States as it continued to boost investments in inside sales and digital sales channels. Meanwhile, many high-tech companies, such as Google and Amazon, actually grew their sales forces. In 2023 companies that prospered with the help of thousands of salespeople in the United States alone included technology companies (e.g., Microsoft, Apple, Verizon, Salesforce), health-care companies (e.g., Thermo Fisher Scientific, Stryker, Pfizer, Johnson & Johnson), and financial services and insurance providers (e.g., Citigroup, Edward Jones, Hartford Financial Services, Aflac). Innovative companies with complex products needed salespeople to thrive.

We're at an unprecedented moment, but at the same time, we've been here before. For more than a century we have seen predictions that salespeople are going away. In 1916 an article in the *New York Times* asked: "Are salesmen needless?" The article quoted an expert who said, "Advertising is producing better results than the old method of personal solicitation . . . The traveling [sales]man is a middleman, and the evolution of business is gradually eliminating the middleman." Yet sales force numbers kept growing.

Fast-forward to 2015, when Forrester Research predicted that one million B2B salespeople would—lost to e-commerce—become obsolete by 2020. Since then, some companies have cut salespeople, but others added many more. Overall, sales force employment remained stable.

What *has* changed over the past hundred years is the *role* of the salesperson. Sales is an ancient profession; for centuries we have relied on salespeople to learn about new products. In the nineteenth century, buyers usually became aware of new offerings when a "traveling salesman" showed up at the door with a novel technology, like a clock or a sewing machine. The salesman helped the buyer understand the product and evaluate what to purchase. He then took the order and later fulfilled it by delivering the goods on wagon or horseback.

In the early twentieth century, advances in transportation, storage, and distribution largely took the task of the physical fulfillment of goods away from salespeople. In the late twentieth century, a proliferation of media options made buyers aware of products before talking to a salesperson. (Also around that time, "salesman" was replaced by "salesperson," reflecting gender diversity in the profession worldwide.) As innovation eliminated some of the job's responsibilities, new ones emerged and entirely new kinds of companies and industries formed. Throughout all these developments, one aspect has remained constant: effective sellers add value for customers and their companies.

This chapter explores different types of sales roles, since what your salespeople do affects what you need to do as a sales manager and leader. Then the chapter discusses the timeless job of adding value and concludes with insights about how salespeople can coexist and thrive alongside digital and virtual sales channels.

Types of sales jobs

When you are a salesperson, you are steeped in serving customers: planning for and prioritizing them, and then finding, engaging, and nurturing relationships with them.

Table 1-1 shows several examples of customer responsibilities for different sales roles and salespeople's expected results at four very different companies. (In chapter 2, we will see how the sales job at each of these companies leads to a complementary role for the manager.) Reflect on how these responsibilities and expectations overlap with those of salespeople at your company. And think about how the sales roles and responsibilities could or should change as the needs of customers, salespeople, and the business do.

The job descriptions in table 1-1 (and most such lists we see) mention customer needs and value but don't emphasize these concepts enough. We strongly recommend that you focus on customer needs, experience, and value in your lists of responsibilities, and in the job description for sales managers. Examples include creating a positive customer experience, helping customers better understand their needs and options, seeking customer feedback about needed improvements, and reinforcing how products and services add value to the customer's business.

Companies have many different sales roles (and even more titles), depending on their situation. A simple environment might have a single sales role that does everything, while more-complex situations typically have several sales roles working together. Here are some examples:

TABLE 1-1

Salesperson responsibilities (examples)

Company (industry)	Sales role, customer responsibilities, and expected results
Amazon Web Services (enterprise cloud services)	**Account executive** • Own the full sales cycle, from identifying opportunities to building relationships to negotiating and contracting • Understand solutions and connect that knowledge to customer ROI • Proactively seek opportunities for expansion (upsell, add-on, cross-sell) • Maintain customer relationships, prepare sales proposals, engage in sales activities • Develop strategies and coordinate cross-functionally to help customers maximize value • Achieve sales quota
W.W. Grainger (industrial supplies)	**Field account executive** • Identify opportunities, negotiate sales, manage needs and cost requirements • Be responsive to customers' real-time needs • Use many communication methods to increase sales through all channels • Achieve or exceed shared metrics of daily calls and customer face-time minutes • Grow revenue to reported thresholds and meet performance targets
Liberty Mutual (insurance)	**Sales agent** • Identify prospects through existing book of business and community prospecting • Use consultative sales techniques to drive new business • Follow up with customers to keep retention high and find cross-selling opportunities • Address customer concerns, coordinating with other departments to ensure quality service • Meet monthly goals for new business sales
AstraZeneca (pharmaceuticals)	**Sales representative** • Develop and maintain in-depth market knowledge of your sales territory • Educate and engage health-care professionals about clinical evidence, product profiles, and prescribing for patients • Capitalize on opportunities using a variety of promotional and personnel resources, and analytics to meet local customer needs • Drive performance and ensure sales forecasts and budgets meet or exceed expectations

- **Territory manager.** Develop business in a geographic territory (prospect, sell, and manage the ongoing customer relationships).

- **Business development manager.** Identify and pursue new business opportunities.

- **Account manager.** Nurture and grow relationships with existing customers.

- **Strategic account executive.** Manage relationships with the most important customers by leading a team of product, solution, and service specialists.

- **Sales engineer.** Work alongside account executives to understand customer needs and configure technically complex solutions.

- **Private banker.** Build and grow relationships with ultra-high-net-worth individuals.

- **Sales agent.** Promote a company's products as an off-roll commissioned seller who works for a third-party agency or as an independent contractor.

- **Channel account manager.** Develop and maintain relationships with channel partners.

While some of the roles above are field-based and others are purely remote (or inside), the reality is that technology has turned most traditional field sales roles into hybrid roles: selling in person while also using the phone and web to connect with customers. At the same time, technology has elevated the role and impact of inside sales. Leveraging technology, inside salespeople are selling complex products costing hundreds of thousands of dollars without ever meeting a customer physically.

How salespeople add value

Before you buy something unfamiliar, you will search for information to boost your knowledge and confidence. And even when buying familiar things, you are likely to check if something new, better, or cheaper is out there, especially with expensive or high-stakes purchases. Business buyers are no different—they have questions at each step of their journey.

- When customers are defining their needs and want to discover the best solution:
  - What is my need or opportunity?
  - What are my options?
  - What are the benefits and costs of each option?
- When buyers and sellers must agree on a solution and terms:
  - Which sellers do I trust?
  - How do I get all the players on my team to agree on a solution?
- When customers want to get the most out of what they purchased:
  - What value did we realize?
  - How can I get continuing benefits from this and future purchases?

To answer these questions, buyers will search online, talk to peers, and turn to the various information channels that sellers provide, including salespeople themselves. A customer will choose to use a salesperson if that individual can answer one or more of their questions. They're especially likely to want help when the situation is complex, there is uncertainty, or complete answers are not readily apparent. Complexity occurs when products or services are multifaceted and customized, customers have heterogeneous needs, or buying processes involve many steps and stakeholders. Sometimes all these factors occur at once.

While salespeople can (and should) add value for customers in complex and uncertain situations, the company also gains value—not only because salespeople increase the likelihood of a sale but also because they gain market and competitive insights.

Defining buyers' needs and closing knowledge gaps

The path to a productive business relationship begins with sellers and buyers developing a shared understanding of what the buyer needs and how the seller can meet those needs. How salespeople close knowledge gaps depends on how well the customer understands their own needs and the possible solutions, as well as on how well the seller understands the customer. Figure 1-1 shows three situations in which knowledge gaps exist (there are many possibilities in between) along with additional steps salespeople must take even after those gaps have closed.

Next, we discuss how salespeople discover, educate, and cocreate to close knowledge gaps in the three cases when understanding is lacking on either or both sides. (The section after that covers salespeople's additional responsibilities once there is mutual understanding.)

FIGURE 1-1

How salespeople help pave a path to mutual buyer-seller value

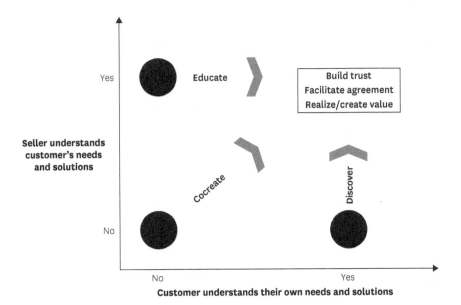

DISCOVER. This is when buyers understand their need or opportunity and are seeking the best solution. An HR leader is looking for health insurance coverage for employees. A chief of staff is looking for a venue for an executive offsite. An architect is looking for the latest in lighting management solutions for a building still in drawings. In these cases, buyers have a reasonable idea of their needs. The requirements could be quite detailed, as is the case in a request for proposal (RFP), or defined more loosely, with room for suppliers to shape needs and solutions. Salespeople work to *discover* what the buyer wants, then help craft the answer.

Discovery involves a range of activities. These include probing to learn the customer's goals, knowledge, and budget, mapping the buyer organization to understand roles and authority, and observing and interpreting customers' nonverbal cues (facial expressions, change in posture, tone of voice) to gain a deeper understanding of their emotions, concerns, and motivations.

The best salespeople know their markets and keep their ears open. They get in on early conversations with buyers as an RFP is being formed, which allows them to help define the buyer's requirements, giving their company an edge in winning the deal. They help assess whether a deal is winnable, or if a competitor already has a lock on it (and the RFP is simply a way to keep the competitor honest). For winnable deals, salespeople shepherd the response, discover buyer influences and unspecified criteria, discern the competitive landscape, and coordinate the effort of their team members.

EDUCATE. This is when sellers have insights that buyers lack. John Deere is known for its farm and construction equipment, but it is also a leader in precision agriculture, a high-tech approach that uses real-time data about crops, soil, and air that is collected by sensors on the ground as well as by drones and satellites. Precision agriculture aids growers in making decisions about plant spacing and their usage of water, fertilizer, and pesticides to improve profitability and environmental sustainability. Deere's salespeople don't only sell equipment—in most cases they must also *educate* growers about the methods and benefits of precision agriculture.

Education often involves sharing knowledge with customers about what has worked (and not worked) in similar circumstances. It is also about bringing customers ideas for addressing needs that they haven't expressed or recognized, or aren't aware that a solution exists for.

Product innovation creates an ongoing need for salespeople to educate customers in numerous industries. It explains why cloud service providers such as Amazon Web Services and Microsoft have hefty sales forces. Players in the medical device industry, such as Boston Scientific and Medtronic, launch multiple products with novel features each year, sustaining the need for salespeople as educators.

COCREATE. This is when sellers and buyers work together to hunt for opportunities and solutions. Sometimes, both sellers and buyers are heading into unknowns. Cocreation requires problem-solving, creativity, and resourcefulness. Companies with innovative offerings relish being in this situation, as it provides a great opportunity to partner with customers and accelerate innovation ahead of what competitors offer. For example, business technology providers often create novel offerings by inviting customers to participate in the design and testing process. If these pilots succeed, they may result in follow-on work and relationships that benefit both parties. To even get started on such *cocreation* efforts, a level of comfort and mutual trust must exist between the buyer and the seller. Salespeople are the ones tasked with earning and managing that trust.

Discovery, education, and cocreation are not all-or-nothing constructs. Both customers and salespeople can be somewhere along the spectrum of understanding needs and solutions. Plus, different decision-makers in a buying organization, as well as different participants from the selling organization, may be starting at different points.

Building trust, facilitating agreement, and realizing value

Whether you begin the buying and selling journey with discovery, education, cocreation, or some combination, the buyer and the seller must align on a solution. Salespeople play a key role in making this happen by building trust, facilitating agreement, and helping both organizations realize value.

BUILD TRUST. In B2B contexts, trust is the foundation for buyers and sellers to work together, especially when purchases are complex and high-stakes. Over time, trust is built by meeting commitments, but earlier in relationships salespeople are stewards of those commitments. Ethical behavior, competence, reliability, and credibility are essential to establish the trust that starts and sustains long and fruitful relationships. Emotional connections foster trust as well.

FACILITATE AGREEMENT. For most complex purchases, both buying and selling are team efforts. A timeless responsibility of salespeople is helping buyers and sellers come together. When our firm negotiated a global enterprise contract with a cloud services supplier, multiple parties were involved. On the supplier's side, there was an account executive (AE), a partner reseller account executive, and a customer success manager. Supporting them were a finance person, a sales manager, and systems architects. Our team was led by our vice president of cloud services and included a director of cloud services, a head of IT system engineering and operations, and a finance specialist. The supplier's AE played a critical role in aligning interests, connecting decision influencers with the necessary resources, and facilitating meetings to achieve consensus, resulting in a positive outcome for all involved parties.

Salespeople also help harmonize thinking within their organization, since having different perspectives in the selling organization can delay deals. For example, a sales manager wants to craft an offering that maximizes the odds of winning the deal, the marketing manager is concerned about product mix, and the finance person pushes to maintain margins. The salesperson can advocate and broker agreement within their company to ensure that all parties are satisfied with the deal while the buyer perceives value.

CREATE/REALIZE VALUE. With many products and services, salespeople have a growing role in helping buyers get the most out of what they purchase.

Consider the role of clinical sales associates at Intuitive Surgical. These salespeople are responsible for helping surgeons "enhance their surgical precision and greatly improve patient benefits." Clinical sales associates "drive utilization of the da Vinci® (Robotic Surgical) System by working with surgical teams to select appropriate procedure applications; [and] drive continuous expansion of the user base by working with key hospital staff and thought leaders to develop a qualified lead funnel," according to the company. Positions such as this one require salespeople to largely work on-site at the hospitals they serve.

Often, mutual value for sellers and buyers accrues over time as the customer benefits and then continues and expands their purchasing. This has resulted in the expansion of roles such as a customer success manager (CSM), responsible for ongoing customer care and growth. An IT buyer at ZS describes the CSM role this way: "She brings ideas about how we can use her products better . . . Every month she spends a full day on-site with us. Every quarter we review our spending and look at other issues that are important to us. These include cost reduction, speed of handling critical problems, security, and the path forward."

Bringing market and competitive insights to the company

Salespeople are on the front lines, working with customers every day to learn their preferences, pain points, and opportunities. They observe market trends and shifts in customer behavior firsthand. They learn about competitor offerings, pricing strategies, and sales tactics, and find out how customers react. By sharing these types of insights internally, salespeople help the organization improve products and services and create smarter strategies for differentiating offerings. Sales managers help channel these on-the-ground insights back to the company.

Salespeople coexisting with digital and virtual sales channels

As the seller's responsibility for helping customers address complexity and uncertainty persists, digital channels and inside sales are taking over many of the tasks that field salespeople once performed. Yet while salespeople stay focused on the complex, they also need to team up with digital channels and inside sales to ensure customer needs are met.

The tasks moving away from field salespeople

Field salespeople are no longer "talking brochures" or order takers. Numerous simple customer-facing tasks once done by them have shifted to digital channels, self-service, and inside sales. Prospect identification and lead qualification is now handled largely by inside and digital resources. Websites, email, video, chatbots, and other tools have taken over sharing product information. Order-taking is moving online as well. In 2000 Dow Corning created Xiameter, a separate online business that sold standard silicones in large quantities with a fixed price and a specified minimum lead time. Salespeople were no longer in the equation. (Xiameter has since become a brand within Dow's business.) Grainger's Zoro (in the United States) and MonotaRO (in Japan) are similar online-only distribution businesses, selling industrial supplies from an extensive catalog.

Leveraging digital and pivoting to hybrid engagement

While digital is replacing some field sales tasks, it is also assisting salespeople with the steps of selling. Customer relationship management (CRM) systems capture a buyer's information, history, and preferences, helping salespeople personalize their approach. AI-based tools provide suggestions about which customers to target and which offering is most likely to resonate. Field salespeople use LinkedIn to build their network and engage with potential customers.

Field salespeople now mix in-person, virtual (video, phone, collaboration platforms), and text-based interactions with customers. Virtual outreach works well in many circumstances. These include when sellers and buyers have a trusting relationship, when buyers are highly motivated, and when offerings are differentiated. Virtual also works well early in the process, when buyers and sellers want to efficiently assess whether pursuing a relationship is worthwhile.

Customizing offerings to customer needs has always been part of a successful sales playbook. Now it's also about customizing communication modes, finding the right mix of face-to-face and virtual personal selling, along with digital outreach and customer self-service. Success requires tailoring interactions at each step to buyers' knowledge and preferences.

———————

We started this chapter with a question: Do we still need salespeople in the digital age? Even as their responsibilities shift to complex situations and as hybrid engagement becomes the norm, salespeople are in no way becoming obsolete. The question we should be asking instead is: How can we enable them to work alongside digital to build increased customer value and trust? The next chapter will explore the role of managers in this new reality.

2.

The Sales Manager: The Force Behind the Sales Force

When a sale occurs, the sales manager is usually not in the room. Their job isn't to close sales—it is to make sure the magic happens by working through and with salespeople. Even as the changing digital landscape reshapes selling, the success of the company depends on sales managers and the effectiveness of their people.

This chapter describes the spectrum of the sales manager's responsibilities for customers, salespeople, and the business. Examples from the four companies whose sales roles we introduced in chapter 1 show how the manager at each one complements those roles. Then the chapter shares insights about the sales manager's place within the broader organization and the connections they need to succeed. The chapter concludes with guidelines for an operating cadence to bring these responsibilities to life.

Three pillars of responsibility

An overview of the sales manager's role (see figure 2-1) captures three key pillars of responsibilities: customer management, people management, and business management. All of these are underscored by the vital job of managing change.

This role involves an immense variety of tasks, ranging from strategy to execution.

Customer management

The first pillar is about helping salespeople ensure customers buy and get value from what they purchase and from their interactions with the sales force. (Chapter 3 is devoted to this topic.) Managers support sellers with customer planning to ensure that plans align with business goals. They also oversee the effective execution of processes by helping salespeople break down longer-term goals into short sprints that move customers through their buying journey.

FIGURE 2-1

Key pillars of the sales manager's role and responsibilities

Customer value		Company results
Customer management	**People management**	**Business management**
Strategize and foster customer engagement	*Build, nurture, and guide the team*	*Achieve goals; align, steer, and improve the business*
• Support customer planning • Ensure effective sales process execution • Nurture customer relationships and participate in complex sales • Bring back market feedback • Facilitate customer relationship transitions	• Hire and onboard • Train, coach, and leverage work-based learning • Manage performance • Motivate and reward success • Retain a strong team	• Adapt company strategy to the local market • Define roles, territories, and goals for salespeople • Manage regional resources, budgets, and operations • Coordinate with other company functions • Foster company culture • Ensure policy compliance • Drive ongoing improvement
	Change management	

Managers often participate in complex sales, engaging with customers in collaboration with salespeople. The power and impact of the role come from managers bringing things that salespeople can't. This includes a broader perspective (wider view of the market, industry trends, competitive landscape, and potential opportunities and challenges), companywide resources (help from finance or technical specialists), and the authority to offer specific deal terms. The broader view also helps managers relate to senior-level customer decision-makers more effectively than a salesperson can.

Even as managers connect the company to customers through salespeople, they also bring back market and customer insights to the company. And finally, if salespeople leave or are promoted or reassigned, it's the manager who must shepherd the customer relationship and transition it to a different salesperson.

People management

The second pillar is about empowering a team of salespeople to win. There's a reason the organization that sales managers are part of is called a sales *force*. A (sales) force creates movement, acceleration, and change in direction (with a customer).

The manager's job is to strengthen the sales team by hiring the right people and developing, managing, and motivating them, while arming them with information and insights. While a single salesperson might interact with fifty customers or prospects, all the salespeople in a large company together might interact with more than ten thousand. The company, with the manager, can provide guidance and support to help salespeople offer a breadth and depth of insight. This is a key priority as analytics becomes an increasingly powerful driver of sales success—a topic that is explored further in chapters 11 and 16.

Each salesperson is unique, with their own competencies, motivators, performance, and potential for future success. Career stage is a consideration as well; someone who is newer to sales needs to be managed differently than an experienced or senior team member. Leading the team effectively requires a personalized approach to hiring and onboarding, developing, managing, rewarding, and retaining. (Section 2 is all about people management.)

Business management

The third pillar is focused on setting direction to produce results. Several interconnected elements collectively drive success. Sales managers must translate the company's overarching goals and strategies into plans and actions that accommodate regional nuances and customer needs and goals. They must define responsibilities, territories, and goals for team members, ensuring that everyone understands how their efforts contribute to overall success—while being prepared to adjust these assignments as company strategies and market dynamics shift. In addition, they are responsible for managing regional resources and budgets, coordinating with other company functions, ensuring compliance with company policies, and fostering a shared company culture within the team. Finally, constant improvement is an important aspect of business management. Managers must continuously diagnose the team's performance, identify opportunities and challenges, and respond as the business landscape evolves.

Sales manager roles: Four examples

Table 2-1 shows how customer, people, and business management come together to define the sales manager job at the four companies we introduced in chapter 1. Refer to table 1-1 to see how the manager role at these companies aligns with the sales role. Although these four manager jobs are similar in some ways, there are also some key differences, including varied emphasis on the three core pillars. Reflect on how these responsibilities and expectations overlap with your sales management role. And think about how your role could or should change as the needs of customers, salespeople, and the business do.

The sales manager's role in the organization

In the introduction, we described a **sales system**—a set of interconnected decisions, processes, and resources that the head of sales is responsible for. A sales manager oversees a local sales system, including the linkages among

TABLE 2-1

Sales manager responsibilities (examples)

Company (industry)	Customer management	People management	Business management
Amazon Web Services (enterprise cloud services)	• Ensure customer satisfaction and accelerate adoption • Develop long-term strategic relationships with key accounts • Maintain a robust sales pipeline • Work with partners to reach more customers • Manage contract negotiations	• Hire and build out an enterprise sales team	• Meet or exceed quarterly revenue targets • Drive revenue and market share in your region • Develop and execute a regional sales plan
W.W. Grainger (industrial supplies)	• Develop relationships with customers and internal partners • Facilitate meetings with branch employees, sellers, managers, and customers	• Coach, counsel, and develop the team	• Drive revenue in assigned geographic area • Plan, solve problems, perform analysis • Review financials to analyze needs, budgets, and earnings
Liberty Mutual (insurance)	• Ensure exceptional customer satisfaction and high retention • Establish long-lasting relationships with customers	• Develop and coach the team • Facilitate an engaging environment in which agents are inspired and feel supported	• Drive sales team to achieve and exceed sales metrics • Generate strategic and innovative ideas to drive new business development • Oversee operational functions of the branch
AstraZeneca (pharmaceuticals)	• Review, modify, and approve strategically targeted, account-specific business plans developed by sales reps	• Lead your sales team • Do in-person field coaching and ride-alongs to support sales reps' development • Work one-on-one with sales reps on product knowledge, territory management, and other selling skills • Create a motivating environment and set an expectation of success • Create a culture of team spirit and innovation	• Be responsible for the overall performance of your region • Collaborate with the home office to develop marketing plans, incentive plans, sales training, and other programs • Work with internal departments to drive performance

customers, sellers, and company strategies and goals. The system has many moving pieces in an always-changing competitive environment. Think about where sales managers are in the middle of the organization chart. They have a team, the people they manage and influence. But they also live in a broader ecosystem, since there are others in sales and in various departments and functions that touch the sales world. So a sales manager must manage *down* by working with salespeople and customers and keeping them connected to company goals, but must also manage *up* and *across* the organization.

Managing up

This goes well beyond having a good relationship with superiors and keeping them up-to-date about activities. It means informing marketing and product strategies by sharing on-the-ground insights, such as what customers or competitors in your region are doing and how their needs are evolving. It means keeping the company informed about issues as varied as sales force morale, successful hiring profiles, or rising stars on the team. Managing up also involves advocating for customers and salespeople to get the resources they need and the recognition they deserve.

Managing across

Managers are not alone as they execute their diverse set of responsibilities. Many people within the company are there to help. Managing across is about working horizontally to build an internal network to help you access company resources and expertise to share with customers and salespeople.

Managing across can involve working with other commercial teams that share your customers. A manager of field-based account executives might work with an inside sales team or product specialist teams, as well as with groups outside of sales, such as customer service, technical support, and customer success. The manager will also work with marketing, collaborating on activities from customer targeting to lead generation to content creation.

Managing across also involves interaction with corporate support roles. The HR department is an important partner for supporting a manager's people management responsibilities, including hiring, training, and motivating the team. And departments such as legal and finance are helpful with issues like customer contracting and pricing.

One of the most important partners is the company's sales operations (sometimes known as "commercial operations") group. "Sales ops" is there to assist with planning, compensation, forecasting, territory design, and other behind-the-scenes activities that are essential for making the sales team great. With the growing demand for data analytics and sales technology constantly evolving, a good working relationship with sales ops can be a key ingredient for success. Sales ops often assumes a boundary-spanning role between sales and the IT department—a function essential for assisting with the many digital tools and data that salespeople and managers need to do their jobs.

A manager's relationships with key people in these and other functions can help with navigating the organization and quickly connecting salespeople and customers to resources and expertise.

Being a change agent

The sales system is never static. The company itself is constantly changing. It might launch new products, enter different markets, or restructure as it redefines priorities, perhaps under new leadership. The external environment is continually shifting as well, as new competitive forces emerge and customer preferences change. Technology, as we explore in section 3, is another force of change. No matter what the company faces, managers are tasked with shepherding whatever is new in their regions. And sometimes managers are asked for input about what the company should do to respond to different shifts. Chapter 20 will further explore the critical role of sales managers in bringing successful change to the organization.

The sales manager's operating rhythm

With the variety in the job, it's easy to lose focus. Discipline is essential to ensure things don't fall through the cracks. A consistent operating cadence, such as the example shown in table 2-2, helps managers focus on the key priorities for customers, salespeople, and the business. Every quarter, every

TABLE 2-2

Typical operating rhythm for customers, salespeople, and business

	Customers	Salespeople	Business
Annually/ quarterly One-on-one planning session (1–3 hours)	• Plan, review, prioritize, course-correct customer strategies	• Review development plans and progress	• Conduct business review • Evaluate results, reallocate resources
Monthly Meeting with the sales team (60–100 minutes)	• Share customer insights	• Recognize success • Provide learning and development opportunities	• HQ shares strategies and market insights with field • Field shares customer and market insights with HQ
Biweekly Joint customer visits with each salesperson (half to full day)	• Develop and discuss insights from each customer visit	• Observe and participate • Coach on skills, activities, and priorities	
Biweekly or weekly Sales sprint meeting with each salesperson (45–60 minutes)	• Review prior sales sprint progress • Assist with planning customer advances for next sprint	• Coach on customer strategies	
Periodically Tasks as needed	• Sell with salespeople • Facilitate customer relationship transitions	• Hire and onboard new team members • Do open-ended random check-ins	• Do administrative tasks • Analyze and reflect
Typical allocation (% of manager's time)	25%–40%	30%–55%	20%–35%
Support change initiatives	Help design and implement changes to sales structures, systems, processes		

month, every two weeks, and every week, doing certain tasks consistently helps keep performance on track.

The right operating cadence and time allocation—across customer, people, and business responsibilities—depend on the situation. Here are some guidelines:

- When the sales process is relatively straightforward and largely entrusted to salespeople, and the manager's role with customers is minimal, success depends on strong people management. Managers should allocate more than 75 percent of their time to people management tasks. Most of that time will be spent with salespeople, working one-on-one or in groups. The 25 percent (or less) that remains goes to managing customers and the business.

- If there are long sales cycles and complex deals involving multiple decision-makers, managers will frequently work alongside salespeople and others in the company to advance toward a sale. Customer responsibilities will take up 50 percent or even more of a manager's time. The 50 percent that remains is divided between managing people and managing the business.

- If a manager has a significant local budget and resources (for example, a local marketing budget) or has to adapt strategy frequently (for example, when launching many products or expanding into new markets), the manager will need to split time equally among customers, people, and the business. Each will get about 33 percent.

The operating cadence and time allocation that works best will change over time; the guidelines above provide insight into what factors could drive an allocation change.

Defining the right cadence and balance of customer, people, and business management is a key capability for sales managers. Next, you'll want to hone critical skills within each area, focusing on those with the highest impact, while aligning everything you do around business strategies. Whatever your type of business, people and customers will be the key focus of your time and attention. We start with your customer management responsibilities—the topic of the next chapter.

3.

Driving Salespeople's Success with Customers

At every level of a company, from frontline employees to top leadership, the goal is to get customers to buy, and sales managers are pivotal in this quest. Managers are entrusted to work through and with salespeople to grow streams of mutual value for customers and the company.

In this chapter, we explore a manager's role in building and nurturing customer relationships by:

- Assisting with sales planning

- Working alongside salespeople to execute sales sprints that are responsive to the market

- Enabling the sharing of customer insights and learnings across their teams

- Facilitating transitions in customer relationships

This is a balancing act for a manager—empowering salespeople while directing them in a way that is helpful rather than overbearing or demotivating.

A manager's operating cadence

A regular cadence of meetings with your salespeople is how you can best direct attention to the key priorities of customers, sellers themselves, and the business, while helping ensure that nothing is missed due to a lapse in attention or process. Here, we focus specifically on the customer-focused tasks in the cadence. (See table 3-1.)

TABLE 3-1

A sales manager's cadence of customer-focused meetings with salespeople

	Customer-focused tasks
Annually/quarterly One-on-one planning session	• Plan, review, prioritize, and course-correct customer strategies • Develop customer plans and goals for next period • Set goals for key result areas, actions, and metrics
Monthly Meeting with the sales team	• Share customer insights • Find areas for innovation and growth with customers
Biweekly Joint customer visits with each salesperson	• Develop and discuss insights from each customer visit
Biweekly or weekly Sales sprint meeting with each salesperson	• Review prior sales sprint progress • Assist with planning customer advances for next sprint
Periodically Tasks as needed	• Sell with salespeople • Facilitate customer relationship transitions and other change initiatives

We start with a brief overview of sales planning and then get into the details of managing sales execution. Later in section 3 of the book, we'll explore how digital capabilities are essential for keeping the plan responsive to market needs.

Assisting with market-sensing and agile sales planning

A sales plan serves as a flexible road map for each salesperson. The plan outlines objectives and goals as well as the tactics for achieving those goals. Even as managers monitor and ensure the plan's execution, the plan must work for salespeople and customers, not just for the manager and the company.

Sales plans: A living road map to guide actions

A sales plan includes a description of the market and the headwinds and tailwinds affecting the business. It defines the targeted customers and prospects, the steps and actions need to serve each one, which sales roles and resources are needed, and the milestones to achieve and by when. Sales plans are constantly updated as customer and market needs and company strategies evolve.

Good plans do three things:

- Provide a road map to achieve sales goals by focusing efforts and resources on the best opportunities

- Put salespeople, managers, and leaders on the same page, ensuring that everyone is working toward common objectives

- Measure progress toward goals and identify areas where adjustments are needed to stay on track

Account planning

Accounts that contribute a meaningful portion of current or potential results each have their own plan. To help salespeople create account plans, ask questions that enhance their understanding of the customer. (See table 3-2.)

Understanding account potential

Understanding the sales potential of customers and prospects is a cornerstone of a growth mindset in sales planning. Knowing the potential of each account helps salespeople allocate their effort for the greatest impact. Two accounts that both bought $200,000 last year should not be considered equal if what they could spend next year and beyond might be different.

Account potential considers factors such as account size, industry, and purchasing budget, along with estimates of how much your company could sell based on your competitive position and the relationship and engagement with the account. Estimates can span a year, multiple years, and even customer lifetime value—the revenue that a customer could generate for a business over the entire relationship.

Having a sense for account potential helps with customer targeting, resource allocation, and deciding where salespeople should deploy their effort to get the best results. It is also important for designing territories, setting fair territory goals, assessing salespeople's success, and matching their rewards accordingly.

Estimating an account's sales potential is typically done at the company headquarters level using customer profiles and other data. Analytics and AI are making these estimates faster and more accurate.

Quarterly business review and planning

In a quarterly business review (QBR), a manager meets with the sales team, or with individual salespeople one-on-one, to discuss the previous quarter and the future. For industries such as manufacturing and software, QBRs tend to include the whole team. For service industries, one-on-one sessions often work better, especially when account managers deal with very different markets. The QBR has two parts:

- **Reflecting on what happened last quarter.** The discussion covers insights about past performance, new opportunities, and areas for

TABLE 3-2

Questions for helping salespeople create and review account plans

	Examples of questions to ask salespeople	Plan elements affected
Industry context	• What emerging market trends or changes affect customer needs and priorities? • What is the competitive landscape and our position? How do we differentiate ourselves? • What tailwinds and headwinds exist?	• Sales strategy and competitive positioning
Customer needs, priorities, pain points	• What are the customer's needs and pain points? What is the degree of urgency? • Do customers have unrecognized needs that our offerings can address? • How do customers realize value from what we sell?	• Goals • Offerings • Source of customer value
Customer potential	• What is the size and scope of the account? • Are there other divisions or departments we could do business with? • What is their budget and buying power? • What do we sell now, and what is the growth potential?	• Goals • Offerings • How much effort and resources to invest
Customer history	• What has the customer already purchased from us? • Through which channels has the customer engaged with us?	• Opportunities and goals • Which sales channels to use
Customer buying process and stakeholders	• Who is involved in the buying decision, what is their role, and what are they looking for? • Where is the customer in the buying process?	• Design of selling process (engagement cadence) • What resources are needed
Customer knowledge	• What is the customer's level of knowledge about the opportunities and solutions?	• Where the focus should be (education, discovery, cocreation)
Customer channel preferences	• Does the customer prefer in-person, remote, or digital communication?	• Which sales channels to use (salesperson, inside sales, digital channel)
Relationship status	• How engaged and satisfied is the customer? • Have we demonstrated value in the past? • Do we connect with stakeholders regularly? • Where can we win?	• Acquisition versus expansion or retention focus

improvement. It also looks at the objectives, the actions taken, and the key performance indicators (KPIs) that measure the objectives' achievement.

- **Revising plans and goals for the next quarter.** The discussion identifies objectives, the next actions to take, and the KPIs for measuring those actions' effectiveness.

Salespeople come into each meeting with a preliminary plan ready to discuss with their manager, and in some cases with their peers. Both the salesperson and the manager have access to the same data for informing the plan. The meeting focuses on overall issues and on key customer progress, opportunities, challenges, and plans.

If a QBR is done poorly, salespeople may spend a lot of time bragging about their wins and complaining about their losses without providing any meaningful insights or feedback. By encouraging honesty and transparency about both successes and failures, you can make the QBR a constructive and collaborative process for enhancing future success. For more, see the sidebar "Checklist of critical tasks for quarterly business review and planning."

Checklist of critical tasks for quarterly business review and planning

Preparing sales plans for the next quarter:

- ❏ Use estimates of unrealized potential to help salespeople identify and prioritize where to focus efforts, both among accounts and within each account.

- ❏ Maintain a list of priority accounts (about 20 percent) that are the most important to retain based on their current business or to grow based on their unrealized potential.

- ❏ For key accounts, have a joint understanding with salespeople about the priorities for retention and growth across various product lines and customer businesses.

❏ For key accounts, know the existing formal and informal relationships. Identify influencers and gatekeepers. Ask salespeople to create and maintain an influence diagram or map. Stay informed about the frequency of salespeople's connections and the strength of the relationships.

❏ Ask salespeople questions to help them create their own account plans; don't micromanage or create the plans yourself.

Reflecting on sales plan progress for the last quarter:

❏ Regularly select random accounts from a short list of priority accounts. Contact the salespeople responsible for those accounts and ask them to walk you through each account's profile, plan, and progress. Provide feedback and brainstorm on how to move forward. Make sure that each salesperson receives one such call at least twice per year.

❏ As you work with salespeople to monitor progress, come into discussions prepared with data. Make sure salespeople come prepared and have access to the same data you have.

❏ Distill takeaways from wins and losses. Focus on factors that you can control.

Ensuring effective execution and enabling change with sales sprints

Execution is a top challenge for most sales leaders. As a VP of sales put it, "We have invested in a lot of initiatives . . . I don't want new stuff . . . I want us to execute well and show results now."

Where do execution gaps come from in a well-trained sales force? Sales is a multifaceted job, with many choices of what to do at any moment. Results, especially with large deals, follow weeks and months of sales activity. Sales managers, marketing managers, and digital nudges often push salespeople in inconsistent directions. They may get pulled into nonsales tasks by customers' demands, such as addressing a request that is better handled by customer service. Salespeople themselves may choose tasks that are easy—such as calling on friendly accounts with modest upsides, or focusing on short-term small wins—rather than advancing larger, longer-term opportunities.

Enabling execution through sales sprints

To execute effectively, companies across industries have implemented **sales sprints**, in which a salesperson or sales team seeks to complete a defined amount of work in a timeboxed period of one to two weeks. Bookended by a one-on-one meeting between the salesperson and the sales manager, a sprint breaks down large, complex strategies into small, manageable tasks, making it easier for salespeople to stay on track.

Action plans in each sprint are built around the buyer's journey, from realizing a need, to shopping for solutions, to completing the purchase, to getting value from the selected option. At each step, the seller's actions (thought of as the seller's journey) are aimed at meeting the buyer's needs and making progress that creates value for both parties. Sales sprints focus on customer advances—the result of specific actions that a salesperson or a manager can take to get commitments that move the customer toward a purchase decision and increase the pipeline's value. (See figure 3-1 for examples.)

Implementing sales sprints at a food manufacturer

At a food ingredients manufacturer, most sales were repeat sales, and a relationship-based order-taking sales culture had taken hold. Salespeople visited customers using a repeatable route and collected orders. With growth stalled, the company wanted salespeople to focus on selling new higher-value products to existing customers and to prospects in new markets. The reactive "route system" had to give way to a proactive "growth system" for expanding the business. The company also planned to change the incentive plan to reward growth rather than volume.

Implementing the change would be challenging. For salespeople, sitting on a large book of business was no longer going to cut it. And the new products were complex and unfamiliar to the team. The company fully expected a jump in turnover of salespeople as the planned changes would redefine the winners and losers.

FIGURE 3-1

Sales actions that lead to customer advances

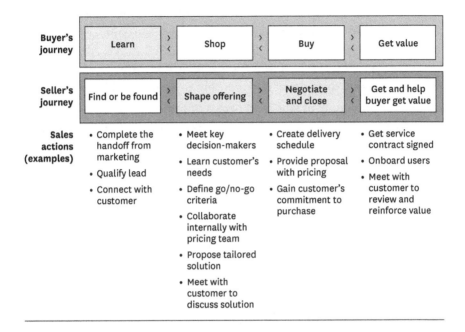

Buyer's journey	Learn > <	Shop > <	Buy > <	Get value
Seller's journey	Find or be found > <	Shape offering > <	Negotiate and close > <	Get and help buyer get value
Sales actions (examples)	• Complete the handoff from marketing • Qualify lead • Connect with customer	• Meet key decision-makers • Learn customer's needs • Define go/no-go criteria • Collaborate internally with pricing team • Propose tailored solution • Meet with customer to discuss solution	• Create delivery schedule • Provide proposal with pricing • Gain customer's commitment to purchase	• Get service contract signed • Onboard users • Meet with customer to review and reinforce value

To enable the shift, the company revamped its approach to sales planning and execution. A sales operations team supported leaders in estimating sales potential at the account level. Sellers were assigned goals that reflected the market profile of their territory. Salespeople worked with their managers, using a process of account planning and sales sprints to make the change stick.

To start, managers worked with each salesperson to break down quarterly goals into key result areas. KPIs emphasized growth and were used to track progress in each area, including:

- **Results:** revenues, contribution margins

- **Customer metrics:** retention rates, current customer business growth, Net Promoter Score

- **Resource allocation metrics:** customer mix (percentage of new customers), product portfolio mix, targeting effectiveness (sales potential versus effort)

- **Pipeline metrics:** customer acquisition costs, win/loss rates, pipeline velocity

- **Activities:** number of sales conversations, demonstrations, or proposals submitted by customer, customer segment, or product

Managers and salespeople worked together to execute the quarterly plans by breaking them down into monthly goals and weekly sprints. Sellers had the autonomy to look both back and forward and then to prepare weekly action plans for progressing toward the goals. In fifty-minute one-on-one meetings, usually on Fridays, salespeople and the manager focused on three questions:

1. **What happened?** They reviewed the previous week, including how the planned actions played out, how they did on pipeline progress and the key result areas, and what they learned.

2. **What next?** They also planned the next week, including the key prospects and customers to focus on, the actions to take, and the customer advances or progress to seek.

3. **How can the manager help?** Finally, they discussed what the manager could do to support the next week's efforts, such as sharing expertise, pointing the salesperson toward helpful resources, or facilitating a connection with a senior-level buyer.

In the sprint meetings, managers acted as a brainstorming partner and a sounding board for the salespeople. Key takeaways from the meeting were documented in a weekly plan that created accountability and focus for the coming week.

Once a month, the weekly sprint meeting was extended to 100 minutes. The extra time was for validating and adapting plans for the next thirty days, with a focus on the largest opportunities and the longer-term actions and resources that were needed. The monthly meetings were critical for keeping plans relevant as circumstances changed.

The weekly sales sprints—combined with the implementation of performance management, coaching, and processes for goal setting that were linked and digitally supported—helped the company make the implementation work. Despite some initial sales force attrition, the changes boosted customer selling time by 30 percent, expanded the number of SKUs sold by 50 percent, and increased overall sales and margins by 15 percent.

Why sales sprints work

Sprints allow both salespeople and managers to take ownership of the actions that drive performance. As a result, the odds of winning go up. Here is what sellers and managers have told us about how sprints drive results.

- **Get specific about the "how."** "The [past approach] was too general and not relevant. Sprints help us get focused on how we will achieve our sales goals."

- **Actionable short-term plans.** "Our quarterly plans before were like checking the box. I never looked at them after I had developed them . . . Sprints make the plan actionable."

- **Know what matters.** "The weekly game planning helps me focus on what is important. Things don't fall through the cracks."

- **Collaborative idea generation.** "We work together to plan what's next . . . I've never had this type of conversation. We generate ideas that move the needle."

Checklist of critical tasks for sales sprint reviews

- ❑ Prepare for the sprint review and expect salespeople to come with customer advances planned for the next sprint.

- ❑ Be ready to help salespeople execute by bringing resources and sharing insights you have access to.

- ❑ Document and reinforce the value of sales sprints.

- ❑ Once a quarter, share insights about improving sprints with your peers.

- ❑ Reschedule reviews only when absolutely necessary.

Sprints to bring about change

Sales sprints can be especially helpful when organizations face changes, whether those are transformational or evolutionary. Many sales organizations have rallied around sprints to make change possible.

Transformational changes

These can include a sales reorganization, an entry into new markets, a shift to new sales channels, and numerous other events requiring major adjustments to how sellers work. For example, to revitalize growth, an environmental testing company restructured its sales organization by redefining its two sales roles. In the old structure, *business development managers* acquired new accounts and *account managers* retained and expanded business in current accounts. In the new structure, *account executives* were responsible for acquisition, retention, and growth at small and medium-size accounts, while *key account executives* handled the company's largest accounts.

The restructuring presented significant challenges. Every salesperson's role would expand to include acquisition, retention, and growth, a shift that would stretch their capabilities and create conflicting priorities. Salespeople were likely to be unsure of their ability to succeed in their new roles. The changes could also confuse or concern customers, especially because account reassignments would disrupt established relationships. Adding to the complexity, the company introduced a new data-supported sales process. Every salesperson had to adapt to an unfamiliar role and a new way of working.

Sales sprints helped team members embrace the change. In weekly meetings, salespeople and their managers collaborated on account plans using data to guide their decisions. For account executives, data-derived lists of target accounts and opportunities helped them book appointments with decision-makers well in advance. And for key account managers, stakeholder maps assisted with getting more connections to the C-suite. The transformation caused some healthy turnover, but sales sprints ultimately helped sellers adapt to their new roles and drive growth.

Evolutionary changes

These involve incremental adjustments and improvements to how salespeople work. They may have new products to sell. They may need to handle a customer's difficult and pervasive situation or respond to a specific objection. Perhaps the company is testing a bundled offering or wants to try out a new marketing promotion. Or maybe a salesperson simply has a novel idea to increase business in an account with untapped sales opportunity. Sales sprints allow managers and salespeople to collaborate on executing all types of evolutionary changes.

One professional services firm had a global client that consistently purchased about $1 million in services annually. The firm wanted to pursue opportunities for the client to benefit from additional services, including in other countries. To amplify the focus on short-term sales execution, members of the account team used weekly sprints to discuss the previous week's actions, steps they would take in the coming week, and additional future actions for advancing the relationship with the client. Within a year, the firm's revenues from the client had doubled.

The manager's role in execution with key accounts

Sales managers often have direct customer responsibilities with large or strategic accounts. Consider how one supplier of home improvement products manages its relationship with its largest customer, Home Depot. Salespeople work with district buying managers and store personnel on issues such as designing product displays and store layouts, tracking sales and inventory, resolving complaints, and providing training to store associates. The supplier's regional sales managers (who also manage the salespeople) spend half of their time building and maintaining relationships with Home Depot's regional-level buyers. The matching of individuals with sales responsibility and buying responsibility occurs at all levels—up to the top leadership—of both organizations.

Relationships are multilevel. In this case and many others, by interacting directly with key accounts, sales managers reinforce the value that's delivered while also gathering feedback from the customer and learning about their needs and challenges.

Here are some examples of situations in which managers bring value to key accounts:

- **When the customer's executives are part of the buying team.** While salespeople work with buyers and users of a product or a service, managers can meet with C-level people to bring strategic insights and communicate the customer's importance in the partnership.

- **When a sales manager's expertise is needed.** In complex situations, managers can help craft solutions or demonstrate how the offering addresses customer pain points and goals.

- **When sales managers have authority.** They can get the attention of the internal product development, engineering, or service team to create and execute a quick solution.

- **When there are multiple salespeople responsible for different products or geographies.** Managers can coordinate and align the selling teams and address potential conflicts.

- **When the company wants to nurture a partnership.** Manager involvement can show customers that they are appreciated and make transitions between salespeople easier.

- **When a key customer is unhappy.** A manager can address the situation quickly.

Checklist of critical tasks for assisting with key accounts

- ❑ Participate in dry runs with the sales team before big sales pitches. Make the dry runs mandatory for important interactions with key clients.

- ❑ Before working with salespeople in customer meetings, agree on how to clearly delineate your respective roles.

- ❑ Before visiting an account with a salesperson, ask them how they plan to reinforce the value delivered to the customer.

❏ Ask the salesperson about the short-term and long-term objectives with the account.

❏ Schedule regular one-on-one conversations with the customer's senior leaders. Get feedback about how the company is doing and discuss industry trends. Talk about issues important to the customer; do not make this about sales or negotiations.

❏ Ask customers how they would like to interact with you and your company. Discover their expectations.

❏ Keep an "idea log" of topics and issues that come up during customer visits. Use these as conversation starters for follow-up discussions and for new business development.

Enabling the sales team to share customer insights

Bringing all the salespeople in the region together every month to discuss customer insights is a great way to foster collaboration, share knowledge, and encourage continuous learning. When marketing or product managers join such sessions, there are even more benefits. The sales team can offer ideas that inform marketing strategy and product design.

Team meetings are more effective if they have an agenda and encourage broad, active participation. One organization uses the principle that no one speaks twice until everyone speaks once. Managers should say very little; a different salesperson can lead each item on the agenda. Hearing one seller's experience can lead to others adding their take, followed by a discussion and a personal reflection by each team member on which ideas resonated for them.

Here are some examples of agenda topics that can generate valuable insights:

- Market trends and competitive intelligence

- Assessments and improvements of customer experience

- Sales strategies and tactics that are working well and ways to improve the sales process

- Opportunities and strategies for new business development and expansion

There is a two-way payoff in these peer-to-peer learning sessions. Salespeople often find it useful to learn from peers who face similar challenges. At the same time, they see their ideas make a difference, particularly when headquarters personnel, including executive leaders and marketers, participate in the meetings. Engagement and motivation are boosted.

An effective way to wrap up the meeting is to ask individual salespeople which ideas they found most useful and what they will do differently because of what they heard. You can also encourage action by documenting key takeaways and sharing your summary with the team.

Facilitating customer relationship transitions

You get a call from one of your top salespeople, who has decided to quit. A few days later, you learn that they are joining a competitor. Your first thought is, "What could I have done to retain them?" Your more pressing thought should be, "How do I keep their top customers?"

In any year, 25 percent to 50 percent of the accounts that salespeople are responsible for will likely change hands as team members leave, are let go, or are promoted or reassigned. Many accounts will be reassigned if the team expands, downsizes, or restructures. The greatest risk is when salespeople are poached by competitors, taking customers with them.

The good news is that customers know that their relationship with the company extends beyond the salesperson. They know it's the company that provides the products, the ultimate source of value. (In many service industries, the person designing the solution can be a dominant part of the value.) Managers have the power of the product and the company behind them. And, during a transition, customers want to hear from a manager.

Identifying risky transitions

You are responsible for minimizing the impact on customers, ensuring a smooth transition to a relationship with a new salesperson, and reducing any negative impact on the business. The manager's role is more significant when accounts are strategically important or contribute substantially to results, when sales cycles are long, and when strong relationships based on knowledge and trust exist between buyers and salespeople.

Planned customer coverage changes

If accounts are reassigned after the sales team expands or following the promotion of a salesperson, customer relationship transitions are easier. The person who covered the account is still available to help, but this does not mean customer transitions should be taken lightly.

Take the example of an industrial distributor with short sales cycles and a high rate of repeat purchasing. When the distributor restructured its sales force, about 30 percent of accounts changed hands. A thoughtful changeover approach was implemented. For key accounts, sales managers orchestrated customer meetings that included the newly assigned salesperson and the former one (who introduced their colleague to the customer). For mid-tier accounts, the handoff happened over the telephone. For smaller accounts, no special steps were implemented. In the months following the transition, reassigned key accounts continued to purchase at the same levels as accounts that hadn't changed hands. The distributor's smallest accounts also maintained their purchasing. But the story was different for mid-tier accounts. Reassigned accounts in this segment purchased 20 percent less than accounts that kept the same salesperson. The telephone handoffs did not work.

At-risk customer coverage changes

The riskier situations are when the salesperson losing an account does not cooperate in the transition. This can happen, for example, if the person joins a competitor. In industries such as wealth management, medical devices, real estate, and insurance, the relationships and trust that account managers (salespeople) have with customers can be so strong that many customers will follow them if they leave. In industries such as professional advisory services, solutions are designed as they are sold, and the account manager adds immense value to the design. Again, accounts are at risk of moving with the person. Even if that doesn't happen, the customer may use the account manager's departure as a reason to reevaluate and consider competitive offerings. The departing seller may also have customer insights and knowledge that get lost.

Facilitating risky transitions

In risky transitions between salespeople, managers should be deeply engaged and ready to act quickly. Having a documented customer transition process and checklist allows you to respond as soon as you know that an account is to be reassigned.

Focus on important accounts and large deals in the pipeline

At one wealth management firm, when a financial adviser departs, managers are expected to reach out to all major accounts within twenty-four hours and to try to meet with those accounts within a week.

As soon as you know that accounts will be reassigned from one salesperson to another, take a few steps:

- Focus your attention on any high-producing customers or accounts that have large deals in the pipeline. Contact key decision-makers right away.

- Make in-person visits soon after. Meet with key players, and then participate in one or more transition meetings that include customer personnel, the salesperson taking over, and the departing person (when possible).

- Arrange for temporary coverage of the seller's accounts until a permanent replacement is found. The interim person can be the manager or another salesperson. The key is to act quickly to reinforce customer attention and care.

- Following the initial transition period, continue to check in with key customers periodically to ensure their needs are being met.

A purposeful transition process can do wonders for customer retention.

Treat account transitions as opportunities

Despite all the challenges that accompany transitions, there is a silver lining. Bringing in a new person with a fresh perspective often has a positive impact even on growing accounts. The same is often true with high-potential but poorly penetrated customers. Use the opportunity to reach out and introduce them to a new salesperson who brings a novel perspective and different product, market, or selling strengths. Many times, we have seen accounts that were considered plateaued or impenetrable come back to life with a new salesperson.

Prepare as if the team member will leave tomorrow

Some defensive approaches help minimize the impact to a relationship when a disruption inevitably occurs:

- For key customers, have a contingency plan ready to implement quickly.

- Build personal relationships with key decision-makers.

- Establish multiple connections between the customer and the company. Connections can be with people (for example, product sales specialists, an inside salesperson, customer service reps, or technical support personnel) and with the company's digital resources, such as a customized ordering website or online customer support.

- Ensure the disciplined use of CRM by salespeople so that essential information about customers is not lost when a seller departs.

The more connections to the company that customers have, both through personal relationships and digital channels, the more likely it is that their loyalty will outlive the departure of a salesperson. Fortunately, in situations where the risk of loss is highest—big deals and long sales cycles—multiple people are usually involved.

———————

A key aspect of your role as a manager is empowering salespeople to plan and execute customer strategies that work when you are not there. This is the people management part of your job, and it's critical to your success. That's why the entire next section of this book is devoted to people management—how to hire, develop, manage, motivate, and retain a team of salespeople who can consistently win with customers.

Talent Management

4.

Personalizing Talent Management

Some great salespeople are born, but all great sales forces are built through deliberate attention to talent management.

Section 2 of this book covers talent management essentials. This chapter provides a foundation by exploring the building blocks and how managers personalize their approach for each salesperson.

The building blocks of talent management

Imagine asking a salesperson, "Are you successful?" If they answer, "Of course I am, I'm making my numbers," that seller is focusing on *results*. If you ask a manager the same question, you might get a similar answer. However, if you ask, "Why is your sales team consistently successful?" you are likely to get a different response, such as "I have a great team." Now the focus is on success being driven by *salespeople's capabilities and motivation*. Further, the manager might add, "My people spend time with the right customers." Now they are talking about *salespeople's activities and behaviors.* And if you ask, "Why aren't you making your numbers?" the manager's answer might focus on results ("My team isn't bringing in enough new business"), the salespeople themselves ("I've lost all my experienced people"), or what the sellers do ("My team isn't spending enough time selling our new products").

These answers point to different parts of the sales system, a chain that links salespeople's capabilities and motivations, their activities and behaviors, and customer value and company results. (A full diagram of the sales system is shown in figure I-1, in the introduction.) Talent management is one key aspect of the sales decisions, processes, and resources that drive outcomes within this system. It is about hiring, developing, managing, incentivizing, and retaining a team of salespeople who can carry out the team's goals. Here's what those tasks entail:

- **Hiring** is the process of recruiting individuals who have the right skills and experience, as well as personalities that align with the company's sales culture and goals, and then onboarding and acculturating them.

- **Learning and development** helps salespeople continuously improve their knowledge and skills. It includes training that provides opportunities for professional growth, coaching to nurture individual strengths and address weaknesses, and work-based learning opportunities such as apprenticeship, mentorship, and peer-based programs that promote learning on the job by doing and observing.

- **Managing performance** requires a personalized approach to working with star and core performers, and with those who have the potential to become stars and core players, at various career stages. It includes tasks such as setting challenging but attainable goals, recognizing and rewarding achievements, providing constructive feedback, and empowering salespeople to win.

- **Sales incentives** are monetary rewards used to direct and motivate sales effort.

- **Retention** is about holding on to high-performing people at every career stage and managing inevitable turnover effectively.

Managing talent is similar in many ways to managing customers. You find and acquire the right customers, bring them on board, serve their needs, and retain them while expanding the relationship. Similarly, you hire the right sellers, develop and energize them, and retain them as they grow more productive, enjoy career success, and drive more value for customers and the company. The mindset you used to succeed as a salesperson can help you excel in your role as a manager.

Using personalization to develop, engage, and retain salespeople

Personalization is a manager's all-purpose tool. It's effective whether you are convincing a great potential hire to join the team, helping a rising star balance the demands of in-person and virtual engagement, motivating a tenured seller to adapt their selling skills to the changing environment, or trying to prevent a top performer from joining a competitor. By understanding key dimensions about each person, including their competencies, motivators, performance, and career stage, managers can tailor their approach for maximum impact.

This chapter explains the relevance of these dimensions at a high level. The chapters that follow will provide more detail and examples of how to put these insights into action to create a robust talent management program for your team.

A key goal of talent management is to create a team of people who possess the necessary *competencies* and who are *motivated* to engage in activities that drive results. A successful sales team can and will do the job. Thus, the first two dimensions of insight are about competency and motivation.

Competency

Competency models define the proficiencies needed for success in a sales role. They guide learning and development, performance management, and hiring. The models help salespeople and managers align around the strengths and the development needs of the salesperson.

A typical competency model uses a set of eight to fifteen measurable role-specific competencies. Most models focus on capabilities, the defined skills and knowledge needed to execute the sales process (e.g., customer insight, product expertise, territory management, selling process skills). Occasionally, competency models include more general capabilities (e.g., problem-solving, time management, digital proficiency). Characteristics (e.g., adaptability, resilience, empathy) can be part of competency models too, but this is less common because they are largely inherent.

Competency models describe each competency, typically with three to five levels of proficiency. (See tables 4-1 and 4-2.)

There are many ways to use a competency model. An effective approach allows each salesperson to self-assess their proficiency while the manager also evaluates the person. When the two parties meet to compare assessments and discuss alignments and differences, both have had time to reflect so the discussion is more balanced and holistic. Once you agree on the capabilities the salesperson is strong in—and those they need to work on—you

TABLE 4-1

Example of a competency model

Competency	PROFICIENCY-LEVEL ASSESSMENT			
	Foundational	Skilled	Advanced	Expert
1. Prospecting and qualifying				
2. Identifying decision-makers; defining needs				
3. Designing solutions; articulating value				
4. Delivering proposals; reaching agreements				
5. Setting up contracts; onboarding customers				
6. Maximizing and reinforcing value delivered				
7. Industry and market knowledge				
8. People, process, and technology				

TABLE 4-2

Example of competency proficiency levels

#7 Industry and market knowledge: Understands customers, segments, and the industry, and uses this knowledge to benefit customers

Foundational	Skilled	Advanced	Expert
• Understands industry, segments, and local markets; acts as industry expert for customers • Knows full portfolio of products and services • Is aware of newest innovations and offerings	*Foundational, plus:* • Has solid understanding of current product and service portfolio • Stays up-to-date on the newest innovations and offerings • Understands how products and services compete within industry • Shares insights with customers to differentiate company from competitors • Brings insights to buyers to shape future strategies	*Skilled, plus:* • Continuously seeks to grow industry expertise • Fosters connections with key customers to build and leverage relationships • Shares insights with customers to nurture partnership • Proactively shares insights with sales leadership, including ideas on how to shape future strategies • Analyzes economic, industry, market, and financial data to anticipate impact	*Advanced, plus:* • Uses industry and product knowledge to assist others • Collaborates with cross-functional teams and their sales leaders to develop plans for using these offerings to benefit customers and the business • Is viewed as a thought leader on how trends shape future strategies, products, etc. • Actively teaches others how to contribute to business growth

can jointly craft a plan for leveraging the salesperson's strengths and finding opportunities to address their weaknesses. Both people preparing in advance helps facilitate alignment and accountability. Assessing competencies is a key component of personalizing your approach to talent management.

Motivation

Motivated salespeople get going in the right direction and with sustained effort. Commitment is an important part of motivation, as it involves following through on a promised course of action. Gauging motivation involves observing someone's effort and looking for changes in behavior. By understanding an individual's motivators and motivation levels, you can personalize rewards such as recognition and incentives, while allowing each person to succeed according to their own goals, strengths, and aspirations.

FIGURE 4-1

Extrinsic motivation programs

	Short term	Medium term	Long term
Cash	Cash prize contests	Annual/quarterly incentive program	Salary Profit sharing or stock options
Noncash	Noncash prize contests Appreciation	Public recognition Group incentive trips	Career progression

There are two types of motivation: intrinsic and extrinsic. *Intrinsic* motivation comes from within and does not need an added reward or consequence. Successful salespeople are intrinsically energized by specific aspects of the job, such as working with customers or solving complex problems. Other intrinsic motivators include a sense of community, meaningful work, and new challenges. *Extrinsic* motivation relies on outside rewards, such as an incentive payout or salary increase, a promotion, or praise from a manager or a customer. Companies use several extrinsic motivators over time spans from the short term to the long term. (See figure 4-1.)

Extrinsic motivation programs are typically made available to all salespeople. But different salespeople respond to various intrinsic and extrinsic motivators to different degrees, and the relative importance of each can change during a person's career and in new circumstances. Understanding team members helps a manager know what actions to take to boost commitment. The manager can then create the right combination of both types of motivators.

Performance

Salespeople who have different levels of success and trajectories of growth face unique challenges. Consider four segments of sellers and the varied tactics you use to improve the performance of each.

- **Stars (high performance, high growth).** Your focus should be on energizing and retaining them—these are the people you especially want to keep.

- **Core players (high performance, stagnant growth).** For these people, the goal is to sustain their performance and prevent complacency from setting in.

- **Potential performers (low performance, high growth).** Your managerial actions should center on learning and development that can help them become stars.

- **Question marks (low performance, low growth).** For these salespeople, the path forward often involves a role change that allows them to be more successful.

Chapter 7 provides more insights about managing people in each of these performance segments.

Career stage

Salespeople's challenges and needs also vary with their career stage. (See figure 4-2.) What you do to help those who are just starting to explore a sales career is different from the actions needed to ensure rising stars continue to gain traction. And for team members who have already demonstrated several years of success (either inside or outside your company), you'll need a management approach that keeps them engaged and growing.

The chapters that follow share numerous ways that personalization brings power to your talent management decisions and processes. To illustrate, consider a few examples that use a lens of career stage and performance to show how you can personalize your approach to talent management. (See table 4-3.)

Making the sales team great requires bringing excellence to your talent management decisions and processes, including those for hiring,

FIGURE 4-2

Career stages and trajectories

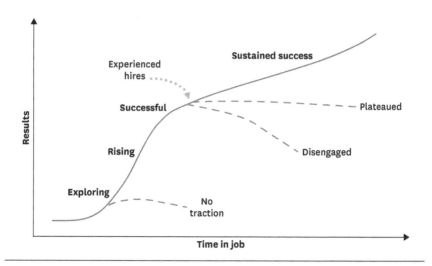

TABLE 4-3

How managers personalize talent management

Career stage	Performance	Manager challenges and actions
Early	**Exploring** (first job in sales)	Help salesperson build confidence and competence. Tap into feelings of excitement, insecurity, and eagerness to learn and succeed.
	Rising (experiencing early success)	Support salesperson in building competence with bigger accounts and developing advanced sales skills. Keep salesperson motivated as the initial excitement of a new job abates and the realities of work set in.
Middle	**No traction**	Quickly discover why salesperson is struggling. If the problem is unsolvable, help salesperson make a respectful exit. If there are many such people, sharpen hiring skills.
	Successful (3–5 years of consistent success)	Provide rewards and recognition, new opportunities, and autonomy. Focus on retention—salesperson is likely to attract the attention of competitors and talent search firms.
	Sustained Success (6+ years of consistent success)	Create new challenges to prevent complacency from taking root. Be on the lookout for potential plateauing or disengagement.
Late	**Plateaued**	Reenergize salesperson who has changed their attitude about work-life balance, resists change, and feels "I have earned it."
	Disengaged	If it's too late to turn the situation around, it could be time to part ways with the person.

developing, managing, incentivizing, and retaining the team. The next five chapters share more about the talent management activities that are part of your people management role. (Later, in chapter 17, we delve deeper into the ways digital is affecting all these activities.) Let's begin with hiring.

5.

Hiring and Onboarding for Speed and Impact

When we ask sales leaders, "What percentage of your salespeople are excellent?" the normal range of answers is only 20 percent to 30 percent. There's no question about it, hiring the right people, and enabling them to succeed, is hard. If you have ten salespeople on your team today, in a year two to five of them will most likely be gone—promoted or off to another job. You'll have to hire their replacements. That's why sustained success depends on your ability to bring quality and speed to hiring.

Salesperson hiring is a responsibility shared between headquarters—typically a hiring manager from sales or HR—and sales managers. The hiring manager's role is to create job profiles, post jobs, screen résumés, and oversee the entire process. Sales managers help find candidates and evaluate their characteristics, knowledge, skills, and cultural fit. They also have the responsibility of onboarding new team members.

This chapter will cover the key components of an effective process for hiring and onboarding sales talent, beginning with your role in that process. The evolving digital impact on hiring will be explored further in chapter 17.

The sales manager's role in the hiring process

The hiring process is made up of five components, with managers playing a key role in each one. (See table 5-1.)

By being involved in hiring, you get in on the early stages of building a successful team. In addition, your input helps improve the hiring process, and interviewing experienced candidates helps you get smarter about what customers and competitors are doing and thinking. Interviews are an incredible source of market insight.

Using a structured process makes hiring streamlined, consistent, repeatable, and easier to improve over time. This leads to better hiring decisions and stronger sales teams in the long term.

TABLE 5-1

Hiring process components and the manager's role

Component	Manager's role
Selection criteria *Qualifications and competencies you seek in candidates*	• Share your input to improve the job profile, competency model, and selection criteria. • Provide insight about how changing customer needs affect these.
Source of candidates *Where you look for candidates*	• Use your professional network to find candidates. • Keep an active bench of candidates. • Celebrate successful job referrals made by your people.
Selection *How you assess candidates on the evaluation criteria and choose who gets an offer*	• Conduct competency-based interviews, role-plays, and other selection methods. • Help make selection decisions.
Attraction *How you ensure that candidates accept offers*	• Create a positive recruiting experience for candidates. • Personally reach out to candidates who have offers.
Onboarding *How you facilitate new hires' entry into the job*	• For new-to-sales hires, build their confidence and competence. • For experienced hires, acculturate and help them master the internal support network.

Defining the candidate selection criteria

A structured approach to hiring begins with defining both the job and what to look for in candidates. There are several sources of insight to consider.

Two key inputs: Job profile and competency model

A **job profile** (or position profile) describes an employee's responsibilities and qualifications (for example, five years of selling experience, a bachelor's degree, etc.). It also provides information about compensation and other perks. The job profile is shared externally (on the company's website, on job boards, etc.) to attract candidates. This helps job seekers determine whether they are interested in the role and whether they have the right background and experience to apply. The applicant pool is narrowed down by eliminating candidates who lack the qualifications listed in the job profile.

A **competency model** (described in more detail in chapter 4) defines characteristics and capabilities that will help a candidate perform the job. These models focus on factors such as customer knowledge and proficiency with the steps of selling. Less commonly, they also include innate characteristics such as resilience, adaptability, and empathy.

Together, the job profile and the competency model inform the list of criteria that will help you evaluate candidates. The list will vary by sales role. (See examples in table 5-2.)

Sales success requires a complex and multifaceted combination of factors, which makes defining the selection criteria challenging. With experienced hires, we suggest including requirements that demonstrate past achievements, such as "proven success in acquiring key accounts" or "documented history of achieving quota." Such objective criteria make your hiring process more robust and reliable.

Learn from top performers

Your successful salespeople are a great source of insights for understanding what you're looking for in candidates. Think about the characteristics and capabilities of the top 20 percent of performers.

TABLE 5-2

Sample of what to look for in experienced hires for two roles

	New business development sales role	Customer retention/ growth sales role
Innate characteristics and motivators	• Is curious • Is empathetic • Handles rejection and is persistent • Has motivation and drive	• Is detail-oriented • Wants to help others and is dependable • Wants to make a difference
Selling capabilities	• Identifies stakeholders • Builds rapport quickly • Influences • Communicates value	• Knows customer's organization, business, and priorities • Has deep customer relationships and access • Reinforces value realized • Leverages data and analytics to find opportunities • Advocates for the customer
Culture fit and adaptiveness	• Orchestrates collaboratively with customer and internal stakeholders • Adjusts approach to customer's situation, knowledge, and needs • Responds to changes in environment, such as competition or technology	

Some companies also use data and research to identify traits of top performers. Health-care giant Novartis pioneered a technique called *performance frontier* to identify outstanding performers and isolate the behaviors that differentiated them. These behaviors shaped the company's sales training, coaching, and selection criteria for hiring. Novartis periodically reexamines the behaviors of outstanding performers in various roles and updates the selection criteria to reflect changes.

Include forward-looking criteria

As customer needs and sales processes evolve, the qualities required for success do too. A great example is the shift to virtual work and its impact. Salespeople who used to work mostly in person with customers had to adjust to hybrid sales models. This meant knowing *how* and *when* to reach customers (some of whom work from home) using the right mix of digital, virtual, and in-person approaches. To assure your new hires of success, the hiring criteria have to reflect current job requirements. If you revisit the list each time you start a candidate search, you'll increase the odds of hiring someone who has what it takes to win both now and in the future. Chapter 13 shares a list of five forward-looking sales competencies that you may want to add to your list.

Focus on experienced or new-to-sales hires?

Your decision to hire experienced employees, new-to-sales talent, or a combination depends on numerous factors: the nature of your products, the requirements of your customers, how quickly you need people to be productive, the availability of training and support resources, and more. Your decision affects how you source, select, and onboard candidates. Consider the contrasting strategies of two technology companies.

In 2019 Google Cloud Platform (GCP) began rapidly expanding its sales force to compete for share of the fast-growing enterprise cloud computing market. GCP's sales talent strategy centered on hiring experienced candidates who could hit the ground running. By January 2020, there were hundreds of job postings for GCP sales roles, typically requiring applicants to have several years of enterprise software sales experience. With new sellers coming from Oracle, Microsoft, Amazon, and others, GCP launched a new onboarding curriculum that immersed new hires in a personalized and peer-to-peer social learning experience, allowing them to ramp up quickly.

In 2023 Dell Technologies offered two- to three-year programs for inside, field, or specialty sales roles, providing comprehensive training and development opportunities for new-to-sales candidates. The company had recruiters visiting university campuses throughout the year to showcase opportunities for interested students. Dell's Sales Academy—an entry point for new-to-sales hires—provided onboarding and training, with an accelerated learning approach in an immersive experience to help people launch their careers in sales.

Hiring experienced salespeople is a double-edged sword. They bring competencies that allow them to become productive quickly with a minimum of training and management attention. Those with a proven track record in the industry may bring customer connections and new ideas as well. They also have realistic expectations of what a sales job involves.

But experienced salespeople cost more. They may come with habits that are not aligned with the organization's values or sales methods. They may be reluctant to change, slower to learn, and more difficult to acculturate. Organizations that haven't assessed these hires for cultural fit and onboarded them effectively have seen high failure rates and turnover—a challenge made even greater as people switch jobs more frequently than they did in the past due to the changing dynamics of the modern workforce.

Sourcing talent

The quality of the people you hire depends in large part on the quality of your applicant pool. So where do you find great candidates?

Identify the best sources for candidates

Most employers source candidates by posting job openings on their own websites and on job boards (such as Indeed, Monster, Glassdoor) and social media platforms (such as LinkedIn, Facebook, X [formerly Twitter]). Online channels give you access to a large pool of potential talent. Job fairs, agencies, and internal placements are also helpful. And the personal connections of sales managers can produce a targeted pool of candidates from competitors, customers, and others.

Although it's common to source experienced talent from your competitors, many companies are finding ways to hire candidates from other industries who bring similar sales skills. For example, renewable energy companies hire from the oil and gas industry. Customer success managers from the technology sector are finding their skills apply to a variety of industries. Medical device firms hire from pharmaceutical companies. One healthcare company discovered that many of its most successful salespeople came from nontraditional backgrounds, such as teaching, and had little or no experience in health care or life sciences. The company changed the criteria for screening candidates, accelerating the rate at which it filled open positions during a sales force expansion.

When sourcing new-to-sales candidates, online channels, job fairs, and referrals are all good options. College campuses are also a fertile ground, allowing you to reach a large pool of potential talent. New graduates typically start out with lower performance than experienced hires do, but improve their performance faster and continue to grow it more steadily over time. Some of the most rapid and sustained growth is seen in hires who come from collegiate sales education programs.

Leverage the power of employee referrals

Most managers agree that employee referrals are the most productive source of new hires. The quality of such candidates is high because the referring employee understands the job and culture and will recommend people they believe will fit. Further, a poor recommendation reflects negatively on the referrer and could create career risk for them. Referrals are fast and keep recruiting costs low. And employees hired through referrals tend to stay with the company longer.

Many companies use referral bonuses, which do help, but there are more powerful (and free) things you can do to encourage more referrals. For example, celebrate successful referrals at monthly regional meetings, calling out the person who brought in the talent. In addition, some salespeople are great social ambassadors through their professional, social, and alumni networks—leverage their help too.

Keep an active bench

The best managers maintain their own applicant pool—a short list of internal and external candidates "on the bench" who could be available to fill vacancies as they happen. Remember, half the people on your team are likely to move on in two years, and sometimes even faster. Keeping an active list of candidates on your radar greatly reduces the time it takes to fill vacancies.

Selecting talent

Selecting the right candidates is a challenging and error-prone process, even when you're starting with a strong applicant pool. The quality of hires is greatly enhanced when you use a structured selection process with multiple screening methods and interviewers. Although no process is perfect, there are several things you can do to boost the odds of choosing the right people.

Adapt your selection criteria for the candidate's experience level

Your list of what to look for in candidates (see "Defining the candidate selection criteria" above) is a key input for the hiring process. This list shapes the interview guide and scorecard you will use. (See table 5-3.)

Your selection criteria will be different for experienced and new-to-sales hires. With experienced candidates, you can screen for mastery of selling capabilities, market knowledge, and success in past roles. And it's critical to screen for culture fit.

New-to-sales candidates have yet to prove they can sell. Therefore, you can't use sales proficiency as a criterion. Focus instead on capabilities such as critical thinking, problem-solving, communication, planning, and organizing. Innate characteristics to consider include integrity, self-control, emotional intelligence, confidence, ambition, adaptability, learning agility, and teamwork.

A question that arises often: Should you hire for *height* or *slope*? Hiring for height means going with the candidate who has a high current level of performance, such as a track record of exceeding targets. Hiring for slope means opting for someone who does not have as strong a track record but who has demonstrated the ability to learn and adapt. You can argue that in a constantly evolving field, the ability to learn and adapt is critical for long-term success. But some organizations are looking to win quickly and so prioritize proven success, as Google Cloud did. To be fair, people with a great track record may have slope too. In a dynamic world, there may be no height without slope.

Use multiple screening methods

No single screening method on its own is very good at predicting job performance. However, a structured process that uses a combination of sev-

TABLE 5-3

Competency-based interview guide and scorecard

Desired attributes and examples of questions	Rating 4=Expert 3=Skilled 2=Proficient 1=Developing
Curiosity • Describe a project you worked on where you did not know much about the topic. What did you do? • How have you learned what a customer was really thinking and feeling when you came into the conversation not knowing them?	
Persistence • Can you give me an example of a time when you kept facing roadblocks? What did you do? • Tell me about a project that took a year or more.	
Adaptiveness • Describe a time when you had to work with a difficult colleague. What steps did you take to address the situation? • Tell me about a situation where you had to try several different approaches until you found one that worked.	
Other • •	
Total competency-based interview score	

eral methods, including those described here, leads to higher-quality hiring decisions.

Selection typically begins with a résumé screen to whittle down the applicant pool. When there are large numbers of applicants, automated résumé screening can search for keywords and qualifications to identify people with, for example, certain years of experience, industry backgrounds, or types of college degrees. Automation makes the initial phase of candidate screening faster and can reduce the unintentional biases that occur when humans do the selection. However, dealing with job candidates who tailor their résumés to match posted job descriptions is a serious challenge in automated processes. Sales aptitude tests, some of which have been vetted in specific industries, can be an added filter, as can simulations that ask candidates to complete specific job-related tasks through an application. Automated virtual interviews that are led or assisted by AI are increasingly common early screening techniques as well.

For the candidates who are short-listed, the manager's involvement might include competency-based interviews, panel interviews, role-plays, and informal occasions such as meals. Each method shows different aspects of a candidate. (See table 5-4.)

Conduct structured competency-based interviews

Most companies rely on interviewing as a primary means of screening sales candidates. Increasingly, recorded video interviews are also used in early rounds of candidate selection. Sales managers are likely to participate in interviewing during later rounds, either in person or over live video.

Hiring decisions are generally better when competency-based interviews (CBIs) are used. A CBI focuses on identifying a candidate's past behavior in specific situations to predict their future behavior. Interviewers ask people to recount experiences in which they demonstrated characteristics, capabilities, and culture fit attributes from the list of selection criteria. (Table 5-3 provides a template with examples for a CBI guide and scorecard.) On the other hand, when interviewers create their own spontaneous questions without a prepared guide, and evaluate candidates based on subjective impressions and judgments, too often selection becomes more about likability than competence. If an interviewer claims, "I just know quality when I see it," believe them only if history shows that their past hires have consistently proven to be winners.

Guidelines for interviewing candidates

- Review the candidate's résumé before the interview. Use an interview guide to help you prepare questions that are specific to their résumé.

- Have an agenda. Welcome the candidate, ask predetermined questions, give the candidate a chance to ask questions, and wrap up the conversation by sharing next steps.

TABLE 5-4

Screening methods and responsibilities

	Example items for new business development role	Résumé screen	Background, references, social media	Aptitude test	Simulation or case study	Competency-based interviews	Informal meetings
Experience and achievements	• 3–5 years selling to key accounts • Top 15% performer	✓	✓				
Innate characteristics and motivators	• Is curious • Is empathetic • Handles rejection and is persistent • Has motivation and drive			✓		✓	
Selling capabilities	• Identifies stakeholders • Builds rapport quickly • Influences • Communicates value				✓	✓	
Culture fit	• Orchestrates collaboratively with customer and internal stakeholders					✓	✓
Adaptiveness	• Adapts to customer situation, knowledge, and needs				✓	✓	✓
Who is responsible?	Hiring manager ————————————————— Sales managers						

- Ask the candidate to describe different situations and tasks, the actions they took, and the results.

- When interviewing multiple candidates, ask the same questions in the same order to strengthen your evaluations and comparisons.

- Have the candidate meet with multiple interviewers to gain different perspectives. Not all interviewers have to focus on the same criteria. However, it's helpful to have interviewers ask some of the same questions and to check for consistency in the answers.

- Allow interviewees to ask questions. These questions will often give you insights into their interest and commitment.

- Rate the candidate and capture your impressions as soon as the interview is over, while the conversation is fresh in your mind.

- Have different interviewers share their ratings with each other before discussing candidates. Otherwise, the opinion of the first person to speak will carry an unduly high weight.

When candidates are skilled at competency-based interviews

Many (perhaps most) applicants are aware of competency-based interviewing and prepare for it. Build on their preparation in the assessment and give candidates who did their homework an opportunity to stand out.

- Ask follow-up questions. For example, if the candidate describes a situation in which they demonstrated a particular skill, have them tell you about when they've used the skill to address a different challenge.

- Ask questions that help you assess different aspects of the candidate's skills. For example, "Can you give me an example of a time when you kept facing roadblocks?" followed by "And when you had to work on a team with strong differing opinions?"

- Observe nonverbal cues for confidence and sincerity.

Create opportunities to observe the candidate

The best selection techniques are often those that allow direct observation of a candidate who is engaged in behaviors related to job success. Here are some ways to observe a candidate's work:

- **Do a role-play.** Provide the candidate with a scenario and ask them to engage in a sales conversation, negotiate, handle objections, or close a deal. Act like a typical customer and offer reasonable questions and objections.

- **Do a case study and a mock pitch.** Present candidates with hypothetical or actual case studies that reflect the challenges they may encounter in the role. Ask them to analyze the situation, develop a sales strategy, and present their approach to you or a panel.

- **Give a take-home assignment.** For example, if you're hiring a new business development role for a key account, give the candidate the name of a company. Have them research the buying decision-makers and come back with outreach ideas in the next interview.

- **Spend time in the field.** This is not possible in many cases (for example, hiring from a competitor), but when it is, have select candidates accompany salespeople on customer visits.

- **Do a job trial or an internship.** In Europe it is common practice to hire employees for a short trial period. There are also companies that require candidates to undergo training before extending an employment offer.

Develop a comprehensive picture with a selection template

A selection template for summarizing feedback across all sources of input is useful for comparing candidates. (See table 5-5.) Have everyone involved

TABLE 5-5

Selection template for summarizing feedback about job candidates

Criterion Scoring model	Typical weight for experienced hires	Typical weight for new-to-sales hires	Your weight	Your score	Your score × weight
Success record: Top 15% performer • Score 10 if similar market and role • Score 5 if different market, similar role	20%–40%	10%–20%			
Competency-based interviews: Score (0–10)	25%–80%	25%–60%			
Aptitude test*: Score (0–10)	0%–20%	0%–30%			
Referral quality: Recommended by high performer • Score 10 if knows well, has worked with candidate • Score 5 if knows well	0%–25%	0%–10%			
TOTAL			100%		

*Aptitude tests are sometimes used as screening filters. Only those scoring highly move to the interviewing step.

in the selection process use a consistent scoring system. Track scores over time and compare candidates (hired and rejected alike) not only across recruiters but also across recruiting cycles.

The relative importance of different types of feedback varies with the situation. A proven record of success is more important with experienced candidates, while an aptitude test might get more weight for candidates who are new to sales. Referral quality is a consideration as well. All other things being equal, bet on a high-quality referral over an online applicant.

Final steps before making an offer

Have your HR team perform some additional checks before you make a job offer. Background checks verify the accuracy of the information the candidate has shared. Social media checks help you assess someone's professionalism, cultural fit, and alignment with company values. And reference checks produce insights from the person's previous employers or colleagues regarding their skills, work ethic, and suitability for the role.

If no candidate fits all the criteria, leave the position open and continue the search rather than hiring the best available option. Hiring too quickly and getting a suboptimal candidate—"warm body hiring"—is something sales leaders consistently regret.

Attracting talent

Attracting prospective employees is part of every step of hiring; it does not begin after making an offer to a candidate. As you are evaluating and interviewing candidates, they are evaluating and interviewing you. Your company culture comes through in every interaction someone has with the company—from the content that prospective employees read online, to the application process, to the interviewing experience, to the offer itself.

Have a candidate-friendly assessment process

A hiring process that leaves a positive impression has several key elements.

A STREAMLINED AND RESPONSIVE PROCESS. Candidates appreciate a process that's efficient and unbiased. Provide clear, timely communication about expectations and timelines, and keep the process moving. The candidate's experience during recruiting communicates how your company operates in every area of its business.

INTERVIEWING RIGOR. While making the assessment process efficient for the candidate, don't skimp on rigor. A demanding interviewing process signals that the company is hiring the best talent; it also validates a candidate's quality, boosting their satisfaction. No one wants to join a club that's easy to get into. At the same time, respect each person's time and keep any work required to a reasonable level for aptitude tests, interviews, and take-home assignments.

INTERVIEWS THAT SHOWCASE OPPORTUNITIES AND CULTURE. This process is not just about evaluating applicants. A key thing on every candidate's mind is, "Do I want to work with these people?" Interviews are occasions to highlight the job's opportunities and the company's culture and values. You can explicitly discuss what success looks like and leads to while pointing to how others have succeeded.

INTERVIEWEES WHO FEEL SUCCESSFUL. Express genuine interest in the candidate's achievements and successes. Structure the interview as a collaborative conversation rather than an interrogation. Throughout the interview, offer positive feedback on their ideas.

The recruiting process should provide candidates with a solid sense of the benefits as well as the challenges of both the job and the company.

Make a good offer and personalize outreach

It's not enough to have attractive compensation. A well-crafted offer and personalized follow-up can make the difference between acceptance and rejection.

MAKE PROMPT JOB OFFERS. Once you've identified your top candidate, quickly extend an offer. Clearly outline the details, including compensation, benefits, start date, and other relevant information. Reinforce the opportunities, the expectations, and the onboarding steps and assistance you'll provide, especially for experienced hires; they'll appreciate an honest assessment of the tailwinds and headwinds they will experience in your company, as well as how you will help them address challenges.

PERSONALIZE YOUR OUTREACH. Once candidates have an offer, let them know that you want them. Continued engagement demonstrates your commitment to their success and fosters a positive experience. Assign the candidate a peer buddy who can coordinate the follow-up. The buddy can, for example, encourage a supervisor to call the candidate, invite the candidate out to a casual dinner or to a company meeting, or ask colleagues to send personalized messages. Giving attention works with customers, and it works with prospective employees too. The little things you do can make a big difference.

Onboarding and acculturating

Your effectiveness as a manager depends on launching new people successfully. You are in the best position to help hires get off to a good start and to accelerate their career at the company. Onboarding someone effectively increases their confidence and motivation and helps them overcome disconnectedness, underpreparedness, and frustration.

Headquarters folks can get salespeople set up with technology and help them learn about company policies and other administrative matters. Beyond this, a staged approach for new hires is helpful; if you throw too much at someone at once, they'll feel overwhelmed. A checklist for the person's first thirty, sixty, and ninety days helps avoid that, while ensuring important steps aren't missed. (See table 5-6.)

Medical device company Boston Scientific has a twenty-six-week onboarding period in which corporate, the manager, and a mentor all play

TABLE 5-6

30-60-90-day salesperson onboarding checklist

	Onboarding goals
30 days	• Understand company culture, mission, values, and strategy • Understand the basics of product offerings, the target audience, and buyer personas • Understand the sales process • Learn CRM and other tools • Shadow manager or colleagues on customer visits
60 days	• Participate in advanced product training, including competitive analysis • Attend training sessions on negotiations • Learn how to use lead-generation channels and follow up on leads • Practice sales techniques • Start building a sales pipeline
90 days	• Take full ownership of sales cycle • Link sales goals to activities and plans • Continue building the sales pipeline • Learn how to self-assess and improve • Conduct a 90-day review with manager

a role. Mentors are experienced salespeople who have the interest and potential to join management someday; helping new salespeople get up to speed is part of their development process. The company also has a formal schedule of what corporate, the manager, and the mentor should do to help a new salesperson onboard successfully.

Onboard new-to-sales hires

Employees who are new to sales are excited, nervous, and eager to learn and succeed. For many companies, sales turnover is extremely high in the first eighteen months on the job. Successful onboarding can begin a virtuous cycle: If new salespeople enjoy the job and taste early success, they are more likely to stay. And if they have a good support system and network, they can weather the inevitable stumbles. Frequent interactions with new-to-sales hires helps them build three key pillars of early success.

COMPETENCE. Good coaching by sales managers guides new salespeople as they learn the company's products or services, gain knowledge of how to work with other parts of the organization such as marketing, and practice effective selling techniques. Through one-on-one interactions, you can help them develop new sales muscles. Your aim should be for them to think, "My manager cares about my growth, understands me, and helps me." It's best to spend their first few months focusing more on the "how" of the job and less on their results. People will become frustrated if you emphasize outcomes before they have the skills they need.

CONFIDENCE AND MOTIVATION. The best way to increase these is to ensure new salespeople win deals. Help make that happen by offering them guidance and support with customer interactions without overshadowing them or usurping their authority. One good approach is to assign them a few easy-to-sell accounts.

A SUPPORT NETWORK. One key aspect of onboarding and training programs is to help new hires form peer support networks. Occasions for in-person peer interaction are especially effective for this. While you provide leadership and guidance, it's sometimes best to get out of the way and allow team members to interact on their own, fostering team autonomy, collaboration, and trust. A peer support system is good for morale and growth.

Onboard and acculturate experienced hires

Salespeople who come from other companies must acclimate to the culture and create internal networks and connections. You can foster their sense of belonging and engagement by helping them build these networks through introductions to others on the sales team and by interacting with them frequently, which helps in the following ways.

CULTURAL IMMERSION.   Acculturation is critical for integrating experienced salespeople into the team. The goal is to help people understand the norms and unwritten rules of the organization. For example, a person who is used to working alone in a competitive sales environment (medical device sales, for example) may struggle to adapt to a job that requires cooperation and discipline (technology sales, for example). The reverse is true as well.

Acculturation is about apprenticeship, not training. It requires spending time with new hires and providing occasions for seasoned people on the team to do so as well, such as in sessions for sharing best practices. Informal gatherings around meals are especially useful for developing teamwork and camaraderie.

At Salesforce, many new hires come with prior sales experience. To help candidates embrace the unique culture, the company starts by screening for innate traits such as competitive spirit and a win-as-a-team attitude. Within ninety days of being hired, candidates participate in a weeklong Becoming Salesforce cultural immersion program. The experience features fireside chats with executives, values-focused breakout sessions, and volunteer projects in local communities.

AN INTERNAL SUPPORT NETWORK.   Experienced salespeople come with skills, but they sometimes underestimate how differently companies operate. Be the guide who helps them understand the company's resources and decision-making processes. Make it a point to connect them to stakeholders and colleagues across the organization. Create opportunities for them to socialize and form relationships, just as you do with new-to-sales hires.

LEARNING FROM EXPERIENCED HIRES. There is much that a manager can teach a new hire. But there is also much the manager can learn from the individual. Someone's early weeks are excellent for developing unique insights that they can bring about markets, customers, sales tools, and management processes. Selected ideas can be shared with others on the team or at the company.

Whether you are onboarding new-to-sales or experienced hires, check in with them frequently throughout the process. Ask for feedback about how things are going and what can be improved.

––––––––––––

The hiring decisions you make have a profound and lasting impact on the performance of your team. By hiring individuals who have what it takes to succeed, you are well positioned to excel at the next building block of talent management: helping your salespeople continuously improve their knowledge and skills through learning and development. That is the topic of the next chapter.

Checklist of critical tasks for hiring salespeople

- ❑ Before a candidate search, update the list of competencies you'll screen for, based on competencies of proven winners.

- ❑ Maintain a short list of internal and external candidates (people "on the bench") to help you fill vacancies as they appear.

- ❑ Celebrate and recognize successful referrals in front of the entire team.

- ❑ Make sure the interviewing process is rigorous, especially for senior hires. No one wants to join a club that's easy to get into.

❑ Have different interviewers share their ratings with each other before discussing candidates. (If you don't, the opinion of the first person to speak will carry an unduly high weight.)

❑ Make sure successful candidates feel that they were successful in the interview; recognize their strengths and ideas.

❑ Focus on attracting candidates not only after the offer is made but also throughout the recruiting process.

❑ Help all new hires get early wins and establish networks.

❑ Especially with experienced hires, spend formal and informal time with them so that they're steeped in company culture.

6.

Empowering Salespeople with Continuous Learning and Development

Complex sales environments, customers' evolving knowledge and expectations, and technological advancements make it imperative for sales teams to stay equipped with up-to-date knowledge, adaptive skills, and a customer-centric mindset. A key to long-term success is continuous learning through skilling, upskilling, and reskilling. An effective learning and development (L&D) program links its content to the sales organization's strategy. Then it delivers that content using a mix of methods that cater to the diverse preferences and lifestyles of modern learners in today's workforce. (See figure 6-1.)

FIGURE 6-1

A model of L&D

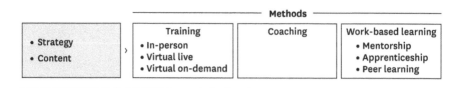

		Methods	
• Strategy • Content >	Training • In-person • Virtual live • Virtual on-demand	Coaching	Work-based learning • Mentorship • Apprenticeship • Peer learning

This chapter begins by sharing insights about the strategy and content of an effective L&D program for your sales team. Then it describes the three prongs of that program—training, coaching, and work-based learning—that serve separate but complementary purposes.

- **Training** is the structured process of helping individuals acquire knowledge, develop skills, and improve competencies. Content can be pushed out to them (such as in a live or a virtual classroom) or "pulled" on demand (such as from a website or library of videos). Training is the dual responsibility of the learner and the trainer.

- **Coaching** is a one-on-one, collaborative, personalized, and ongoing process in which a coach helps a learner discover their strengths and weaknesses and enhance their skills. A coach asks questions, actively listens, and supports the salesperson in self-discovery and problem-solving. Sales managers are usually the coaches for their salespeople.

- **Work-based learning (WBL)** includes a variety of experiential methods in which learning happens on the job by doing and observing. We take an expanded view of WBL that includes formal programs, such as an apprenticeship, and less formal methods, such as seeking out advice from mentors or peers.

This chapter describes your role as a sales manager in blending all these L&D opportunities for your people, and concludes with some insights about current trends. You will also want to reference chapter 17 to learn more about how digital is bringing change to all three methods.

Of the three L&D methods, sales managers spend the most time as the head coach for their people. With training and WBL, by contrast, your role is to orchestrate and provide feedback while others take the lead. Thus, the coaching section is the most detailed of this chapter and includes how-to, practical advice. The training and WBL sections are more observational, designed to help you understand the possibilities so you can guide your people toward the right learning opportunities.

Although this chapter focuses on your role in guiding the learning and development of your team members, L&D is important for your own success as well. Many of the ideas we share can also support your personal development.

Strategy and content

An effective sales L&D program focuses on both the collective needs of the organization and the personal development plan of each team member.

Organizational strategy and L&D content

The organization's changing L&D needs are driven by forces in four areas—offerings, sales strategy, opportunities to leverage digital, and a desire to propagate local success more broadly. Here are examples of each.

- **Offerings.** When Google Cloud Platform hired a large number of experienced sellers from Oracle, Microsoft, Amazon, and others, the L&D program for new hires focused on offerings and solutions for key markets.

- **Sales strategy.** When steel manufacturer Deacero revamped its sales strategy, salespeople had to shift their approach with customers. Instead of selling what was in inventory, they had to proactively prioritize accounts, anticipate market needs, and sell value. L&D and change management programs focused on building key account management skills and solution selling muscle. (More on Deacero in chapter 20.)

- **Digital leverage.** UCB, a biopharmaceutical company, launched a digital platform that gave salespeople access to data about opportunities, next-best-action recommendations, and other insights. Training and coaching helped sellers learn how to use the system and embed it in their customer cadence.

- **Propagating local success.** At ZS, the most successful client teams bring the full range of our offerings to their clients. We conduct workshops in which these teams share insights about how other client teams can familiarize themselves with new offerings and identify opportunities where clients can benefit from them. The sessions also cover strategies for integrating ZS solution specialists into sales discussions and delivering solutions.

Personal development plans

A salesperson's L&D plan specifies content, delivery channels, and methods (a mix of training, coaching, and WBL) that are tailored to the individual's needs. Factors that influence the plan include the salesperson's career stage, sales role, and gaps in capabilities (defined by the competency model described in chapter 4), as well as gaps in their skills and knowledge that could emerge as role requirements evolve. An L&D plan is developed in collaboration with each team member and their manager and can be informed or supplemented by external assessments. The plan is a living blueprint that usually is updated quarterly.

- **Collaboration between manager and sales team member.** The process is anchored by one-on-one meetings in which the manager and salesperson discuss the salesperson's career goals, aspirations, and areas where they seek improvement. Together, they review performance data, feedback from colleagues and customers, and a self-assessment the salesperson has completed. They outline specific objectives, focusing on how these goals align with those of both the individual and the organization. This approach ensures that the development plan is personally tailored, realistic, and linked to tangible outcomes. (A trend toward self-directed learning, as discussed at the end of this chapter, is giving employees a greater role in creating their personalized development plan.)

- **Utilization of external assessments.** The collaborative process can be enhanced by leveraging third-party tools or services to assess the skills, strengths, and areas for development of sales team members. These assessments provide unbiased insights about emotional intelligence, leadership qualities, and other competencies that might not be fully captured through internal reviews.

The L&D plan outlines a tailored learning pathway that allows the salesperson to pursue their goals. This might include a combination of online courses for skill development, in-person workshops for practice and feedback, mentorship programs for guidance and insight from experienced professionals, and shadowing opportunities to learn specific roles or tasks. For example, the learning pathway for a salesperson aiming to improve negotiation skills might include role-play exercises, negotiation workshops, and one-on-one coaching from a negotiation expert. Progress along these pathways is regularly reviewed, allowing for adjustments based on feedback, new goals, or changing business needs.

Learning pathways typically include all three prongs of your L&D program—training, coaching, and WBL.

Training

Training programs are structured and repeatable. They are part of the solution for addressing many sales force challenges—whether launching a product, seeking to boost new business development, or getting more usage out of the CRM system. Training has lasting power when it is reinforced through coaching and WBL. It also has an evolving palette, with solutions delivered in a variety of media and methods.

Salespeople in Apple's retail stores ("geniuses," in the company's parlance) participate in a training program called Pathways throughout their first year. Learners are empowered to assess their own skill level, suggest what training they need, and determine when they are ready to work independently. Geniuses are encouraged to use the Loop, an internal platform that facilitates peer-to-peer learning. For example, an Apple employee who has successfully addressed questions about iPads' power capacity can share a video clip offering advice and tips. Each employee starts their shift by checking Hello, an app that provides briefings on important news of the day. This keeps all employees aligned with Apple's vision and helps the company stay connected to its workforce.

In many cases, sales L&D programs are developed and delivered by an internal department or an external company. The trainer can be a sales manager but is more often another person, either from inside or outside the company. In some circumstances, the manager is the trainer. For example, pharmaceutical company Novartis rolled out a Performance Frontier program to help salespeople learn skills that differentiate high performers from average ones. Trainers from headquarters held "train the trainer" sessions for sales managers. That way, managers were seen as advocates of the program, making all salespeople more likely to adopt the skills learned.

Instructor-led and on-demand training

Effective instructor-led training, whether in person or virtual, minimizes the time learners spend passively listening. An experiential learning model that is active and problem-centered—through case studies, role-playing exercises, and discussions—will foster salespeople's ability to apply knowledge in real-world contexts. The mindset of training has expanded from "Here's what salespeople need to know; we'll teach you," to one of "Here are examples of situations you will face and how you can respond."

Many organizations have replaced much of their in-person classroom training with virtual instructor-led training. This makes it easier and less expensive to rapidly reskill and upskill remote and geographically dispersed workers. Effective virtual training does not simply replicate what is done in person. It leverages features such as breakout sessions, whiteboarding, online polls, and chats, and daylong sessions can be broken into multiple shorter modules.

However, virtual is not a cure-all. It can be challenging for trainers to keep learners' attention and to observe nonverbal cues and adjust their approach. And in-person training is still the best option for fostering teamwork and cultivating culture.

Much of sales training has gone digital. On-demand learning platforms provide access to training content anytime, anywhere. Self-service resources, such as online courses, tutorials, and podcasts, empower individuals to select learning materials that are relevant to their needs. Driven by digital, changing work dynamics, and evolving business needs, workplace training is undergoing a significant change. (More about this in the "L&D trends" section at the end of this chapter and in chapter 17.)

Combining training methods to reinforce learning

Often, the most effective learning happens when a combination of training methods is used. When a global digital marketing company wanted to help its salespeople elevate their consultative selling skills, salespeople first completed online training modules. Next, they participated in in-person classroom workshops led by an instructor, which included customized role-plays. This reinforced the new skills through practice, feedback, and coaching. After the workshops, employees had access to on-demand refresher content, and a mobile app delivered periodic skills-based questions to people in the field, tracking their correct answers on a leaderboard. This approach made learning fun and helped make the content stick. Coaching is also critical for reinforcing concepts learned in training—as we explore next.

Coaching

We often hear from sales leaders that coaching is a manager's most important role. While training provides salespeople with a foundation, personalized coaching supports the application, adaptation, and continuous development of skills in a real-world context. It also positively affects retention.

Most sales managers got promoted because they were good at selling. And experience as a salesperson helps managers earn the respect of the people who report to them. But being a great salesperson does not automatically make you a great coach. The history of sports is full of legendary players who made unsuccessful coaches. Although sales coaching is like sports coaching in many ways, there are differences. In sports you're off the field, never on; in sales you're mostly off the field, but sometimes you work with customers alongside the salesperson. Unlike in sports, you do not see every play. The objective of sales coaching is to improve the play even when you are not around.

Importantly, coaching works. Even the best athletes receive it, whether in a team sport such as basketball or an individual sport such as tennis. Coaching helps the B and C players, but it also helps the A players; it is difficult to see our own blind spots. Further, the changing world necessitates constant upskilling and periodic reskilling.

What sales managers need for effective coaching

Successful coaching is founded on a solid base of knowledge and personal characteristics. It involves a methodical process of discovering, diagnosing, and facilitating change.

Foundational knowledge

To coach an athlete, you don't have to be a great player, but you do have to understand the game. Similarly, to coach a salesperson, you need foundational knowledge of core aspects of their role. This includes a grasp of local market dynamics so you can help the person align their actions with the company's strategy. You must know your products and services along with the needs, preferences, and behaviors of the target customers. You need to understand the sales process and how to manage the pipeline and territory. And you need to be proficient with the technologies and tools that salespeople are using.

Effective coaching also requires insight about the seller, including their experience, knowledge, skills, and performance history. (See chapter 4 for more on talent management.) Further, you can increase your effectiveness if you understand how the salesperson learns (for example, by hearing, seeing, doing) and their preferred modes of communication (such as being direct or collaborative).

Characteristics of an effective coach

There are several characteristics needed. These include a people-first leadership style, characterized by empathy, adaptability, and a genuine care for the well-being of others. A good coach is open to change and capable of responding effectively to new situations and challenges.

A common mistake that managers make is doing too much telling and not enough asking. Statements that undermine your coaching effectiveness include: "I always do it like this . . ."; "You should do the following . . ."; "This works for everyone . . ."; "I'll take the lead here . . ."

By asking questions, you develop salespeople's self-awareness, which helps them diagnose their deficiencies and take ownership of their performance. Questions such as the following enhance your coaching effectiveness:

- "What is the agenda for the customer visit? What do you think are some of the roles we should play?"

- "What are your thoughts on the advance we are trying to achieve with this customer today? How do you think we can achieve it?"

- "I know you can do this better. Can I observe the visit and give you feedback later?"

- "Let's brainstorm some obstacles or barriers. What can we do to overcome them?"

A sales manager's coaching model

Armed with foundational knowledge and the right personal characteristics, sales managers execute two key coaching steps—*discovery/diagnosis* and *activation*. Executing these steps well builds salespeople's knowledge, skills,

FIGURE 6-2

A model of coaching

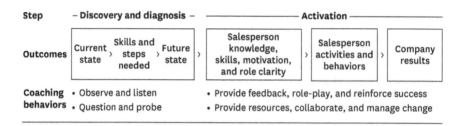

Step   – Discovery and diagnosis – ———————— Activation ————————

| Outcomes | Current state | > | Skills and steps needed | > | Future state | > | Salesperson knowledge, skills, motivation, and role clarity | > | Salesperson activities and behaviors | > | Company results |

Coaching behaviors
- Observe and listen
- Question and probe

- Provide feedback, role-play, and reinforce success
- Provide resources, collaborate, and manage change

motivation, and role clarity. This leads to a positive change in their activities and behaviors, which ultimately drives company results. (See figure 6-2.)

Discovery and diagnosis is where the coach works with the salesperson to pinpoint improvement opportunities. It involves observing the seller's behavior and listening, especially during customer interactions. It's also about asking questions and probing to help the salesperson uncover issues, opportunities, and solutions. When discovery and diagnosis are successful, both the manager and the seller understand the current state, the desired future state, and the skills and steps required to go from one to the other.

Activation is the actionable part of sales coaching. It is where you work with the salesperson to implement improvements and new strategies. This phase translates the insights gained during the discovery and diagnosis phase into tangible results. Activities include:

- Offering constructive feedback to guide improvement

- Role-playing scenarios to enhance skills and build confidence

- Encouraging the salesperson to strive for their goals and maintain a positive mindset, especially when facing challenges

- Providing the necessary tools, information, support, and resources

- Collaborating with the salesperson to demonstrate new approaches or to advance the customer relationship

- Managing change with the seller so that they own it

A cadence for coaching

Coaching is an ongoing process. Every one-on-one interaction between a manager and a salesperson is an opportunity to coach, whether it's a quarterly business review, a sales sprint check-in, or an unplanned, informal discussion. An important component of coaching is the manager ride-along, where you accompany the salesperson on customer visits. These in-field sessions should have a regular cadence; typically they happen one to two times a month per salesperson and last from half a day to a full day. The objectives and frequency depend on the person's career stage and performance. For example, a medical device company that places substantial emphasis on coaching uses the following guidelines:

- **Star performers:** three half-days a month to recognize, monitor, learn, and assist

- **Rising performers:** four half-days a month to boost customer knowledge, sales skills, confidence, and effort allocation

- **Low performers:** two half-days a month to assess and improve or redirect

Ride-along sessions usually include one or more joint customer visits, followed by a debrief. (See table 6-1.) Almost always, these meetings are best done in person, not over the phone or even over videoconference. In the words of one sales manager, "You can't coach from behind a computer screen. You can't do it in a classroom." The most effective approach comes from observing people in action and then probing to help them discover ways to improve.

Don't discount the value of ride-alongs. If you think, "My winners are already successful, I just let them be," that's a serious mistake. As one manager put it, "Don't starve the eagles and feed the chickens." Remember, even the best athletes have coaches.

TABLE 6-1

Coaching steps for ride-along sessions

Step	Manager and salesperson	Manager	Salesperson
Plan	• Schedule joint customer visits • Set objectives (One to two times per month per salesperson)		
Prepare	• Discuss objectives, roles, and plans for visits (salesperson leads discussion)	• Review objectives	• Review objectives • Prepare plans and supporting materials
Execute	• Visit customers using agreed-upon roles and plans	• Lead short debrief after each visit	• Ask manager for a short debrief after each visit
Coach and debrief	• Discuss ideas for improving performance • Set new performance objectives • Agree on next steps	• Ask salesperson to analyze performance • Document feedback in short email to salesperson	• Share thoughts on performance • Summarize key takeaways of the day

Checklist of critical tasks for coaching salespeople

❑ Spend the most time with rising performers, but spend time with high performers also.

❑ Aside from in-field coaching, also coach team members on account planning and strategy.

❑ For each salesperson, maintain a cheat sheet with the key sales actions to emphasize; they should align with the objectives you agreed on during their performance reviews or in prior coaching sessions.

❑ Before a coaching debrief, script the discussion (opening, messages, examples, exercises, next steps). Reflect on someone's potential objections to your points and plan how you will respond.

❑ When making critical observations, frame them in a supportive way, using sentences such as, "When I was a salesperson, I also used to . . . until I found out . . ."

- ❏ Observe the seller's body language for signs of objection to or disengagement from your feedback; when needed, do something different to engage the person.

- ❏ Check that you are not taking up all the airtime in the meeting. Use pauses and probing questions to allow a two-way dialogue.

- ❏ Spend more time coaching when your environment is evolving, helping salespeople navigate changing waters.

Work-based learning

As sales jobs grow more complex, WBL approaches bring training and coaching to life with hands-on, on-the-job practice. Such programs integrate learning into people's jobs through formal apprenticeship and mentorship programs, as well as through less formal exchanges of information, such as those among peers.

Apprenticeship

In apprenticeship programs, a senior salesperson brings a new seller on customer visits and involves them throughout the sales process. The experienced person is not a coach or a trainer. Rather, their role is to provide opportunities for the apprentice to learn by observing and by gradually taking on more-complex tasks with increasing autonomy. Apprenticeship is a great way for new salespeople to adapt to the company's ways of working and to learn nuances such as how to collaborate, when to lead, and when to hold back. It also helps the more experienced person develop the mentorship and coaching skills they will need to advance and take on leadership roles.

Mentorship

Mentorship is a professional relationship in which an experienced and knowledgeable salesperson (the mentor) provides ongoing guidance, support, and coaching to a less experienced seller (the mentee). Mentors offer ideas on how the mentee can improve in their current job, as well as general career advice. Although a mentor can be from outside someone's company, here we focus on internal people who facilitate WBL.

The mentor-mentee relationship isn't supervisory in nature—the manager remains the supervisor. The dynamic is designed to help the mentee develop their skills and accelerate their career in an environment of mutual trust. Mentoring is usually voluntary for both sides and can occur informally or be officially assigned. A novelty gift company assigned two mentors to each new salesperson. One mentor had been in the sales role for one to two years and could relate to the challenges of being new. The other had more experience and could share deeper wisdom.

Blended approaches

Learning is quickly lost unless it is reinforced and used. That's why it is so important to align training, coaching, and WBL. Further reinforcement through performance management helps ensure that people's learning leads to lasting behavior changes. Learning is also reinforced by information support—for example, by providing salespeople with leads and customer insights to complement training on new business development.

One company had a three-stage L&D program to help new hires develop a core set of sales competencies (see table 6-2). The initial classroom-based training was reinforced by virtual follow-up sessions, and then manager-led coaching and case study exercises. Salespeople were also expected to use self-study guides and e-resources to reinforce learning, while digital tools supported specific tasks, such as territory management and targeting. Further, an apprenticeship program assigned new employees to a more senior salesperson who could offer on-the-job guidance.

Although training, coaching, and WBL are all important and work together, the mix can vary by circumstance. To learn about compliance issues, a training program is appropriate. To learn about new products and strategies, a training program backed by coaching works best. When there is high variety in customer contexts, a dynamic environment, or a focus on change and transformation, WBL approaches should be part of the mix. An L&D planning matrix helps you make decisions about the content and the best methods for sharing and reinforcing it. (See table 6-3 for an illustration.)

TABLE 6-2

L&D program for new sales hires

	Stage one (first week on job)	Stage two (after two months on job)	Stage three (after six months on job)
Content: Needed sales skills	• Core product knowledge • Selling skills • Territory management	• Targeting • Selling to groups • Building relationship versatility	• Negotiation • Situational leadership • Collaboration
Training: Length, format, and follow-up	• Three days • Classroom • Virtual (four one-hour sessions over four weeks)	• Two days • Classroom • Virtual (four one-hour sessions over three weeks)	• Two days • External workshop • Virtual (four one-hour sessions)
Coaching and work-based learning: Methods	Manager-led • Coaching to reinforce skills • Case studies • Guided discussions with peers at quarterly sales team meetings Self-managed • Self-study guides, web resources, and tests • Tools for territory management and targeting • Apprenticeship: guidance from an experienced salesperson		

L&D trends

In the L&D world, there has been a decided shift away from classroom-based, top-down programs. Innovative learning strategies such as peer collaboration, self-directed learning, and on-demand microlearning are reshaping professional development. These strategies ensure that content remains timely and relevant, while making it possible to keep up with the fast-evolving needs of learners.

Reliance on peers and external resources

There is a noticeable trend toward learners increasingly relying on peers and external sources for their development, rather than solely on formal corporate L&D programs. With the rapid pace of change in many industries, employees often find that their peers, who are dealing with the same challenges, can provide the most current and practical advice and insights.

TABLE 6-3

L&D planning matrix*

Learning content	Training	Coaching	Work-based learning
Product and service offerings	60%	30%	10%
Market insights	30%	30%	40%
Customer insight	20%	50%	30%
Sales planning	60%	10%	30%
Sales execution	40%	40%	20%
Technology and tools	30%	10%	60%
Policies and compliance	80%	20%	—

*Percentages reflect the relative emphasis on each L&D method in this situation.

To support this trend, organizations are providing platforms and resources to help employees connect with peers and access external learning opportunities. Many companies set up online communities to help salespeople collaborate and share knowledge. Members can post questions and comments, while the company monitors content to avoid any spread of erroneous information and ensure the site stays current and focused. One company asked high-performing experienced salespeople and managers to record videos of themselves giving advice about specific job challenges. The videos became part of a library that any salesperson or manager could access when needed.

Emphasis on self-directed learning

Self-directed learning empowers individuals to chart their own learning paths, while ensuring alignment with both individual and organizational goals. Learners enjoy the flexibility to focus on areas of interest or necessity at their own pace, fostering deeper engagement and better learning outcomes. Organizations nurture self-direction by advocating its benefits, offering varied and accessible learning resources, and fostering a culture that encourages continuous growth and self-paced advancement. Organizations must also provide a supportive framework that makes guidance and resources readily available. Managers act as a sounding board and help ensure that each individual's development plan aligns with company goals.

On-demand microlearning for just-in-time training

Microlearning aims to provide learners with quick and targeted learning experiences that are relevant to their immediate needs. Consider the case of a large B2B telecommunications provider. The company traditionally conducted technical sales training through multiday in-person or virtual sessions. The long planning time required to implement these sessions made it difficult to keep content aligned with the pace of product innovation and customers' ever-changing needs. So, the company embraced a microlearning, just-in-time approach. Online modules (videos, games, infographics) were developed to deliver content in bite-size, focused chunks. Sales engineers could access these modules on demand to get the exact information required to solve a customer's problem. If they encountered a new problem or found a better solution, they could share their insights with others by posting on a message board. Some content was made available to customers as well, allowing them to address issues quickly without a sales technician. A microlearning approach caters to the busy and fragmented schedules of sales teams. By delivering more digestible content precisely when it's needed, team members can apply what they learn immediately and retain it better as well.

More L&D trends are covered in section 3 of this book. Chapter 13 discusses digital-age sales competencies, and chapter 17 explores the impact of digital on L&D.

———

Continuous learning is critical for salespeople and managers, and the best organizations embed it into their cultures. Sellers who are constantly learning are more successful, engaged, motivated, and likely to stay in their roles. And their continued growth is reinforced by the managers who coach them and support their ongoing learning. L&D is a key tool that managers use as part of performance management, which is the topic of the next chapter.

7.

Managing Performance to Drive Results

Successful sales managers tailor their performance management approach to each salesperson. People have varied strengths, weaknesses, and preferences, and each person operates in a specific customer and market environment. Recognizing and understanding these differences will help you manage and motivate your salespeople while supporting them in taking accountability for their success.

In this chapter we discuss the following topics:

- How to implement an approach to performance management that links inputs (salespeople and their activities and behaviors) to desired outcomes for customers and your company

- How to customize your approach to managing each salesperson, based on their current performance level and their potential to grow

Sales performance: Managing inputs and outcomes

The goal of performance management is to ensure that salespeople engage in activities and behaviors that drive personal performance and company results. Tailoring your approach begins with understanding who each person is and what they do (inputs) as well as their performance and results (outcomes). These insights come from several sources. (See figure 7-1.)

A performance management cadence

Your goal is to help each salesperson stay on a continuous path of success. The typical cadence of planning, performance reviews, coaching, and meetings with your team consists of the following:

- **Annual and quarterly one-on-one planning sessions.** Meet individually with each salesperson to review their development plan and progress, set goals and expectations, and develop and refine their approach for meeting those goals and expectations.

- **Monthly meetings.** Work with team members (either individually or as a group, virtually or in person) to discuss collective goals and progress, validate and adapt plans, recognize successes, provide

FIGURE 7-1

A model of sales performance management

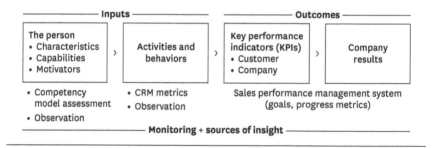

learning and development opportunities, and share customer insights and best practices.

- **Biweekly joint customer visits.** Accompany each salesperson on customer visits. Debrief, provide feedback, and coach the person on their skill development.

- **Biweekly or weekly sprint meetings.** As you meet with each salesperson to review their progress and to plan customer advances (see chapter 3), supplement the discussion with coaching on customer strategies.

The conversations during this cadence can be supported by documents and data gathered from the sources highlighted in figure 7-1. The data should be visible to both the manager and the salesperson. (AI and analytics are making this kind of data increasingly valuable, as we will explore in chapter 11.) Dashboards and reports track progress on key performance indicators about outcomes, including someone's performance, company results (e.g., sales, profits, and goal attainment), and customer results (e.g., satisfaction, retention, and renewal rates). Metrics track the inputs as well, such as time spent with customers, proposals sent, and pipeline progress— the daily effort of people's jobs. Self-assessments and your assessments of salespeople's competencies (as specified in competency models) are also part of these ongoing discussions.

Besides setting the right cadence, don't underestimate the value of agenda-free and unplanned check-ins. These conversations with your salespeople allow you to listen, discover opportunities, provide support, build trust, foster collaboration, and improve morale and motivation. Check-ins show your team that you are not just a machine pushing for results.

Four types of performers and how to manage them

As you assess each salesperson, it's important to keep in mind that outcomes are consequences. A manager's actions influence the inputs that lead to the consequences.

FIGURE 7-2

Strategies for managing salespeople in four performance segments

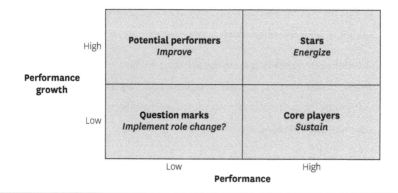

There are many factors that combine to affect someone's outcomes (including career stage, level of competence, effort, and growth), and each combination suggests a set of tactics for managing performance. Here we describe four broad segments of salespeople based on two key dimensions: performance and growth. (See figure 7-2.) The sections that follow summarize managerial actions—include training, coaching, motivating, and rewarding—for improving and sustaining performance within each segment.

Energizing your stars

Star salespeople bring in a disproportionate share of results. They are also in high demand: you want to recruit your competitors' stars; they want to recruit yours. LinkedIn, Glassdoor, and other online platforms help these people know their market value. Often there are highly variable rates of retention for stars across companies in the same industry—which is why energizing your top performers *does* make a difference. (Retention strategies are explored further in chapter 9.)

You'll need the support of your company to ensure stars have competitive compensation and benefits as well as opportunities for personal development and career growth. In addition, there are some basic tools for getting stars to stay and perform:

- Recognition and appreciation

- New challenges and opportunities

- Support with time and resources

- A positive work environment that fosters open communication and collaboration

Beyond these core approaches, you can use some frequently missed techniques to keep stars engaged and motivated.

Being fair

Fairness matters for salespeople at all performance levels, but it has an out-size impact on star performers. Consider the case of Susan, a top performer, and James, a medium one. Both sellers end the year at 125 percent of their goal and earn equal incentive payouts. Later, Susan learns that James was given an easier goal, and rightly sees it as a lack of *outcome fairness*. Rewards and recognition are motivating only when they are perceived to match people's effort and skill. Now let's take another situation. Susan is overjoyed at being tapped to advise on a new product launch in a category she knows exceptionally well. She later learns that she was picked at random from a group of all salespeople who made their goal. The knowledge demotivates Susan due to a lack of *process fairness*; the decision was made in a nonobjective and irrational manner.

Workload fairness is also frequently lacking for top performers. Too often, we observe sales managers giving a disproportionately large share of their region's goal to their stars—the ones they can rely on to deliver. While this may lead to a higher likelihood of achieving the goal for a few quarters, it is an unsustainable strategy. Placing an unfair burden on high performers may cause them to feel resentful, burn out, or look for a new job. When individuals are given higher goals, they must be compensated commensurately with higher rewards.

Spending time with strong performers

Some managers use the mantra, "I take a hands-off approach with my high performers. I spend my time with people I need to help, direct, or push."

Although this approach can boost performance in the short term, it is a serious mistake through the lens of retention. You must spend time with strong performers—learning from them, recognizing their achievements, and monitoring them to understand their evolving needs. Observe what motivates them and watch for signs of disengagement.

Providing visibility and an opportunity to influence

Medical device company Boston Scientific hosts "meet the experts" events at which salespeople who excel in certain areas share their expertise with the rest of the team. High performers are also invited to participate on an advisory board that meets twice a year with senior company leaders. These top performers provide input on strategic issues while getting visibility that can enhance their careers. Salespeople on the advisory board also help communicate important messages to the rest of the sales force, especially in moments of change.

Improving potential performers

Potential performers are the people who could grow into stars, given the right nurturing and opportunities. The best approach to managing them depends on their career stage.

Early-career team members

These salespeople are still exploring selling as a profession, so focus on building their competence and confidence. They are constantly asking themselves two questions:

- Can I really succeed here?

- Is this the right career for me?

Early success begins a virtuous cycle. When new salespeople enjoy the job and taste early achievement, their confidence builds and they are more likely to excel and stay. Conversely, early setbacks can be a motivation and retention killer. You can keep winning streaks going (and turn losing streaks around) through ongoing skill development. Effective tactics include:

- Focusing on skill progression, starting with product knowledge, communication, and time management before moving on to customer understanding, relationship management, pipeline management, and negotiation

- Coaching on skills and behaviors first, and then, as someone's success builds, shifting to results as well

- Sharing market insights that help new salespeople develop a deeper understanding of the market and competitors

- Nurturing self-discovery, rather than using directives

There are some industries in which new salespeople routinely struggle to get off the ground. For example, with some types of insurance, sellers' earnings come primarily from commissions, and many find it difficult to build a book of business. At one insurance company, many new agents (as salespeople are typically called in the industry) had a hard time. They sold supplemental policies to employers and earned all their pay in the form of commissions on sales. Since more than 60 percent of new agents left before completing their first year, the company's investments in recruiting, training, and managing were being poorly spent. To help agents find early success, sales managers began focusing on three priorities:

- **Account assignments.** Managers began giving new agents a few existing customer accounts that were easy to close. This increased the odds of making a sale quickly, thus boosting people's belief that they could succeed in the job.

- **Training and coaching.** Managers also doubled down on training and coaching agents during their critical first year, helping them master the skills they needed. Occasionally managers would help close deals while they coached, but did so in a way that let the new person feel they contributed.

- **Incentives and motivation.** The company began offering agents an "early success" bonus for achieving a sales milestone within their first month. Agents received frequent digital nudges about their progress toward this milestone.

With these efforts, first-year agent performance and retention improved significantly.

Established sellers

These potential performers are the rising B players who have what it takes to become A players. Provide them with the right opportunities, management, and attention to allow them to master new challenges and skills. Some of these salespeople may be former A players who have lost their edge as the sales environment changed. For example, a salesperson who excels at in-person interactions may need to get comfortable talking to customers virtually. A manager can help the person build new capabilities and reemerge as a star.

New but experienced hires

While early success still matters for new but experienced hires, the effort to energize and retain this group hinges more on acculturation. Salespeople who come from other companies need support in acclimating to the culture, as well as in building internal networks and connections to foster their sense of belonging and engagement with the organization.

Sustaining core players

Core players produce good results but show little or no growth. A frequent challenge is that they may become content with their current level of performance, so they ease up on the throttle. A variety of terms are used to describe this situation—plateaued, complacent, quiet quitting, coasting, disengaged—but the result is the same: missed opportunities with customers. The good news is that you can anticipate their disengagement and prevent it, or take action to turn things around.

Is disengagement always bad?

Consider the following scenario. A career salesperson has been working for fifteen years. He has contributed consistently but no longer has the intensity he once had; now he has other priorities that include family, hobbies, and community. He's able to maintain acceptable performance with less and lower-intensity effort.

So why not let him do it? After all, he has earned it. But someone's lack of intensity usually comes with consequences. Suppose sales will grow 20 percent a year for the next four years if this salesperson stays engaged. If he plateaus, customers stop getting the needed attention, opportunities with new products and services are missed, and few new customers are acquired. Or say territory sales growth drops to 5 percent per year. Over four years, the gap compounds and 35 percent of territory sales will be lost! On top of that, the company's position in the marketplace weakens while competitors' positions grow stronger. Plus, disengagement is contagious. Other salespeople see it as an aspirational model of success: "If I work hard for another five years, maybe I can reach the same level of comfort."

In the early 2000s, a US technology distributor faced the consequences of disengagement. As the market for technology skyrocketed, the company's veteran salespeople amassed lucrative territories of customers who purchased repeatedly. These veterans didn't have to work hard and felt no urgency to acquire new buyers. Meanwhile, the distributor struggled to hold on to new sellers, who found it difficult to develop a book of business. Things got worse when market growth slowed and scrappy digital competitors moved into the legacy markets, meaning the sales force had to sell new products to new customers. Veterans kept collecting their paychecks, while the company's profitability plummeted.

We've seen this drama play out multiple times, and it never ends well. The typical situation involves a confluence of factors: a seller in an advantageous position in a growing market, an incentive plan that rewards sales (as opposed to growth), a large volume of repeat sales from existing customers, and a "let winners run" mindset in which successful salespeople are minimally supervised. But turbulence hits when the market shifts and growth slows. Leaders then regret not taking preventive action years earlier.

Pay attention to pockets of disengagement

Disengagement on sales teams usually starts with a few salespeople. A formerly successful seller thinks, "I've been in this job a long time, I'm earning a decent income, and I'm tired of working hard." Managers tolerate the attitude because the disengaged person is generating reasonable results. And if the salesperson controls relationships with key customers, there is risk if the manager interferes. The longer the manager waits to act, though, the harder it becomes to turn things around. You can guard against this risk by building relationships with key decision-makers and ensuring important customers have many connections to the company, thereby preventing the complacent salesperson from having excessive control. If pockets of disengagement are tolerated, complacency may dominate the sales culture before long.

Preventing disengagement from starting

The tactics discussed earlier for energizing stars are also effective at sustaining the performance of core players. Here are some other possible actions:

- **Make changes to job responsibilities.** Salespeople who face constant challenges in their jobs and who come to expect and embrace change have little opportunity to feel disengaged. New products and promotional programs naturally bring novelty. Adjustments to customer assignments bring new challenges. Occasional special assignments keep people connected and stimulated.

- **Ensure that incentive compensation isn't contributing.** Plans that pay salespeople based on their goal attainment, sales growth, or new business development—rather than for their total sales—can keep people focused on growth and new opportunities. Although managers usually don't control the incentive plan directly, your input helps sales heads and others who influence the plan's design address problems early, before complacency can take root.

At the life insurance company Northwestern Mutual, signs of complacency often emerge after salespeople have been in the job for twelve to fifteen years—long enough for someone to master the job, build a book of business, and earn a good income without working very hard. Sales managers find that recognition is more effective at motivating this group than offering additional money is. New products also help keep these salespeople engaged and continually expanding business with their existing clients.

Implementing role changes for question marks

For salespeople who are low performers and are not on a growth trajectory, the key is to act quickly. If these individuals don't have the characteristics required for success—and the problem cannot be reasonably corrected through training, development, support, or other managerial actions—retaining them too long has a great cost to both the organization and the individuals themselves.

As soon as you recognize that someone is mismatched with their job, act quickly. Communicating about the situation clearly can help the person see that their strengths aren't aligned with their role and that they have more potential to succeed elsewhere. Typically, these conversations are more easily accepted when the sales force is downsizing or reorganizing, since many people will be losing their jobs or switching roles. But even when such changes are not happening, it's important to have these discussions. Change is not only the right move for the company; it's usually the right long-term solution for the employee as well. Good performance management helps you identify issues early on, and regular, frank communication with a salesperson about their effectiveness ensures that they will not be caught by surprise. Further, support from the HR team can help you deal with situations in a respectful and legally sound manner.

If you have many salespeople in this category, you'll need to improve your hiring process (see chapter 5). By honing your skills at selecting the right candidates, you'll spend less time dealing with low performers, leaving more time to develop and motivate your currently and potentially strong team members. The vast majority of your performance management efforts should be directed at energizing your stars and core players while developing your potential performers to help them become stars.

The framework in this chapter gives you a good starting point for thinking about how to manage your four categories of people. But keep in mind that each salesperson is unique. Consistently improving and sustaining their performance requires tailoring your approach to the needs of the individual. Salespeople in any segment may learn best in different ways; some may be energized by overcoming challenges (for example, landing new customers), while others want recognition, and still others are motivated by money. Monetary incentives are almost universally used as a tool for managing and energizing salespeople—and that is the topic of the next chapter.

Checklist of critical tasks for personalizing performance management

- ❏ For each salesperson, keep a list of two to three areas of focus for improving or sustaining their skills, motivation, and performance.

- ❏ Do not determine someone's performance solely on their sales results; consider their behaviors, values, and contributions. Use objective criteria that are based on metrics, data, and firsthand observation.

- ❏ Spend more time with top performers than with low performers.

- ❏ Proactively seek opportunities to give personal and public recognition of salespeople's success.

- ❏ Be on the lookout for signs of complacency, and be proactive in eradicating it. The best way to prevent complacency is to stop it before it takes hold.

- ❏ Focus on getting new-to-sales team members early wins to boost their confidence.

- ❏ Connect new but experienced hires to the culture and organization.

- ❏ Be proactive and initiate timely, frank, and honest discussions about performance issues.

8.

Motivating Sales Teams with Incentives and Goals

Most sales forces use incentives—monetary payments, usually on top of a base salary, that reward people for achieving and exceeding goals. When sales efforts produce results that can be measured, incentives are an effective way to motivate your team. They become even more important when salespeople work mostly unsupervised.

After salaries, incentives are usually the largest single item in sales force costs. When things go wrong, no program gets as much scrutiny and blame from employees and leaders. And when the sales organization faces new challenges, adjustments to incentive programs are often on the short list of potential solutions. Yet incentives are hard to get right. While they can motivate, provide direction, and align costs with sales, they can also encourage behaviors that are not in the best interests of the company and customers, especially when they're a large component of pay.

Although incentives are an essential part of the sales manager's toolbox, they are only one instrument you can use to direct and motivate sales effort. Incentives have much more power when they are reinforced by other decisions and systems—for example, strong L&D and performance management programs, which are discussed in chapters 6 and 7, respectively.

This chapter covers five topics to help you collaborate with your sales operations team to design a sales incentive program and set goals:

- Understanding what incentives do

- Assembling the building blocks of a plan

- Linking an incentive plan's design to your sales strategy and environment

- Setting goals that motivate

- Assessing an incentive plan's health and performance

Understanding what incentives do

A well-designed sales incentive plan balances four objectives:

1. **Motivate.** Three aspects of an incentive plan motivate salespeople to put forth extra effort. First and most obviously, salespeople's earnings should be linked to their performance. Many plans have higher tiers of payout rates as salespeople reach higher levels of performance. Second, a motivating plan is fair. Fairness requires transparent criteria for earning rewards, equitable treatment of salespeople, achievable goals, and a clear connection between performance and rewards, which includes appropriate rewards for exceptional performance. Third, a motivating plan is simple. If a plan is too complicated, salespeople may not understand it, won't know what they need to do to earn incentives, and may ignore the plan altogether.

2. **Provide direction.** By specifying the kind of results that warrant rewards, an incentive plan guides salespeople in how to spend their time. For example, the company can communicate its priorities by varying incentive payouts for different product lines, or by differentiating payouts for sales to new customers versus existing customers.

3. **Be fiscally responsible.** A well-designed incentive plan keeps costs in line with results. Stronger company results lead to higher payouts in a predictable way. Results include measures such as revenue, profitability, and customer satisfaction.

4. **Adapt to evolving needs.** A plan must also be flexible enough to change in response to shifting market conditions, product lines, and company priorities. Periodic reviews and adjustments keep the plan aligned with the company's financial goals and the market's realities.

Complexities of designing incentive plans

Designing an effective plan can be challenging. It's difficult to strike the right balance between motivation, direction, cost-effectiveness, and flexibility. A simple plan is motivating but may not direct salespeople's attention to strategic customers or products. Conversely, a plan that attempts to encompass numerous customer and product priorities may become overly complex, potentially undermining its motivational power as well as its flexibility to change. Balancing motivation and fiscal responsibility can also be tricky. High payouts that motivate increased sales effort can inadvertently lead to excessive costs or overselling.

Unpredictable market dynamics add another layer of complexity. Windfalls can lead to salespeople being overcompensated, while unexpected challenges can demotivate them. Moreover, sales teams and markets are diverse. For example, designing an incentive plan that works for both a growing territory and a saturated one is not easy.

Further, different types of cash rewards can be used to motivate sales teams over varied time horizons. Incentive plans link payouts to medium-term outcomes, such as achieving quarterly or annual goals. Sales contests can direct attention to shorter-term objectives, while stock options and profit-sharing plans focus on longer-term outcomes such as sustained performance and retention. This chapter explores what most companies consider their core sales incentive program—a plan that links a specified payout to specific medium-term outcomes.

The building blocks of incentive plans

Designing incentive plans involves combining various building blocks, including plan types and metrics and the amount of pay at risk.

Plan types and metrics

Figure 8-1 provides several simplified examples of incentive plans and describes the circumstances in which each is appropriate. The plans are of different types and use different metrics to determine payout.

The design process brings various features and metrics together in a way that helps you achieve business goals. There are numerous possibilities. For example, you can:

- Tier payouts by accelerating or decelerating them with higher levels of performance

- Use multipliers to link individual, team, or company performance

- Use a quota-based bonus plan for goal achievement, then pay commission on sales above quota

Amount of at-risk pay

A plan can put a large or a small amount of pay at risk (versus what is paid as salary). Several factors affect how much that amount should be. The maximum size of the at-risk portion depends on the extent to which sales efforts produce results that you can measure. The higher the measurable impact, the more pay can be at risk. Then, other factors come into play. Your desired sales culture and industry practices both influence at-risk levels. The targeted split between salary and incentive (which is expressed as a ratio—

FIGURE 8-1

Plan types and examples

Plan type	Simplified examples	Appropriate circumstances
Commission	Pay 3% of sales *Other example of commission plan:* Pay 10% of gross margin to goal and 15% above goal	• Largely unsupervised salespeople with short sales cycles • Part-time direct sales forces • Partners and agents • Launch and early-stage growth products with unpredictable sales
Quota-based bonus	$20,000 bonus at 95% of quota* $30,000 bonus at 100% of quota* $10,000 bonus for every 5% over quota* (*Usually a sales quota, but can also be a quota for other results metrics, such as gross margin)	• Complex sales process with longer sales cycle (account management role) • Products with carryover sales • Diversity of customers and market potential across sales territories • Reasonable ability to forecast territory sales
Matrix	**% goal achieved** **Current customers** % goal achieved / New customers vs. Current customers: |	90%	100%	110%
90%	0.4	0.6	0.8
100%	0.8	1.1	1.4
110%	1.2	1.6	2.0 | *Multiple of target pay (Target pay = $25,000)* *Other examples of matrix plans:* Goal achieved for all products vs. strategic products Sales vs. price discount offered	• A need to balance multiple sales priorities • A need to balance conflicting priorities (e.g., sales and price discount)
Management by objectives (MBO)	**MBO** — **% MBO target pay** Complete level-two sales skills training — 20% Conduct four meetings with key decision-makers — 30% Achieve distribution in eight of top ten accounts — 50% **Achieve all three MBOs** — **100%** *Other examples of MBOs:* Create and execute strategic account plans Boost Net Promoter Score	• A need to bring attention to leading indicators of sales • A need for focus on specific objectives that are not part of main incentive plan

salary portion:incentive portion) varies widely by industry and company. For example, channel partners are typically paid using a 0:100 commission-based plan; there is no salary. The same is true for many life insurance sales agents who work largely unsupervised. Industries that want to balance incentives with other tools may target a 50:50, 60:40, or 70:30 ratio. Usually, in such cases, a quota-based bonus plan determines the amount of the incentive payout. Still others may forgo incentives completely (100:0) if there is compliance risk or danger of overselling.

When the incentive portion is large (above 40 percent of target pay), the plan has a dominant influence on how salespeople spend their time. This creates a challenge for managers seeking to direct their salespeople's effort. For example, if you ask the team to focus on strategic products and customers, but incentives are earned on sales of *all* products and customers, employees are likely to ignore your message. Many sales organizations find that the sweet spot for balancing motivation with managerial control is a targeted incentive portion of around 30 percent of total pay.

Linking incentives to the sales strategy and environment

An effective incentive plan motivates the sales team to engage in the right activities for achieving business goals. Here are some examples:

- To increase sales of specific products, boost payment for sales of strategic products, new products, and high-margin products.

- To direct focus to account acquisition, pay more for sales to new customers.

- To drive customer retention, pay incentives for customer retention or renewal.

- To boost the profitability of sales, pay on gross margin or average selling price, or vary payouts by product group (e.g., a higher commission rate for premium versus core products).

- To improve customer satisfaction, tie a portion of the incentive to the achievement of goals for customer satisfaction or Net Promoter Score.

- To encourage team selling, link incentives to team, regional, or company goals.

- To jump-start sales in a selected period, increase the pay rate for, say, the first month of the quarter (a "fast start" emphasis) or a timeboxed period (a blitz).

A good incentive plan addresses the complexity of the environment while reinforcing the activities expected of the sales role and acknowledging the company's confidence about the accuracy of its sales forecasts.

Designing for complex environments

In industries such as office products or standard chemicals, when the sales process is simple and sales cycles are short, a typical incentive plan is linked to short-term individual goals. However, in industries such as cloud services, customized manufacturing equipment, and specialty chemicals, products are multifaceted, customers are diverse, buying is done by multiple decision-makers, deals are larger, and sales cycles are longer and involve multiple salespeople. In these cases, large short-term incentives for individuals can distract from what it takes to succeed. Further, it's difficult for the company to isolate the impact of a single salesperson because that impact unfolds over time and is shared with multiple roles and digital channels.

In complex sales environments, monetary incentives are still important, but plans differ from those used in simpler situations. A typical incentive plan pays for longer-term performance (e.g., quarterly or annual) and often includes features such as the following:

- Shared credit for sales; for example, if an account executive and a solution specialist work together to make a sale, both get credit even though they have separate territories and incentive plans.

- A team-based component, such as a bonus shared by all employees if the team reaches or exceeds its goal.

- An individual component linked to management by objectives (MBOs) for activities, or leading indicators that reflect a salesperson's contributions to team outcomes. Each salesperson works with their manager to set MBOs.

In addition, tools other than incentives generally get more emphasis in complex environments. In simple situations, incentives are often the primary lever for motivating salespeople, such as to bring in new customers. But in complex situations, it usually takes more. For example, in addition to offering an incentive, headquarters might highlight the importance of new account acquisition by supporting salespeople with customer insights (opportunities, decision-makers) and providing customized sales collateral. And managers might get more involved in the sales process.

A holistic sales management approach matches the incentive plan, and other tools for directing and motivating sales activity, to the complexity of the situation.

Matching plans to roles

One company that sells customized software as a service (SaaS) has four sales roles. Each role has its own salary:incentive ratio, metrics, plan structure, and other features. (See table 8-1.) The time frames of the incentive plans also vary to match the impact cycle of each role:

1. Sales development representatives generate and qualify leads (inside role).

2. Account executives acquire customers.

3. Sales engineers work with customers and account executives to tailor solutions.

4. Customer success managers help customers realize value and grow their product consumption.

TABLE 8-1

Incentive plans for sales roles at a SaaS company

Category	Sales development representative (SDR)	Account executive (AE)	Sales engineer	Customer success manager
Role	Generate and qualify leads	Acquire customers	Support customers and AEs with demos and solution design	Help customers realize value and grow usage
Salary:incentive ratio	80:20	50:50	70:30	75:25
Metrics	• Number of leads • Revenue from customers who started as SDR leads	• Total bookings • Revenues	• Product-specific bookings • Total bookings	• Net promoter score • Renewal success • Consumption
Plan structure	• Quota bonus • Role-specific MBOs	• Quota bonus • Commission	Quota bonus	• Quota bonus • Role-specific MBOs
Payout to top earners (90th percentile)	1.3 times target incentive	2.5 times target incentive	2.0 times target incentive	1.5 times target incentive
Payout frequency	Monthly, quarterly	Monthly, quarterly	Quarterly, annually	Quarterly, annually

The effectiveness of the entire process is achieved by paying incentives on a combination of metrics—some that reflect success at the selling stage that the individual is responsible for, and others that reflect downstream results. In table 8-1, sales development reps are paid for the number of leads they generate. But the quality of leads is important too. Quality is captured by a downstream metric—revenue generated by the leads—that affects incentive payouts for the entire customer-facing team.

By aligning the sales incentive plan with the specific requirements and objectives of each sales role, you help maximize motivation, performance, and overall effectiveness of the sales team.

Dealing with unpredictability

Most incentive pay in sales is linked to goal achievement, and goal setting is a perennial challenge. In unpredictable environments (those with competitive activity or first-of-their-kind products, for example), even the best forecasting data and goal-setting methods cannot predict sales well. Several strategies for designing incentive plans can mitigate the demotivating downsides of goals being too high, as well as undeserved payouts if goals are too low.

TIERED SUCCESS MEASURES. This is the most critical adaptation for uncertain environments. Rather than setting goals that focus on a single number, you can define multiple levels of success for salespeople to aim for. For example, incentive pay could start at 75 percent of a success goal, a success range begins at 100 percent, and an excellence range begins at 125 percent. Payouts could accelerate as someone hits each level, and the more uncertain your forecast is, the lower the percentage at which payout begins should be.

SHORT TIME FRAMES. If goals turn out to be unreasonable, short time frames ensure the sales force is affected only for a limited time and the impact is minimized. However, there is a flip side, especially with a longer sales cycle: a shorter time frame produces more variability in performance, and a longer time frame provides more opportunity for variability to average out.

FLATTER PAYOUT CURVES. If sales are unpredictable, you can start payout at a low or no threshold, pay out at one rate up to quota achievement, and accelerate the rate moderately (1.5 or 2 times) beyond quota. Or, you can pay a commission.

PAYOUT CURVES THAT ADJUST WITH COMPANY RESULTS. You can link an individual's incentive payout to their performance relative to the rest of the company, as well as to overall company performance.

MBOs. Management by objectives can be based on skills, activities, or results.

EARNINGS CAPS OR DECELERATORS. Caps (limits on the amount of incentive pay a person can receive) and decelerators (mechanisms that reduce the rate of incentive payout) can be justified in unpredictable environments to protect the company against excessive incentive costs if goals are set too low. However, we generally do not recommend caps and decelerators because they can dampen the motivation of top performers. If you do use them, consider offering a special reward, outside the main incentive plan, to a top performer who gets limited by a cap or a decelerator and who truly deserves the reward.

A biotechnology company changed its sales incentive plan as forecasting accuracy improved over the course of a product's life cycle. For several months leading up to the launch of the company's first product (into a new and largely unknown market), salespeople earned incentives linked to MBOs for prelaunch activities, such as developing account plans and contacting customers to create awareness. For the first year after launch, the company had reasonable confidence in its national sales forecast but lacked data for creating accurate territory-level forecasts. Salespeople earned a commission on total territory sales, plus a small bonus if the national goal was achieved. By the following year, the company could predict sales more accurately by territory. Salespeople earned incentives for attaining territory goals, with payouts starting at 75 percent of the goal and accelerating beyond 100 percent.

Setting goals that motivate

The majority of sales incentive plans connect payout to the achievement of quantitative sales goals or quotas, as well as to MBOs linked to capabilities, activities, or intermediate results that drive sales. Goals help you customize incentive plans for each territory and market. Sales leaders point to setting goals as a persistently difficult challenge, yet doing it well is essential for directing and motivating your team and controlling compensation costs.

Effective goals: Achievable, transparent, and equitable

Leaders often push for higher goals (while salespeople push for lower ones), but counterintuitively, higher goals can lead to lower sales. If a salesperson's goal is so high that they view it as unachievable, they may start to feel disengaged, leading to lower sales than if the goal been set at a reasonable level. On the other hand, if someone's goal is too low, they will achieve it easily, without putting forth any extra effort—the company essentially pays out free money. Setting challenging but achievable quotas and MBOs is essential for an incentive plan to be both motivating and fiscally responsible. If 25 percent of the team do not make their goals, you can attribute that to their skill and effort; if 75 percent don't, the goals were too high.

In addition to being achievable, effective goals are both transparent and equitable. Transparency is realized by using goal-setting methods that salespeople trust. Equitability is about the absence of perceived biases, which can vary with the type of incentive plan. With commission plans, such as those in the insurance industry, salespeople expect to make more money as they build a larger and larger book of business. In fact, junior sales team members aspire to reach the same level of success and pay that their senior peers have achieved. With quota-based bonus plans, salespeople expect that quotas will account for differences in factors they cannot control, such as territory difficulty, market conditions, and past performance.

Using measures of sales potential to set quotas

When setting quantitative goals or quotas fairly across a sales force, having data on unrealized potential in accounts or territories is critical. (But keep in mind: if the company goal is too high, no quota allocation method will fix that.)

Territory potential or market opportunity tries to capture what you could sell in the future. Some industries have measures of market opportunity readily available. For example, in the airline and pharmaceutical industries, there are data companies that sell information on sales of all competitive products by account or local market. In other sectors, creative approaches are required to develop good surrogate measures. A greeting card company used US Census Bureau data to estimate the opportunity at retail stores by looking at population and average household income within a three-mile radius of each store. One company, which sells insurance and financing as part of a bundled service offering on retail sales of motorcycles, uses customer demographic characteristics, competitors, the presence of local credit unions, and the onset of spring weather (triggering an increase in motorcycle sales) to predict territory opportunity. Direct and indirect measures of potential are improving every day, enabling increased accuracy and fairness in quotas. A team at headquarters, such as a sales operations group, typically helps with developing these measures.

Quota-setting formulas

Sales organizations use many different methodologies to set quotas. These range from applying a simple percentage growth expectation to using sophisticated forecasting and analytical techniques. Effective quota-setting formulas combine two key components: carryover and growth.

Carryover is the expected repeat sales that will happen with little or no sales effort. It's usually calculated by applying a percentage to the prior period's sales. The percentage varies by industry. In a recurring revenue environment, such as with cloud services, the carryover percentage can be more than 100 percent if customers will naturally grow their usage. With capital goods, it can be zero if every sale is a new sale. In other cases, the carryover percentage is somewhere in between, since some customer churn is expected each period.

Growth is the expected sales beyond carryover. It's important to consider how much unrealized opportunity there is in a territory when assigning the growth portion of the goal. For example, if a sales territory has 1 percent of the nation's accessible opportunity, that territory is assigned 1 percent of the nation's growth goal.

These concepts are easy for salespeople to understand. You can use advanced analytics and AI to make estimates of carryover and the allocation of growth more precise. But if you do this, it becomes more difficult to explain the logic to salespeople. You will need to balance the value of added precision with the cost of added complication and reduced transparency.

Strengthening your message by using MBOs

Achieving sales quotas is one measure of success. But often, you want to also direct sellers' attention to additional measures. That's where MBOs—specific, relevant, and time-bound goals that reflect a spectrum of inputs and outcomes—are useful.

For example, a pharmaceutical company discovered that patients who participated in education programs were more likely to take their medicines consistently, leading to better long-term health results. The company linked a modest portion of salespeople's incentive pay to an MBO for patient training. Employees earned bonuses if they met or exceeded expectations for the delivery of patient training programs with high attendance and strong completion rates, which drove product adherence.

At a manufacturing company, salespeople earned most of their incentives through a quarterly quota-based bonus plan focused on achieving goals, but they could earn up to an additional $5,000 for MBO achievement. The company provided a menu of thirty-six possible MBOs, and managers worked with their salespeople to craft a set of them that was specific to each employee. The quarterly payouts and MBOs for one person were as follows:

- $2,000: Boost first-quarter sales according to a 1-10-10,000 system; in the first month of the quarter, accumulate at least ten orders of more than $10,000 each

- $1,500: Acquire at least five new accounts

- $1,500: Improve margins by reducing discounting at least 1 percent

MBOs can reflect a range of inputs and intermediate outcomes in four categories. Here are some specific examples in each category:

- **Competency:** achieve proficiency in Sales Navigator; lead a best practice sharing session

- **Activities and behaviors:** adopt or provide feedback on more than 80 percent of suggested next best actions; share or comment on social media posts at least once per week

- **Customer or company KPIs:** achieve ten new customer sign-ups; grow pipeline by 20 percent; achieve a +10 points boost on Net Promoter Score; renew at least 90 percent of accounts

- **Company results:** achieve more than $100,000 in new product bookings; grow revenues in the education customer segment by 25 percent; reduce discounting by 2 percent

In many successful use cases, MBOs are jointly defined by managers and salespeople, fostering collaboration and a sense of ownership. Sales organizations set MBOs annually, semiannually, or quarterly. Changing them quarterly provides flexibility and brings two advantages. First, you introduce novelty and new challenges for salespeople, keeping them engaged and motivated. Second, in fast-paced industries or markets, quarterly updates ensure that objectives remain aligned with current market conditions and the latest strategic shifts. However, MBOs can be onerous to manage and administer, so the advantages of frequent change must be weighed against the costs.

Assessing an incentive plan's health and performance

We often ask sales leaders, "How good is your incentive plan?" When things are going well, a frequent response is, "We're making our numbers; the plan is great." When things are not going well, the common lament is, "Our goals were too high." However, there are better ways to answer the question. A structured approach helps you assess a plan's ability to motivate and direct salespeople while being fiscally responsible.

Is the plan motivating?

When incentive plans are effective, they encourage salespeople to earn extra pay and drive company results. Motivating plans generate high engagement and excitement, and they're fair and simple.

ENGAGEMENT AND EXCITEMENT. These two metrics help you understand the impact of a plan on salespeople's effort.

- **Engagement index.** This is the percentage of employees earning incentive pay. The simple assumption is that if salespeople have not reached a threshold to earn incentives, they are not engaged and will not stretch themselves to do more. You can also track the rate of meaningful engagement—the percentage of people who are earning an incentive amount that is large enough to have an impact, say 75% of the target incentive.

- **Excitement index.** This is the rate at which salespeople are earning incentive pay. The assumption is that if employees are earning it at a higher rate, they are more excited about the plan and will push themselves harder to achieve more.

To understand these metrics, consider the two incentive plans shown in figure 8-2. Plan A focuses on engagement—more salespeople are likely to hit a threshold of 60 percent of their goal, as compared with the 80 percent threshold of plan B. However, plan B focuses on excitement—its steeper payout curve means that once salespeople are engaged, they earn incentives at a faster rate.

FIGURE 8-2

Comparing two example incentive plans

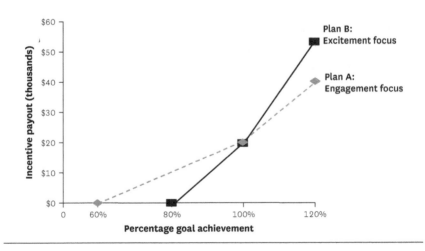

When designing an incentive plan, there is a trade-off between engagement and excitement. High engagement distributes money across more of the sales force, while high excitement gives top performers more potential upside. A commonly used benchmark is that for a sales force in which at least 30 percent of salespeople's pay comes from incentives, at least 90 percent of the sales force is engaged, and at least 65 percent of employees are meaningfully engaged, meaning they make at least 75 percent of the targeted incentive pay (the pay they would earn at 100% goal achievement). In plans in which salespeople earn a commission on every transaction, engagement is obviously 100 percent, assuming everyone sells something.

FAIRNESS. Plan fairness is also important for motivation. With quota-based bonus plans, you can test to see if quotas are biased based on territory factors that salespeople can't control, such as starting volume or market share, required growth, or market opportunity. For example, if salespeople in territories with high starting market share are systematically failing to meet their quotas, that indicates that the quotas did not consider how thoroughly the market is penetrated. In those cases, employees who have territories where growth is inherently harder are being unfairly penalized. In another example, if quota achievement is negatively correlated with the prior year's sales growth, salespeople who previously performed very well (and thus raised the baseline for their territory) may be in an unfair position. Their disproportionately tougher quotas make it harder for them to achieve similar success again.

SIMPLICITY. Uncomplicated incentive plans are more motivating since they are memorable and keep salespeople focused on what's important. If a plan is overly complex, employees may ignore it or, worse, look for ways to game it so that they make money without contributing to the intended goals. In most cases, a simple plan links payouts to a maximum of three or four metrics. And each metric has a weight of at least 20 percent—large enough that salespeople pay attention to it.

Does the plan direct effort appropriately?

In addition to measuring a plan's power to motivate employees, engagement and excitement metrics also help with assessing how well the plan directs sales effort. At one high-tech company, salespeople had goals for four major products and started earning commissions on sales when they hit 75 percent of each product's goal. The commission rate accelerated for sales beyond the goal. The company tracked engagement and excitement indices across the four product lines. (See table 8-2.)

The benchmark was that at least two-thirds of salespeople should be engaged on each product. Two products fell short, especially product B, which was new and strategically important. Most sellers were not making money on product B, and the excitement index for it was low. In hindsight, it was clear that the product's sales goals were too aggressive, and in fact, the overstretched goals led to most employees giving up and focusing on products that earned them accelerated commissions.

Engagement and excitement can also be calculated by market to see if there is sufficient focus on strategic priorities, such as new customers or an important new industry segment.

Is the plan fiscally responsible?

Being fiscally responsible means a plan keeps total costs aligned with overall results while paying salespeople appropriately for their performance.

At the company level, incentive expenditures should be commensurate with sales and profit outcomes. If, for example, the company is 5 percent

TABLE 8-2

Assessing incentive plan engagement and excitement by product

	Product A	Product B	Product C	Product D
Engagement: Percentage of salespeople earning incentive pay	89%	43%	60%	100%
Excitement: Average commission rate salespeople earn	4.2	1.5	2.0	7.9

below goal, and your incentive costs are 25 percent above target, there is a misalignment—the company misses its goal, but salespeople find a way to make money. Misalignment can also happen in reverse if the company does well but incentive pay is low.

At the salesperson level, an incentive plan should pay for performance—and enough pay should go to your top people. To assess this, look at payout by sales percentile. The right allocation depends on your situation. As illustrated in the earlier table 8-1, one SaaS company's plan called for ninetieth-percentile performers to earn between 1.3 and 2.5 times target pay, depending on the sales role.

Assessing plan performance

Companies use metrics such as engagement, excitement, and payout by percentile to assess how well an incentive plan performed. This provides insight into how to adjust the current plan to perform better in the future. These diagnostics can also be used to prospectively test how well a proposed plan is likely to perform before it is implemented.

As an example, suppose you want to choose between the two plans in figure 8-2. Plan A focuses on engagement whereas plan B is designed to create excitement. Testing helps you see how the quality of the national forecast affects the plans' results. If you are unsure of the forecast's accuracy, plan B is the better option. If you are confident about the accuracy, plan A, or even a payout starting at 95 percent of the goal, could work.

Prospective testing helps you analyze various scenarios to understand a plan's consequences across a range of potential future outcomes. For instance, what if the national sales goal is overly ambitious—will salespeople still be motivated by the plan? Conversely, what if goals are achieved too easily—will plan costs spiral out of control? A common mistake is to assume that if the company comes in at 100 percent of the goal, incentive costs will be equal to target pay times the number of salespeople. In fact, this is rarely the case—performance variations among salespeople can skew the total payout, making it higher or lower than the target. It's quite possible for a company to come in at 95 percent of the goal while the average payout is 20 percent or more above the target. It helps to do the calculations so that as you consider plan revisions, you understand what could happen under various scenarios and can make more-informed decisions.

Your incentive program is one of the most important levers you have for aligning salespeople's effort with company strategy, energizing your team, and keeping compensation costs in line with results. Incentives (and compensation more broadly) also have a large impact on your ability to attract talent and to retain high-performing salespeople—the topic of the next chapter.

Checklist of critical tasks for incentives and goal setting

- ❏ With complex sales, stay away from overly short-term rewards.

- ❏ Use diagnostics to assess the health of your incentive plan regularly. Before you change the plan, use similar diagnostics to prospectively assess how the new plan is likely to perform.

- ❏ Keep the incentive plan simple, with no more than four success measures.

- ❏ When sales are unpredictable, use multiple levels of success to energize salespeople.

- ❏ Do not overstretch goals.

- ❏ Build commitment by involving salespeople in defining MBOs.

- ❏ Use rewards in combination with other levers, such as learning and development, information support, and management directives.

9.

Managing Retention and Turnover

Salesperson turnover is one of the more difficult and bothersome problems you'll face as a sales manager. Its impact becomes even more evident when you lose one of your stars, especially one you have invested in and nurtured.

Let's start with some stark statistics. We estimate that:

- Three-quarters of B2B sales forces have annual turnover rates between 25 percent and 50 percent, when you include promotions and reassignments in addition to voluntary and involuntary departures.

- The turnover rate for salespeople is two to three times that of employees in other jobs at their companies.

- More than half of all salespeople are looking for new jobs at any point in time.

While turnover is a fact of life, the level you experience it at is not. You can reduce and manage it. Because while salespeople are the face of the company to customers, you are the face of the company to your salespeople. Managers directly impact people's job satisfaction, motivation, and success, and have a substantial influence on how long people stay in the job. The steps you can take to reduce turnover do work—even when it's hard to know how much of it you have prevented—and you must be resolute in taking them.

In this chapter, we will focus on:

- Understanding turnover costs and dynamics

- Using tailored retention strategies

- Succeeding in high-turnover environments

Understanding turnover costs and dynamics

Managing turnover starts with knowing how much it hurts you, separating the good turnover from the bad, and understanding which factors, especially nonmonetary ones, can keep people on your team.

How high are turnover costs?

Suppose that if a successful salesperson stays in the job, sales grow by 20 percent per year for the next five years. Now suppose that salesperson leaves. Territory sales drop by 10 percent in the first year, and it takes two years for a new salesperson to build the business back up to a 20 percent annual growth rate. Add that up over five years, and the turnover of a single salesperson has lost you 30 percent in total sales. (See table 9-1.)

Make your own assumptions and do the math for your situation. Then multiply that loss by the number of salespeople who leave each year. (And remember that the sales loss due to the departure of a star is several times the annual cost of an average seller.) On top of lost sales, add on the cost and time spent recruiting, onboarding, and developing new people for the team. These costs vary widely but often add up to tens of thousands of

TABLE 9-1

Estimated sales loss due to turnover

		Last year	Year 1	Year 2	Year 3	Year 4	Year 5	Total	
No turnover	**Sales**	100	120	144	173	207	249	**893**	
	Growth		20%	20%	20%	20%	20%		
With turnover (replacement in year 1)	**Sales**	100	90	99	119	143	171	**622**	
	Growth		–10%	10%	20%	20%	20%		
							Sales loss due to turnover	**–30%**	

dollars per person. If that wasn't bad enough, consider how sales losses also erode your competitive position.

It's worth a lot to hold on to good people.

Separating good turnover from bad

A company was struggling with high turnover of the sales force, losing 30 percent of its sellers each year. The company asked an outside HR consultancy to dig into the reasons salespeople were leaving. Table 9-2 shows the results that came back.

The "overall" column in table 9-2 is revealing, but it does not tell the full story. Turnover statistics are much more useful when they consider the performance of the people who are leaving. Not all turnover is undesirable. In fact, it can be good when low performers with little potential for future success leave the company. Turnover is bad only when it involves strong performers or people who have the potential to be strong performers in the future.

The good news for this company is that the turnover rate is lower for upper-half performers (25 percent) than for lower-half ones (35 percent). In fact, most salespeople who left due to lack of recognition or low pay were lower-half performers. That means the pay and recognition systems seem to be working; they encouraged less successful sellers to leave. But managers at this company are not off the hook just yet. Even if many departures

TABLE 9-2

Reasons for salespeople's departure

	Overall	Upper-half performers	Lower-half performers
Annual salesperson turnover rate	30%	25%	35%
Primary reason for departure	Percentage of departures	Percentage in upper half	Percentage in lower half
Poor management	23%	52%	48%
Lack of recognition	21%	26%	74%
Low pay	20%	27%	73%
No growth opportunities	13%	70%	30%
Lack of challenging work	10%	45%	55%
Burnout	9%	40%	60%
Other	4%	50%	50%

are considered good turnover, as we will discuss later in this chapter, good turnover is usually caused by bad hiring. Further, those leaving because of poor management were an almost equal mix of upper- and lower-half performers. Some of this turnover is clearly not good.

Many companies opt for annual engagement surveys, providing a yearly snapshot of employee sentiment and engagement. This approach allows organizations to track changes over time. Such surveys are most valuable when engagement drivers are examined by performance cluster.

What makes people stay?

People leave because they find better alternatives. But the economics of alternatives are not the whole picture; people stay in a job for other reasons too. They stay because they believe in the organization or have an emotional attachment to their job or their coworkers. They may also feel a sense of obligation to the company or their manager.

These nonmonetary reasons are influenced by factors relating to:

- **The job:** attributes such as variety, impact, autonomy, personal growth, and feedback

- **The organization:** characteristics such as culture, support, and fairness

- **The individual:** attributes such as personality, values, and work attitudes

Sales managers have a direct impact on the first two. And through hiring, you can influence which individuals join.

One aspect of salespeople's job-related stickiness is tied to their success. Even when a region ends the year at 100 percent, statistically, only about 50 percent of salespeople will make their goals. The people who miss the goal will likely feel unsuccessful and therefore are at risk of leaving. It's up to you to help salespeople feel valued and successful.

Reducing turnover is, in many ways, embedded in the performance management cadence. As you build the competence and confidence of your people while managing their activities and results, you must also be thinking about how to ensure they stay.

Using tailored retention strategies

It's easy to jump to the conclusion that increasing pay will reduce turnover. But in reality, more-holistic solutions are possible when you dig deeper into turnover dynamics. Pay is only part of the answer.

Retention (and performance management) approaches are most effective when they are tailored to each person's situation as well as to their unique motivators and needs. A good way to start thinking about turnover is to identify the characteristics of the salespeople who are leaving. The best solutions depend on the profile of those who depart, including their performance (star performer, core player, potential performer, or poor performer) and career stage (experienced with the company, experienced new hire, new to sales).

Figure 9-1 shows some practical solutions for preventing future departures among these various segments. From this, you can tailor retention approaches to each person's unique motivators and needs.

FIGURE 9-1

Ideas for preventing future turnover of salespeople

	Experienced with the company	Experienced new hire	New to sales
Star Recognize success and engage	Don't set their goals so unfairly high	Spend more time individually and in groups to help them learn the culture	Apply less performance pressure early on
Core player Energize and support	Spend time; don't let them disengage		Invest more time in coaching and helping them win early
Potential performer Develop and improve	Coach, coach, coach	Help them figure out the company and culture	
Poor performer with poor fit Make role change	Change how people are selected in the hiring process		

Consider some examples of tactics that sales organizations have employed to improve retention across various segments of performance and career stage.

Stars and core players: Recognition, engagement, and support

Stars and core players are the salespeople you least want to lose, but holding on to them can be the most challenging. They are in high demand in the job market, and their success is often evident to customers and competitors.

- Financial services firm Plante Moran had a "re-recruiting" program that helped it limit annual turnover to half the industry average. Managers envisioned what they would do if valued employees were to announce they were leaving. Then, managers did exactly that, without waiting for such announcements. Re-recruitment efforts often involved one-on-one meetings to make staff members feel important and valued. Managers attended workshops where they shared ideas for re-recruitment. Employees also had buddies who offered advice and experienced mentors who provided career coaching and planning.

- When Canadian company London Life Insurance bought most of the Canadian operations of the Prudential Insurance Company of America in 1996, it made a great effort to retain the acquisition's 850-plus salespeople. Immediately following the deal's announcement, the company flew Prudential's sales force to its headquarters. Executives spent two days welcoming them and addressing their major points of uncertainty, including which products they would sell, who they would work for, where they would work, and how they would be paid. Ninety-two percent of Prudential's salespeople signed new contracts with London Life.

Potential performers: Develop and improve capabilities

Turnover of potential performers is often highest among new salespeople who, despite having talent, are unable to reach a threshold of success quickly. These people could be successful if given the necessary opportunity, guidance, and support. Here's what that can look like:

- A global technology company discovered that new sales associates were much less likely to leave if they made their first sale within ninety days. So, the company revamped its new hire training program to focus on accomplishing this single task. Early training covered easy-to-sell, fast-moving products. Training on more-advanced products happened only after several months of success in the job.

- In a direct marketing sales force, many potential performers left within their first six months. In exit interviews, these salespeople reported frustration at the lack of attention from managers. Although managers were responsible for onboarding, they also had selling responsibility, and a substantial portion of their incentive pay was based on their own performance. When the company changed the incentive formula to emphasize metrics such as new employees' goal achievement and year-to-year district revenue growth, retention improved, ultimately driving sales growth.

Poor performers with poor fit: Improve hiring

Poor recruits become turnover statistics. By honing the skills you need to select job candidates with the innate characteristics required for success, you will reduce turnover in the long term. Plus, you will spend less time dealing with nonperformers, leaving more time for current and potential strong performers. Here's how some companies have done it:

- Valquip Corporation, an industrial valves and controls distributor, cut sales force turnover in half when it began using a psychological test to screen job candidates. To get hired, people had to exhibit strong drive and interpersonal skills.

- An automotive dealership reduced turnover (which was over 50 percent per year) by doing more-thorough background checks on candidates and scrutinizing transfer requests, making it harder for dealers to transfer a "problem hire" to another dealer.

- A computer manufacturer reduced hiring mistakes by evaluating sales candidates while they spent a day shadowing someone at the company. This also ensured candidates understood the responsibilities, expectations, and challenges of the job.

Turnover reduction plan

Of course, sales managers have the most power to reduce turnover on their teams, and you should always have a reduction plan in place. Start by making a list of your current team members and any recent departures. Develop a profile of each person that includes their current performance, potential performance, career stage, and what motivates them (for example, new challenges, recognition, social interaction, learning opportunities, or monetary rewards). You can adapt the profile categories to fit your situation. Then answer some questions about why each person left (or might leave) and what actions to take to improve retention. The answers will inform your action plan for driving retention.

For salespeople currently on your team, ask:

- Why might they leave?

- What could encourage them to stay?

- What actions should you take?

For those who left, ask:

- Why did they leave?

- Would you rather they had stayed?

- What could you have done?

Succeeding in high-turnover environments

No matter what managers do, they cannot keep every good salesperson. With platforms such as LinkedIn, each seller's success is visible to the world, and successful ones are always in demand, especially in growing industries.

Four approaches can help you reduce sales loss due to turnover effectively (see figure 9-2).

1. Minimize the sales loss that occurs if salespeople disengage before they quit or are let go.

2. Shorten the time to hire a replacement.

3. Minimize the customer and sales loss that may occur during a transition from the departing salesperson to the new one.

4. Get replacement salespeople up to speed faster.

By executing on all four of these well, you can shave off at least half the downside of losing a good seller. Let's look at each approach in turn.

Minimizing sales loss from disengagement

Anyone quitting a job began thinking about leaving well before they actually did. We call this the withdrawal period—the time from when a

FIGURE 9-2

Reducing sales loss due to salesperson turnover

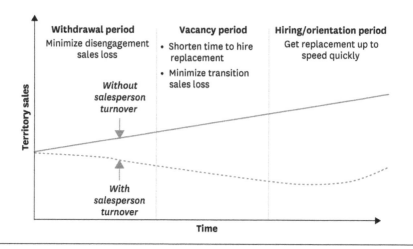

salesperson first considers quitting to when they hand in their notice. Here's what you can do.

DETECT WITHDRAWAL. How do you know when the withdrawal period is happening? If you're talking to your salespeople several times each week and traveling with them on customer visits every two weeks, you have many opportunities to detect disengagement. Telltale signs include diminished enthusiasm and urgency, little effort being put into longer-term opportunities, appointments being rescheduled, reduced involvement in team activities, and indifference to things the salesperson once cared about.

FOCUS ON RETAINING THE SALESPERSON AND THEIR CUSTOMERS. When you detect disengagement, there are two things you can do. First, intervene to try to head off the unwanted departure. In some ways, salespeople are constantly assessing whether to stay or leave. They have a sense of the value of staying, but they may be underestimating it. They are also assessing the value of leaving, but may be overestimating it. Try to diagnose their motive: Are they running away from their current job, or are they heading to the promise of a different opportunity? If you can address what they are running away from, retention may be possible. Solutions can include providing new challenges and role changes. Creating a special compensation deal for someone may be tempting, but it's a dicey route—while it could keep one good performer, the perceived unfairness can hurt the retention of the rest of the team. Learning about the competitors you lose salespeople to (for example, what compensation, benefits, career advancement opportunities, and work culture they offer, and what their retention record is) can help you highlight your own organization's unique strengths and be more persuasive at convincing good salespeople to stay.

Second, even as you try to get someone to stay, pay attention to their customers that may be at risk. Some effective actions for this are covered in chapter 3 and are summarized later in this chapter.

Detecting a potential departure early helps on both fronts. It increases the odds you can persuade a good salesperson to stay, and even if that effort is unsuccessful, it gives you more time to prepare for a smooth transition of customer relationships before the salesperson leaves.

Speeding up the time to fill a vacancy

A sales force of 500 people with 30 percent turnover will have 150 vacancies a year. You should look critically at how long it takes you and your company to fill open roles. We estimate that 10 percent to 15 percent of B2B sales positions are unfilled at any time; this is because for most companies, it takes four to six months to fill a job opening. But you can do better. Proactive recruiting can shorten the vacancy period and reduce lost sales.

ALWAYS BE HIRING. Be constantly on the lookout for potential recruits, especially when you recruit internally or from competitors. A good best practice is to maintain a list of viable job candidates before an opening occurs. This might include employee referrals, candidates who rejected past offers, employees in other functions, and past contacts maintained through LinkedIn or other methods. Having a list of candidates to jump-start the recruiting process can accelerate the time to hire a salesperson.

KEEP A "BENCH." To help fill vacancies faster, one medical equipment company actively recruits, hires, and trains new people all the time—before vacancies occur. This creates a bench of candidates who are ready to jump into sales positions quickly when needed. Bench programs work best in large sales forces. If the sales force is small, training needs are modest, or the cost of maintaining a bench is too high, a steady pace of constant recruiting can create a "virtual" bench with several candidates always close to the offer stage.

Minimizing sales loss during a transition

We discussed this in chapter 3 and will recap it briefly here. When a salesperson leaves, customer effort and attention can suffer. The departing seller may have insights and knowledge that get lost—which is particularly problematic when sales cycles are long or when the departing salesperson is leaving on unfriendly terms or going to a competitor. If the person has close ties with a customer, focus on transitioning that relationship to a new salesperson, which greatly reduces your risk of losing it.

PAY ATTENTION TO CUSTOMER COVERAGE. As soon as you know a salesperson is leaving, act quickly to arrange for temporary coverage of their accounts until a permanent replacement is found. The interim person can be you or another salesperson. If the departing person is promoted or moving into a new role within the company, they can assist with the transition as well. At one wealth management firm, when a financial adviser departs, managers are expected to reach out to all key accounts within twenty-four hours and to try to meet with them within a week.

CREATE MANY CUSTOMER CONNECTIONS. Having multiple connections with a key account can help to minimize sales loss during a salesperson's departure. When selling cycles are longer and deal sizes are large, a manager should already have some connections with buyers. When multiple decision-makers at the customer deal with multiple people from your organization (technical specialists, customer support people, and an inside sales team, for example), any single break or change in the team is unlikely to rupture the entire relationship. Digital capabilities also help. CRM systems capture essential information about customers and sales activity. After a departure, there is less loss of customer knowledge and the intimacy that goes with it. In addition, a customer's loyalty to resources other than a salesperson, such as a convenient ordering website or stellar technical support, can outlive the personal relationship.

Enhancing the performance of replacement salespeople

Onboarding is an effort that is squarely in a manager's wheelhouse. There is a lot you can do to help new salespeople get up to speed quickly and become fully productive. (See chapter 5 for a full exploration of onboarding.) As a refresher, for people who are new to sales, focus on building their competency, including selling skills and knowledge of products and customers, along with boosting their confidence. For experienced salespeople coming from outside the company, enhancing their performance is about acculturation and helping them get to know the internal resources and networks.

In both cases, large doses of joint customer visits will go a long way. And the strongest booster for new hires in both groups is to help them complete sales. This improves their confidence and motivation, leading to a virtuous cycle of success. Effective onboarding and learning and development programs can accelerate the time it takes for new salespeople to become productive, which will lessen the inevitable losses caused by turnover.

Checklist of critical tasks for retaining salespeople

❏ Track turnover statistics by salespeople's performance and career stage. Vary your approach to addressing turnover depending on the characteristics of those who are leaving.

❏ When seeking to boost salesperson retention, look for solutions that go beyond money.

❏ Regularly re-recruit star salespeople. Imagine what you would do if they were to announce they were leaving, then do that.

❏ Focus on helping salespeople who are new to your company succeed quickly.

❏ Be on the watch for signs of disengagement. Intervene early to head off unwanted departures.

❏ Reduce the risk of sales loss when a salesperson departs by ensuring customers have many valuable connections to your company.

The Digital Transformation of Sales Management

10.

Leveraging the Growing Power of Digital in Sales Management

Gone are the days when sales management was primarily about hiring charismatic people, training them, pointing them toward customers, and paying them for results. Sales leaders now leverage a blend of digitally derived insights and their own judgment and experience when making decisions. Moreover, in a world of elevated customer expectations, along with an explosion of data, technology, and analytics, sales success requires combining the strength of personal connection with the power of digital.

We use the term "digital" to mean the use of technology, data, and analytics to design and support business processes and decisions. The earliest use of digital in sales was about keeping the lights on—automating manual processes, improving record-keeping, and increasing efficiency.

Now the impact of digital is everywhere, with an expanded scope in sales effectiveness—for example, using analytics to suggest which accounts salespeople should target and what message they should deliver. Data-driven decisions and digital channels have immense potential to create mutual value for both customers and selling organizations. As a result, digital is transforming sales from an art into a science, enabling you to improve almost every strategic and tactical decision and process.

Digital has reshaped the sales landscape for practically every business. For example, the purchase of simple products has moved almost entirely online. But at the same time, companies with innovative and complex offerings are expanding their sales forces. Often, these salespeople must be equipped to sell products that are built with an ever-evolving set of digital components, leading to growth in product-related services. Analytics and AI are helping companies reach customers in a more coordinated and customer-centric way, while also creating opportunities to improve almost every aspect of sales. Underlying all this change is a workforce dominated by digitally native workers who came of age well after the dawn of the internet era. Today's buyers are equipped with information and insights long before engaging with sellers. And when the Covid-19 pandemic forced businesses to swiftly adapt to an all-virtual environment, the growth in digital urgency and proficiency among both buyers and sellers accelerated dramatically.

Digital power comes with complications. There are always too many choices about how to leverage digital. The change to business processes can be substantial and challenging to implement. And there is constant change.

Digital's impact on sales decisions and processes

The first two sections of this handbook tackled the fundamental decisions and processes that connect companies to their customers and result in sales. This section explores the impact of digital, especially in four key areas:

1. **Customer strategy.** Digital helps sales and marketing organizations work together more effectively to define who to sell to, what value to offer, and how to connect with customers.

2. **Organization design.** Digital increases the number of sales channels, giving you more opportunities to balance the effectiveness and
   efficiency of customer coverage, while making organization design
   more complex.

3. **Talent.** Digital helps organizations recruit, develop, manage, and
   motivate sales force members, ensuring they have the knowledge,
   skills, and drive to succeed.

4. **Channel and customer engagement.** Digital enables sales and
   marketing organizations to work together to deliver and synchronize selling activities that drive value for customers, channel
   partners, and the company.

In every area, digital can boost the speed and impact of decision-
making, while helping to improve sales management processes. The chapters that follow provide practical insights and frameworks to help you
bring digital capabilities to the areas that matter most for your business.
Here is a summary of section 3's chapters.

Chapter 11: Making faster and better decisions with analytics and AI

Sales organizations are using analytics and AI to improve their approaches
to customer engagement, talent management, organization design, team
management, and more. By gleaning insights from large volumes of data,
analytics and AI help sales force members make better choices while boosting speed, efficiency, and agility. Leaders must determine when and how to
combine data-driven insights with their own judgment, considering factors
such as decision stakes and the reliability of the models that produce the
insights. And as sales leaders themselves become more data-driven, they
must help their teams do the same.

Chapter 12: Designing the sales organization for the digital age

Digital has dramatically increased the number and variety of sales channels that selling organizations use to reach customers. There are now an

array of digital channel options, as well as inside and field salespeople and channel partners. Meanwhile, digital is blurring the line between field sales and inside sales. These changes create an opportunity to better match sales channels and communication methods to the needs of customers and the size of opportunities, while directing attention to key priorities and enabling greater market coverage. Digital also allows selling organizations to be nimbler and organization redesign, from territories to sales force sizes, to be more fluid and continuous.

Chapter 13: Unlocking five digital-age sales competencies

In a world of informed and digitally savvy customers, salespeople must acquire new skills to bring value. Five forward-looking competencies are increasingly important for success in the digital world. First, salespeople need to be able to anticipate the customer's tomorrow. Second, they must collaborate inside and outside their organizations to help buyers address complexity. Third, they need skills for leveraging digital and virtual channels for customer interactions. Fourth, they must be able to use data and analytics to bring value to buyers. Fifth, they must adapt to constant change to keep up with the rapidly evolving customer and digital landscapes.

Chapter 14: Synchronizing sales channels for maximum impact

As the number of sales channels and communication methods grows, so do the challenges of optimizing customer communication and enabling collaboration across channels and roles. Synchronization can involve two levels of integration: coordination, which keeps the various channels informed about customer interactions, and orchestration, which provides a centralized point of control. Digital capabilities and sales managers both have a role in enabling the needed collaboration, ensuring that customers can switch between channels without inconsistencies or disruptions. Communication and channel strategies must become more agile, so it's possible for sales teams to adapt continuously as customer needs, knowledge, digital savvy, and preferences evolve.

Chapter 15: Accelerating and streamlining selling with a digital customer hub

Customers are interacting with more digital channels and sales roles, so seller decisions—such as which buyers to contact, what to offer, and what channel and communication methods to use—benefit from coordination and real-time insights. Increasingly, companies are addressing these challenges and opportunities with a digital customer hub (DCH), an organizational entity that brings together expertise and digital assets (technology, data, analytical tools, communication channels) to enable seamless and effective customer engagement. Sales leaders support the success of a DCH by keeping everyone's attention focused on creating value for customers, helping the sales team adapt, and championing DCH usage.

Chapter 16: Amplifying the power of salespeople with digital assistants

The ability to make customer interactions relevant and personalized to each situation has always been a salesperson's distinctive weapon. Now, sellers have the opportunity to enhance this ability by combining their judgment with input from AI-enabled analytical and verbal-visual digital assistants. The assistants, which are usually integrated with the CRM system, mine both quantitative and qualitative data to quickly offer suggestions and increase salespeople's impact. Sales leaders can help drive the adoption of digital assistants by shaping their capabilities and building a support system for the users. They also help manage the risks and uncertainties while learning to use AI themselves.

Chapter 17: Boosting talent management with digital

Digital capabilities have become essential for supporting constant talent management needs. Aspects of talent management in sales have been based on data for some time now, with digital systems supporting key processes. Today companies are using more-advanced digital capabilities, including AI, to improve talent decisions and processes for hiring, learning and development, performance management, and incentive programs. Some companies are even linking disparate talent systems to create an always-on talent support platform—what we call a digital sales talent hub (DSTH)—which allows leaders to speedily adapt talent strategy and quickly hire better people, develop stronger sales force skills, and enhance sales team motivation.

Chapter 18: Managing a recurring revenue business

Besides redefining practically every aspect of selling and sales management, digital also reshapes the very offerings that companies sell. More organizations are relying on recurring revenue to drive their success. This is common at companies that sell digital products (such as software as a service) and increasingly so at those that sell physical products that are digitally enabled for subscription services or consumption-based pricing. Sales strategies for a recurring revenue business require a fine balance between keeping and growing current customers and acquiring new customers. Customer-facing roles must focus on customer success while balancing account acquisition with ongoing account management and continuous business improvement.

The impact of digital on sales management is significant and exciting, and the implementation of digital sales initiatives is challenging and ongoing. Success requires you to embrace digital fully while judiciously weaving it into the human elements needed to create a cohesive buyer experience and enable effective decisions and processes.

A good place to start is to understand the power of analytics and AI—capabilities that are front and center in the journey to digitalize sales management. That is the focus of the next chapter.

11.

Making Faster and Better Decisions with Analytics and AI

We are in an era of digitally assisted decision-making in sales. Relying on experience and intuition is not enough. Analytics and artificial intelligence are transforming every sphere of decisions, including those affecting customer engagement, talent management, the design of the sales organization, and how teams are managed. Analytics and data are not new to sales, yet recent advancements in digital and AI are taking these capabilities to a new level, allowing sales organizations to create more-personalized experiences for their customers and salespeople, leading to stronger relationships, greater flexibility, and enhanced competitiveness.

Analytics involves the use of data, statistical analysis, and algorithms to gain insights, make predictions, and inform decision-making. AI takes these capabilities a step further with its ability to learn, reason, problem-solve, and make decisions autonomously—essentially simulating human intelligence. And like humans, AI can get better at these tasks over time. Both analytics and AI process vast amounts of data, uncover patterns, and extract and communicate insights for improving business performance—and they do this with unprecedented and growing power and speed.

Analytics and AI are particularly well-suited for sales. Selling is transaction- and interaction-intensive, producing large volumes of data about customers, results, and activities. Some of this data is structured (organized in rows and columns), while some is unstructured (text of email chains, recordings of video calls). Traditional analytics is good at making sense of structured data. AI can glean insights from both structured and unstructured data.

This chapter lays the groundwork for the rest of section 3 by exploring the concepts of analytics and AI and providing examples that illustrate their relevance and impact. Six topics are covered:

- The value of analytics and AI for sales

- Understanding the basics of AI

- Empowering human judgment

- Becoming data-driven

- The role of sales operations in bringing analytics and AI to sales

- How analytics, AI, and delivery platforms are evolving

These digital tools are useful to all salespeople and sales leaders, and their impact is only growing, as we explore next.

Using analytics and AI to drive sales actions and impact

Analytics and AI are relevant at every level of the organization while supporting both customer-facing and internal decisions and processes:

- Salespeople get insights about how to manage their customers, territories, and time more effectively.

- Sales managers make better talent decisions and help the sales team realize customer opportunities.

- Sales heads enhance their decisions, design and operate better processes, and diagnose issues to sustain a high-performing team and improve it continuously.

- Companies use data and data-derived insights as the fuel to enable collaboration across departments. For example, sales, marketing, and customer service work together on customer care, and sales and HR partner to build strong teams.

A range of outputs

Analytics and AI can produce many kinds of outputs: descriptive reports about what has happened, insights to uncover causes or predict the future, answers to support decision-making, and recommended actions embedded within workflows. (See table 11-1.)

Addressing any sales force issue usually requires you to use several of these capabilities. For example, to decide where to add headcount, you might start with a report of sales trends by territory, then examine insights about where the most unrealized opportunities are, followed by considering an answer suggested by an optimization model.

Some outputs, such as a report or a recommended next action, are delivered digitally and instantly. Other outputs are produced by an analyst working for several days with statistical or AI models and tools. These might include insights about success profiles or funnel analysis. Other analytics projects could last weeks or months, such as sales force sizing or territory design.

Understanding the basics of AI

For sales force members to be good users of AI, it's helpful to understand what AI does, how it mimics human intelligence, and some risks to be aware of.

TABLE 11-1

Range of sales analytics and AI outputs

Type	Examples
Reports: Provide an understanding of the past	• **Product sales distribution.** See trends of product sales across regions or channels to identify top-performing and low-performing areas. • **Customer segmentation.** Group buyers based on demographics, purchasing, and channel preferences to find attractive segments. • **Sales ranking.** Produce a list of salespeople sorted from highest to lowest quarterly goal achievement.
Insights: Uncover the causes of outcomes and predict the future	• **Sales funnel analysis.** Examine sales funnel stages to identify where leads drop off and investigate possible reasons for the drop. • **Customer churn analysis.** Investigate why certain customers are canceling subscriptions or ceasing to purchase products. • **Sales forecasting.** Use historical sales data, market trends, and seasonality to predict sales for the next quarter or year. • **Recruiting channel analysis.** Track hiring metrics to learn which sources produce the best hires.
Answers: Support decision-making	• **Sales force size.** Use optimization models to determine the most profitable answer based on estimated impact of salespeople on sales. • **Sales territory design.** Use the distribution of account workloads and opportunities to create sales territories. • **Goal setting.** Allocate sales goals to sellers based on past sales and remaining opportunities.
Embedded recommended actions: Use analytics to seamlessly support workflows	• **Lead scoring.** Prioritize prospects based on their value and likelihood to convert into paying customers, helping salespeople focus their efforts. • **Customer suggestions.** Recommend the next best action to advance a customer relationship. • **Upsell and cross-sell opportunities.** Provide recommendations by examining purchasing patterns across similar customers. • **Coaching.** Use AI-based tools to provide feedback in real time based on language, tone, inflection, and other elements of communication.

AI makes inferences and predictions from data, going beyond the capabilities of traditional analytics. For example, AI can examine millions of data points about past sales to all customers, then infer upsell and cross-sell opportunities or predict which customers are likely to churn before it's too late to remedy the situation. AI can share these insights using natural language. And it can do all this quickly, often fast enough to assist in real-time decision-making. AI can make these predictions even when data is incomplete. It is always on, constantly refreshed with new data, and perpetually learning from feedback. Thus, its recommendations can continually get better. The best AI is invisible and runs quietly in the background. Only the data scientists and machine learning engineers who work behind the scenes see the complexity of the algorithms. But remember: AI itself is not the star of the show; what's important is the benefits it delivers to users, customers, and the company.

How AI mimics human intelligence

The power of AI comes from a machine's ability to perceive, think, and act seemingly like a human—and often, better and faster than a human. Several examples show how these ideas apply to sales:

- **Perceive.** AI "perceives" by interpreting natural language, speech, and visual information, such as facial expressions. For example, it can analyze text (such as a social media conversation) and audio or video (such as a recorded Zoom call) to gauge the sentiment of a potential customer. This information can help sales teams tailor their approach and messaging.

- **Think.** AI "thinks" by using machine learning, which includes gaining knowledge from examples (supervised learning), finding patterns in data (unsupervised learning), and adapting to user feedback (reinforcement learning). For example, it can use historical data to score leads based on their behavior and characteristics, allowing sales teams to prioritize those with the highest likelihood of converting.

- **Act.** AI "acts" autonomously, often without human intervention. For example, it can trigger an order to replenish inventory or create a summary of what happened at a meeting. Sometimes the AI acts through a conversational interface with a person. AI-powered chatbots can engage with website visitors, answer common questions, and schedule appointments with salespeople. AI-driven sales assistants can provide teams with information and insights in real time during calls or meetings. The timely suggestions increase the odds that the meeting will advance the prospect toward a sale.

Generative AI

Generative AI (or gen AI) is a subset of AI that quickly creates content, such as text, images, audio, or video. The content mimics the characteristics or the patterns of the media that the AI model is trained on. Training happens by feeding the model large amounts of data that it organizes and learns from. A huge advantage of gen AI is its user-friendliness: a well-trained algorithm can respond to simple plain-language prompts from a user. Applications of gen AI in sales include summarizing text from email or video calls; creating a customized email, presentation, or offer that is likely to resonate with a customer; and powering a chatbot that streamlines customer service.

AI risks

AI offers numerous benefits and opportunities, but it also comes with risks and caveats. Sales leaders must be aware of—and ensure their teams are on guard for—the possibility of biases and errors. AI relies on data to train its models, and inaccurate or biased data can lead to erroneous and unfair predictions and decisions. For example, if AI is used to create a hiring profile, the profile will reflect biases in past recruiting. With gen AI, models can produce different answers to the same question at different times, creating regulatory and compliance risks. In addition, by making a flawed inference, gen AI can come up with statements that are not true. Additionally, you must be concerned about data privacy. This issue exists with any use of personal data, but there's greater risk with AI because it can take action without the filter of human judgment. Your IT and legal teams can help you navigate these complications thoughtfully and put safeguards in place to ensure your use of AI is responsible and beneficial.

Empowering human judgment

As the use of analytics and AI-based models becomes ubiquitous in sales decision-making, so does the question, "How much should we rely on the data-driven insights that models produce?"

There are many factors to consider. Data accuracy and completeness can be high or low. Models that turn data into insights can vary in quality. Errors in some decisions can have mild consequences, while others have a long-term impact.

Effective decision-making requires you to have a sense of when and how to adopt, incorporate, or reject data-driven insights. The answers to two questions can help:

- How high are the decision stakes?

- How reliable are the data-driven insights?

Exploring stakes and reliability

High-stakes decisions are those with wide and lasting impact. Done poorly, high-stakes decisions lead to a significant loss and are difficult to reverse. Examples could include deciding which channels to use for a new product, designing an incentive plan, and developing the hiring profile for a new sales role. Low-stakes decisions, meanwhile, have a smaller downside and are easier to reverse. A salesperson's purchase suggestion to a customer, for instance, can be revisited if it does not work out.

The reliability of data-driven insights depends on the completeness and the accuracy of your data and knowledge base, as well as on how effectively the model crunches the data to produce insights.

Consider a range of examples illustrating how decision stakes and model reliability influence the ways that sales teams use insights.

When a salesperson uses an incentive calculator to estimate their future pay, the answer can (mostly) be relied on. When a sales manager uses a gen AI system to summarize a meeting, the result is likely a good draft, one that's usable with minor editing. These are situations with *low-to-modest decision stakes and high model reliability.*

But what happens as the decision stakes go up or model reliability goes down? Consider three examples of increasing complexity.

When an AI-based "next best action" system advises a salesperson on what to do with a customer, the advice requires a modest amount of scrutiny and supervision. The data on which the model is based may be reasonably good, but it is never complete and is mostly about the past. Thus the model's input is best combined with a salesperson's experience and knowledge to help reach a decision: accept the recommendation, reject it, or modify it. This is a situation with *modest-to-high decision stakes and moderate model reliability.*

Now consider a more complex example. When an AI-based model scores LinkedIn candidate profiles for their fit with a sales job, the model's insight is useful but certainly needs to be judged by a person. Candidate scores are only somewhat reliable because people craft their own LinkedIn profiles, so they may be biased and incomplete. Decisions about who to hire have *high stakes* while candidate scoring models have *moderate-to-low reliability.*

Now consider an even more nuanced example. Say a model makes recommendations for the size and structure of the sales force—decisions that have a lasting impact and will be hard to reverse quickly. Reaching a decision requires analyzing massive amounts of data: sales forecasts, customer potential estimates, sales funnel dynamics, market trends, geographic distances, and more. It's impossible to make sense of all this information without help from a model. Yet the model's inputs, such as estimates of customer potential, are imprecise. Forecasts and market trends are also uncertain. So although the model is essential for helping you evaluate scenarios and think through the best choice, your oversight and judgment must play major roles in reaching a decision. The situation involves *high decision stakes* and the model has *good, but far from perfect, reliability.*

Judging the reliability of data-based insights

Several strategies can help you evaluate data-based insights, which in turn will determine how much attention you should pay to them.

USE THE SNIFF TEST. Does the insight look reasonable? Draw on your experience and external benchmarks to make sure. For example, if a data- and model-based analysis suggests that you double the size of your sales team to three hundred people, you can assess the reasonableness by reflecting on whether competitors of similar scale have sales forces in this range.

DIG INTO WHETHER THE RECOMMENDATION CAN BE EXPLAINED. A recommendation about a cross-sell opportunity, for example, is more convincing if it comes with an explanation of how the model got to the conclusion, such as "because companies in the same industry, of similar size, and in comparable situations have frequently adopted this solution." A suggestion about sales force size and structure is more credible with details about how it affects coverage of specific customer groups and plausible predictions of the resulting sales.

GET A SENSE FOR THE DATA QUALITY. Is the data reasonably relevant, accurate, complete, and timely? If recommendations about who to hire come from LinkedIn profiles, you know that the data can be, intentionally or unintentionally, inaccurate or incomplete. On the other hand, if an algorithm plans a salesperson's route to cover multiple customers in a day, the underlying data (GPS location, traffic conditions, and schedule) is accurate and timely. Timeliness is a key consideration. When data is mostly retrospective, you must assess if the recommendation applies prospectively. Timely sources include CRM data, customer interaction data, market intelligence, and social media monitoring; less timely sources include market research on customer potential or competitive intelligence from a year ago.

ASSESS THE QUALITY OF THE MODELS. This may be hard to do, but you can instead get insight about the people who create the models. Different modelers given the same data will produce different outputs in complex decision situations. The modeler's prior experience and knowledge of both the industry and the sales context have a large impact on model design and performance. Model building is an art!

Models and decision-makers enhance each other

Using data-based insights can help shape your managerial judgment, and repeated use of models over time can make you a better judge of their output. When we're implementing AI-based recommender systems with salespeople, we often see that within two years, adoption rates of the recommendations grow from 40 percent to 80 percent. Models improve as users provide feedback about key decision factors that the models haven't captured. At the same time, users get more proficient with using the models.

Data-driven decision-making is not just about using information and models to confirm your assumptions. In fact, it's counterproductive to seek out data that supports your beliefs while ignoring contradictory information. To mitigate the risks of biasing your decision-making, you have to recognize the value of nonintuitive insights while honing your expertise in using data-driven approaches. Almost always, a judicious combination of model insights and judgment will do better than either alone.

Building a data-driven team

Analytics and AI do not only create insights that lead to higher-quality decisions. They also enhance decision velocity—the speed, efficiency, and agility with which organizations and individuals can make choices. But for many sales organizations, the shift from a judgment-based decision culture to one that judiciously combines data insights and judgment is a major one. Sales leaders should take several steps to make themselves and their people more data-driven and agile decision-makers.

MODEL AND COACH THE RIGHT BEHAVIORS. If you want your team to be data- and evidence-driven, you have to be data-driven yourself. Rather than making decisions by asking, "What do I think?" first ask, "What does the data show?" Your people will see you doing this and will emulate you. Further, when you're coaching someone and they say to you, "We should do the following . . ." your instinct should be to ask them, "What does the data say?"

USE DATA TO EMPOWER THE SALES TEAM, NOT TO CONTROL IT. Salespeople believe they know what their customers want. If you use data and analytics to keep tabs on salespeople—for example, by monitoring sales activities and AI-based recommendations, and pressuring salespeople if they don't follow up on each recommendation—they will come to view data as a means of tracking, measurement, and enforcement, and will push back against a potentially valuable tool. Instead, empower your people by arming them with insights for improving the customer experience and driving mutual value. For example, the company can give each salesperson a list of their high-potential, low-penetration accounts to point them to where effort is needed. Then you can coach each person on ways to act on the information, but give them autonomy to use the insights as they see fit.

BOOST CROSS-SILO COLLABORATION THROUGH INFORMATION. Data helps to bridge organizational silos. For example, customer-facing departments such as sales, customer service, and marketing can work together more effectively when everyone sees the same information. Similarly, sales and HR personnel can more easily team up to improve and accelerate talent processes (such as hiring, training, and performance management) when all parties are working with the same data about salespeople and their performance.

To create a data-driven sales culture, a key obstacle that must be overcome is the often-large disparity in capabilities, mindsets, and priorities between the sales organization and functions with digital expertise, including those in programming, data science, software architecture, and other technical specialties that bring analytics and AI initiatives to life. Sales teams want to identify new sales opportunities, bring innovations to customers, and get results quickly. Digital teams (often housed within IT) have priorities that are equally important but potentially conflicting. These include controlling costs and risks, developing enterprise capabilities, and ensuring longer-term sustainability. To help bridge this gap, your sales operations team is invaluable.

Spanning the sales and digital boundary with sales ops

The sales operations team helps the sales team with all things digital. According to *SPIN Selling* author Neil Rackham, when Xerox first established a sales ops group in the 1970s to take on activities such as planning, compensation, forecasting, and territory design, group leader J. Patrick

Kelly described his responsibilities as "all the nasty number things that you don't want to do but need to do to make a great sales force."

Today, sales ops has increasing power and impact as your partner in bridging the gap between your sales world and the digital world of analytics and AI.

Strategy, operations, and change management

At its core, sales ops works with sales leaders to design, operate, and improve the organization by bringing analytics and AI to decisions and processes. These range from the strategic to the operational. As an example, a global health-care company expects the following from its sales ops leader:

STRATEGIC

- Contribute to the one- and three-year business vision as a member of the executive leadership team

- Evaluate sales force strategies, plans, goals, and objectives

- Contribute expertise to optimize sales force and territory sizing, structuring, and alignment

OPERATIONAL

- Oversee sales performance analyses and reporting, territory alignment, and customer profiling and targeting activities

- Administer quarterly incentive plans and goal setting

- Manage sales force automation and CRM systems and processes

- Provide data, analyses, modeling, and reporting to support quarterly sales reviews

Another description of the job, this one from software development company GitLab, emphasizes bringing "a strategic vision and innovative approach in creating, managing, and executing strategic programs that will drive key revenue, margin, and growth opportunities globally."

As bridges between sales and digital, members of the sales ops team should understand and empathize with sales while also understanding the complexities of using and evolving digital tools that leverage analytics and AI. The digital world is dynamic. In fact, sales ops groups are undergoing a change in the skills and mindset needed, seeking new competencies, for example, in data science, AI, and user experience. These boundary spanners must implement and champion constant change—a topic that is discussed in more detail in the final chapter of this book.

The evolution of analytics and AI

Initially, data and analytics in sales supported basic operational needs. Now, the impact of analytics and AI is pervasive across all decisions and processes. Further, digitalization that began in sales has grown to have an impact beyond it. CRM platforms serve not just sales and marketing but also customer-associated teams across the organization, including content generation, product development, finance, supply chain, and event planning. Modern CRM systems are enabled by analytics and AI and embedded in work processes. Beyond capturing customer interactions and helping salespeople plan customer appointments and routes, CRM systems have become the centerpiece for delivering a truly omnichannel experience for customers, enabling personalization and channel synchronization. CRM is just one example of the evolution from keeping the lights on to making an impact. Systems supporting other sales processes, such as talent management, are making the same journey.

These enormous changes, which are growing out of sales organizations and having an impact across traditional silos, are enabled by technological advancements and improvements that make systems easy and natural for users. They include the following:

- **Cloud-based, connected from anywhere.** Most digital systems now operate in the cloud. This allows users to access data and tools anytime, anywhere. It also facilitates rapid upgrades and scalability.

- **Data capture across channels.** Early systems captured sales data through ordering and fulfilment systems, while CRM relied on salespeople to manually enter data. Modern systems get data from multiple customer touchpoints and channels automatically—they are always on, scraping information not just from customer-sales interactions, but from sources as varied as customer interactions with social media sites and chatbots. What's more, digitally enabled products can send data on their usage directly to the CRM. With more complete and accurate data, the systems make better predictions, identify buying signals, and provide a holistic view of customers' behaviors.

- **Merging sales and customer knowledge with digital capabilities.** In the past, humans were the experts and digital was the number cruncher. Now, an expert system has both the knowledge and the ability to analyze data and provide insights and even answers. These systems can do this in real time, especially with tasks that happen repeatedly, such as tailoring content for customers or coaching. As expert systems become more sophisticated, analytics and AI are becoming ubiquitous.

This chapter lays the groundwork for understanding analytics and AI and their wide-ranging impact on sales. The chapters that follow build on this to share more examples of how the capabilities are enabling better sales decisions that drive success for customers and companies alike.

12.

Designing the Sales Organization for the Digital Age

Microsoft, a technology behemoth, and W.W. Grainger, a leading distributor of industrial supplies and safety products for businesses, serve very different markets and are different in scale. But the same digital forces are reshaping both companies' sales channels, the paths they and their customers use to connect with each other. In the hunt for effectiveness, sales roles at both are becoming more specialized, with focused responsibilities to bring expertise to key tasks. And in the hunt for efficiency, both organizations are using less costly channels (such as digital and inside sales and partner resellers at Microsoft) to take over certain sales tasks that these channels do well.

This chapter describes the various channel choices, using Microsoft, W.W. Grainger, and other sales structures as examples. Then the chapter explores four key issues that are greatly affected by digital when designing a sales organization for maximum impact:

- Choosing the right channel structure

- Specializing sales roles and channels to balance effectiveness, coverage, and cost

- Leveraging inside sales and its growing power

- Dynamically adapting the sales structure and size

Choosing the right channel structure

Companies can use many channels to reach and respond to customers. These include both direct channels (the company's own sales force and website, for example) and indirect ones (intermediaries such as distributors and resellers).

Direct and indirect channels

With direct channels alone, there are numerous options. (See table 12-1.) Personal ones include field sales roles (which have morphed into hybrid roles, in which salespeople connect with customers in person as well as virtually and digitally) and inside roles (salespeople interacting with customers mostly virtually and digitally.) There are various digital channels, including email, text messaging, and social media, to name a few. A website typically serves as the online face of a B2B company and is often the first point of contact for prospects to get information; companies use websites to capture leads and host webinars. Further, they use e-commerce platforms to support online purchasing, and chatbots to provide real-time customer support and even to initiate sales conversations.

Channels are categorized as "pull" or "push" depending on who's asking for or providing the information. Sometimes customers start an interaction with a seller by pulling information from their channel of choice. Other times, the seller initiates contact by pushing information, either digitally (email, text, etc.) or through a salesperson.

Besides these direct channels, there many indirect channels. Different industries use different types of channel partners, including independent

TABLE 12-1

Direct channel choices

Sales roles and channels	Personal channels		Digital	Who initiates interaction?	
	Field/hybrid salesperson	*Inside salesperson*	**Digital**	*Seller (push)*	*Buyer (pull)*
Account executive (sales)	✓	✓		✓	✓
Solution/product specialists	✓	✓		✓	✓
Account management	✓	✓		✓	✓
Customer success	✓	✓		✓	✓
Trade shows	✓			✓	✓
Customer support	✓	✓	✓	✓	✓
Website (information)			✓		✓
Website (e-commerce)			✓		✓
Email			✓	✓	✓
Social media			✓	✓	✓
Online advertising			✓	✓	✓
Webinar	✓		✓		✓

organizations that sell the product without taking ownership of it (such as agents or brokers) and resellers that purchase and resell the product (such as distributors and retailers). Channel partners can bring a variety of benefits. Among these are market expertise, customer relationships, faster and broader market access, reduced cost and risk, and an ability to bundle your offering with complementary products and services.

Having more channel choices allows sellers to better match connections to customer opportunities, needs, knowledge, preferences, and buying steps. At the same time, using many channels introduces design and coordination challenges.

Channel structure at W.W. Grainger and Microsoft

Let's look at the channel structure of W.W. Grainger and Microsoft. A simplified version of the structure at each company is shown in figures 12-1 and 12-2.

FIGURE 12-1

Sales channel design at W.W. Grainger

	Large to midsize customers	Smaller customers
Go-to-market business model	High-touch solutions Customized services and curated product offering for complex operations	Endless assortment Expansive assortment at competitive prices for less complex operations
Relationships	Sales and service reps + digital	Primarily digital
Order origination	Digital (75%), phone (17%), branch (8%)	Website
Order fulfillment	Distribution center (70%) Inventory management (17%) Pickup at branch (13%)	Distribution center Third parties

Source: Adapted from W.W. Grainger's 2022 annual report.

FIGURE 12-2

Sales channel design at Microsoft

	Large enterprise customers	Corporate and medium customers	Other customers
Account management and revenues	Account executives (AEs) Account technology strategists	Partner resellers, supported by AEs	
Solution design	Solution areas specialists (such as Azure, Modern Work, Data and AI), Solutions sales professionals (such as Technology Solution Professionals)	Partner resellers, supported by Microsoft specialists	
Customer support and renewals	AEs, inside sales, and digital		
Value realization	Customer success managers		

W.W. Grainger

The company sells a large assortment of industrial products, including motors, lighting, material handling, tools, and safety supplies, along with inventory management services. It has a distribution system that includes 390 global branch stores, distribution centers, field salespeople, inside sales and service reps, and an array of digital channels. Most of Grainger's revenues come from a multichannel "high-touch solutions" business that serves the complex needs of enterprise customers, such as a large multilocation manufacturing operation. In this business, Grainger partners with customers to create solutions for managing the total cost of industrial supplies, including product, ordering, inventory, and stockout costs. Although many parts of this business are sales force–driven, routine ordering is mostly done by the customers digitally or is automatically executed based on inventory levels. With two million product offerings available in high-touch solutions, 75 percent of orders are digitally placed.

Grainger also has a large and growing "endless assortment" business, which is all digital with no salespeople. The service, which caters to customers who know what they want or can find what they need online, uses an e-commerce website featuring eleven million items.

The company's business of distributing physical products is heavily infused with digital, both for high-touch solutions and for endless assortment customers. Still, a customer can also pick up products directly from Grainger's branch stores.

Microsoft

It sells a broad line of solutions including software, cloud systems and services, computing devices, and other products to consumers and all types of businesses. The diverse range of offerings caters to the evolving needs of a global customer base. Using various combinations of key account managers, field salespeople, inside salespeople, digital channels, and channel partners, Microsoft tailors outreach to the individual preferences and requirements of its business buyers. While salespeople play a key role in connecting with corporate and medium-size customers, many interactions with them are virtual or digital. Much of the push and pull sourcing of these customers is over the web, supported by inside sales. And digital outreach and inside sales are used for renewals and customer support across all segments. Further, the customer success managers who support value realization for Azure, Microsoft's cloud computing platform, engage with customers mostly remotely, even at large enterprise accounts.

Digital is transforming the way companies across industries connect with their customers. Let's delve into the critical factors that will shape your decisions about how to specialize your sales roles, how to leverage inside sales, and how to craft a flexible sales organization that adapts rapidly to change.

Specializing sales roles

When B2B companies are small or have a limited product line or a narrow profile of target customers, salespeople can sell the company's full product line and perform all the steps of the sales process for all types of customers. But the vast majority of B2B sellers have more-specialized roles. Companies like Microsoft, which sells a range of complex products to many different markets, have sales roles that are specialized on three dimensions:

- **Market specialization** assigns sales duties by the type of account or market; for example, industry vertical sales teams. Another example is a structure that uses field sales for large accounts, inside sales for midsize accounts, and digital channels for small accounts.

- **Product specialization** (or solution area specialization) divides up sales responsibility so that different roles or channels handle different product or service offerings.

- **Activity specialization** partitions tasks according to the sales process step; for example, digital channels generate leads, account managers close deals, and customer success managers help buyers realize value.

Specialization allows a sales organization to match roles and channels to customer needs and the size of an opportunity, helping you achieve four outcomes:

- **Impact.** For companies such as Microsoft, the breadth and complexity of solutions, coupled with the diversity of customers, makes it impossible for a single salesperson to master the competencies needed to sell all products, execute all selling steps, and serve all types of customers effectively. Specialization builds and leverages their expertise.

- **Attention.** Specialist sales roles guarantee a focus on strategic priorities. Product specialists direct effort to specific products. Customer success managers (a type of activity specialization) ensure there is concentrated effort on helping customers realize value and expand usage. Market specialists help drive the growth and penetration of targeted industries.

- **Efficiency.** Using less expensive resources, such as digital channels, inside sales, or channel partners, helps deliver what customers need while keeping the cost of sales in line with the opportunity. Less costly channels can cover small accounts, sell simpler products, and execute selling steps such as generating leads and securing renewals. This allows more-expensive field salespeople to focus on high-value customers, products, and tasks.

- **Coverage.** Digital and inside sales channels can reach smaller and remotely located customers. A channel partner can reach buyer segments in which the partner has established relationships or geographic coverage.

Along with these benefits, specialization adds complications. As you increase the number of specialized sales roles or channels, you also increase the need for coordination—and introduce the possibility of confusion about who is responsible for what. And it becomes harder to adapt as business needs change. The question of whether and how to specialize depends on the extent to which the benefits outlined above outweigh the increased complexity you will have to manage.

Specializing by market

Market specialization can be by industry, customer size, or geography. It is the most common type of specialization and brings value in several ways.

You can drive impact with customers in certain segments (e.g., industries) who value a salesperson with deep knowledge of their issues and needs. You can bring attention to key markets and types of customers (e.g., time-consuming new accounts) that are likely to be overlooked if left to a generalist salesperson alone. And you can increase efficiency if smaller or remotely located customers can be served more profitably by less expensive resources, such as inside sales or digital channels.

Large companies that serve diverse customers tend to specialize by market. For example:

- Microsoft segments its sales force by customer size and industry.

- Grainger's high-touch solutions business serves large customers that value a personalized, hands-on approach. The endless assortment business, which is separate, serves customers that value convenience and price.

- Caterpillar has dedicated sales teams for construction, mining, agriculture, and other industries.

- American Express has dedicated sales teams for serving small and medium-size businesses and separate teams for large corporate clients.

Market specialization builds focused expertise and helps you provide tailored solutions. By aligning sales teams with specific customer types, industries, and geographies, companies can better understand their clients' pain points and deliver more effective and relevant products or services. This approach also enables more-targeted marketing efforts and customer relationship management strategies, thereby enhancing customer satisfaction and retention.

Specializing by product

By dividing up sales responsibility for diverse products among different roles and channels, you can realize several benefits. You can drive impact with customers when focused expertise is needed for complex offerings. You can bring attention to products that are likely to be overlooked if a generalist salesperson must sell everything. And you can drive efficiency if simpler products can be sold more profitably by less expensive resources, such as an inside sales team.

There are two prevalent models of product specialization. The first, solution specialists, is a model Microsoft uses for complex offerings. These specialists add a layer of expertise to assist account executives and customers with solutions that cut across offerings, making selling a team effort. For example, a solution for a Microsoft customer could use Azure, AI tools, a collaboration platform, and a CRM system. Several product specialists have to come together to configure a complete solution. In the most complex situations, the Microsoft team can include dozens of product specialists.

Another model is common in the medical products and pharmaceutical industry. Sets of products are covered by different account executives, and each account has multiple primary leads who are knowledgeable about and responsible for different products. For example, a medical diagnostics sales organization that sold a broad, complex portfolio of research and diagnostic products had four separate product specialty teams, which shared hospitals as customers. Three of the teams worked mostly in person at hospitals, while the fourth was an inside team that sold simpler products. This structure provided autonomy and product focus for salespeople while ensuring key products got adequate attention, expertise, and effort.

Specializing by activity

By partitioning activities or selling step responsibilities and giving them to different roles and channels, you can accomplish several objectives. You can drive impact with customers when selling activities (such as designing solutions) are complex and require focused expertise. You can bring attention to any selling activities (such as acquiring new accounts) that are likely to be underemphasized by a generalist salesperson, who may get distracted by other responsibilities. And you can drive efficiency if there are selling activities (such as placing orders) that can be performed less expensively by more-efficient channels without sacrificing effectiveness.

Specialization by the stage of the sales journey has been in the making for decades. Now, with the infusion of digital and the growth of inside sales, it has become even more prevalent. It is easier to implement when the sales process is sequential. For example, digital channels and inside sales handle prospecting and lead qualification. Once a promising lead is identified, the baton passes to a business development team, professionals who possess the finesse to translate initial interest into tangible opportunities by understanding customer pain points, presenting tailored solutions, and navigating the negotiation process. After acquiring a customer, account managers or customer success managers enter the picture to nurture and grow the relationship. These specialists possess an intimate knowledge of the customer's needs and business objectives, enabling them to offer personalized solutions and exceptional service.

Specialization by activity is increasingly used with nonsequential buyer journeys as well. With easy access to digital channels, buyers more often move nonlinearly between purchasing steps. A buyer might first learn about your offerings from your website, then talk to someone on your business development team, and then go back to your website to view a webinar. This sequence is unpredictable; the customer is in control and chooses the channel that brings the most value at any point in time. An always-available and easy-to-access website is convenient for getting product information, while a human expert is better for answering complex questions and brainstorming solutions. You don't know which path the customer will choose, yet you must coordinate or orchestrate across the channels to create a seamless customer experience. (More about this in chapter 14.)

Facilitating collaboration by mirroring specialists

While specialized sales roles bring advantages in effectiveness, focus, and efficiency, they also bring friction. The more specialists there are, the more difficult it becomes to coordinate customer interactions. (Chapters 14 and 15 share management and technology solutions for addressing this challenge.) In these cases, companies can use sales force design to facilitate collaboration among different sales roles. By "mirroring" territories, the specialists or teams that execute different aspects of the sales process are responsible for a common set of accounts. For example, an account executive, an inside salesperson, a solution specialist, and a CSM might work together to serve the same set of customers. Many-to-one mirrors are also a possibility; for example, a solution specialist might be assigned to work with two or more AEs. The purpose of mirroring is to minimize the number of people that each specialist works with, making it easier to coordinate efforts, share information, and ensure a consistent customer experience.

Leveraging inside sales to increase reach and reduce costs

Field sales and inside sales have traditionally had their own domains. Field salespeople did the heavy lifting, working with customers in person. Inside salespeople sold over the telephone and web and were responsible for the uncomplicated products, simpler sales tasks—such as lead generation and renewals—and small and remotely located customers.

In the digital world, inside sales continues in its past role, but has also expanded into serving larger customers with complex needs. Also, inside salespeople who once performed only simple tasks are doing more-complex steps, including assessing customer needs, crafting solutions, and closing sales. (It should be noted that field sales is also tapping into the tools of inside sales, as field salespeople take on hybrid roles that involve a mix of in-person, virtual, and digital interaction with customers.)

Not surprisingly, most B2B companies have ramped up their inside sales investment. For example:

- AstraZeneca replaced virtually all its field sales force support for its mature brand Nexium with a three-hundred-person inside sales team. The team took care of most doctors' basic needs for samples and information at a substantially reduced cost.

- IBM invested in social media training, tool kits, and personalized digital pages to help its inside salespeople generate leads and manage account relationships. This resulted in a significant increase in the number of high-quality inbound leads.

- SAP refocused its large and growing inside sales team on working with channel partners rather than directly with customers. This was part of a strategic initiative aimed at increasing channel sales to 40 percent of the company's total sales by 2015.

When appropriately utilized, inside sales reduces the cost of sales 40 percent to 90 percent, relative to field sales, while revenues are maintained or even grow. Benefits include:

- Reduced cost per contact and increased number of contacts per day

- Increased revenues in accounts that were low priority for field sales but are high priority for inside sales

- Greater access and faster response times for customers

- Increased effectiveness through specializing inside salespeople by industry, product, or activity, without the increased territory size penalty that specialization creates for field sales teams

- Flexibility to scale up the size of inside sales teams without relocating sellers

- Easier coaching and development for inside salespeople, whose customer interactions are easily observed and usually recorded

The growth of inside sales continues to outpace that of field sales, as buyers get more comfortable collaborating remotely, videoconferencing and augmented and virtual reality (AR/VR) technologies become easier to use and more powerful, freemium and subscription businesses steer more customers to buy from digital and inside sales channels, and richer data and analytics allow inside sellers to bring buyers customized content and offerings.

Task division between field and inside sales

Most B2B selling models include both inside and field sales. So, how do you know if your organization can do a better job of leveraging inside sales as part of your overall selling model? An effective approach is to partition the sales job and divide responsibilities along the three dimensions of specialization described earlier in this chapter:

- **Product specialization.** Use inside sales to sell transactional offerings and solutions that have lower buyer risk and don't require on-site assessments or collaboration. Use field sales to sell more-complex products and services that require a consultative approach and customization.

- **Activity specialization.** Use inside sales to supplement field sales activities in large accounts, especially early in the process (e.g., lead generation) or late in the process (e.g., repeat purchases). Use field sales for tasks that benefit from a high-touch approach.

- **Market specialization.** Use inside sales for the entire selling process in small-to-medium- size businesses that have straightforward needs and moderate-to-low potential, or to reach accounts in remotely located areas. Use field sales to manage large accounts with complex needs and buying processes, and more opportunity.

When focused on the right products and services, sales process steps, and customer or market segments, inside sales can drive huge efficiency improvements with little or no loss of effectiveness. As customers get more comfortable buying this way, the impact will become even greater.

Dynamically adapting the sales structure and size

Sales organizations are not known for rapid change. At most companies, major changes in their design occur because of major events, such as shifts in the product portfolio or market disruption. Between these events, stability is the norm. While salespeople customize their approach and offerings to each customer's needs, macro-level sales structure elements remain static. Sellers are anchored by a repeatable and proven process. Territories define their customer, product, and task assignments, allowing salespeople to develop expertise and build long-term customer relationships.

Yet meeting the needs of today's buyers requires more-frequent change. Sellers routinely adapt to buyers as their needs, knowledge, and preferences shift. But it is difficult to take agility to the next level, for example, by varying roles or sales force size. Changing sales organizations at the macro level every two years or even every year is not enough. Consider three strategies to bring change when your portfolio and the market demand it.

Leverage turnover

Most B2B sales forces have to replace between 25 percent and 50 percent of their salespeople every year, due to voluntary and involuntary departures as well as promotions and reassignments. But turnover doesn't need to only be a challenge—it can also be an opportunity to resize and redeploy. With digital tools, it is possible to make a real-time assessment of an about-to-become-vacant territory's potential, historical performance, and customer needs. This helps determine whether the territory should be filled or whether it's better to reassign its accounts and either eliminate the headcount or redeploy it to an area with greater opportunity.

By proactively managing territory vacancies, you can use attrition as a tool to continually keep your sales force's size and deployment aligned with market and company needs.

Create flexible layers

Agile organizations balance continuity and adaptability by designing sales roles that are stable on some dimensions but flexible on others. The structure might include a mix of customer-focused roles and specialized roles. The customer-focused ones bring continuity; salespeople in these positions have more-stable customer assignments, so they can become intimately familiar with their buyers' preferences and pain points. This allows for more personalized and effective engagement and encourages long-term relationships that foster trust, loyalty, and repeat business, contributing to sustainable revenue growth. The specialty roles bring flexibility; salespeople in these positions have a looser alignment to specific customers but perform the same task consistently, such as qualification, product demos, or pricing. The size of the team also shifts more easily without negatively affecting customer relationships.

Constantly experiment and assess

It's challenging for leaders to make changes in a timely manner while also assuring they make the right decisions. Ongoing experimentation can uncover insights for balancing speed and quality in your decision-making. By trying out new concepts on a small scale, organizations can see what works before making broad changes. One technology company introduced various types of technical sales specialists in select territories and then monitored KPIs to measure the impact on sales velocity. The company also has an innovation manager who focuses on running and learning from the various ongoing experiments.

Build a digital foundation to bring agility to change

To create the agility required for adapting sales roles and channels, you need to have a real-time view of how your current coverage is working, where there are gaps, and where there is misaligned capacity. To support such insights, having a digital data and technology infrastructure is foundational. Some organizations have centralized these capabilities in a digital customer hub, also referred to as a demand center or a digital customer platform. The hub houses integrated data and uses analytics to create predictions about each customer's needs and coverage requirements, along with an assessment of channel productivity. (DCHs will be covered in depth in chapter 15.) By aggregating this data by territory and geographic market, you can see which salespeople are overworked or underutilized, and which regions are underserved or have slack capacity. The assessments allow the ongoing realignment of sales roles and channels to match customers' ever-evolving needs.

With sales roles becoming increasingly specialized, and reliance growing on inside and digital selling, companies are finding that new competencies are required for salespeople to execute their roles. In the next chapter, we discuss how success profiles are changing, including the five competencies your sales team needs to thrive in a digital future.

13.

Unlocking Five Digital-Age Sales Competencies

A sales leader at an asset management firm reflected, "Our inside salespeople are doing a better job than our field salespeople. And they make one-third as much." In the pharmaceutical industry, where half of doctors will not see salespeople in face-to-face meetings, one sales leader told us, "We need a different breed of salesperson with a higher digital quotient."

In every industry, what it takes to succeed in sales is changing. The rise of digital has led to more informed and self-sufficient buyers, the proliferation of sales channels, and a growing array of data and tools for improving decisions. Together, these trends are redefining the profile of a successful seller. The focus is shifting even more strongly from closing the sale to mining for mutual value. Organizations face a brave new world where every field salesperson is both a key account manager, coordinating multiple stakeholders from the selling and buying sides, and an inside salesperson, proficient with digital and virtual channels and data-directed selling.

The classic dimensions of a winning salesperson remain relevant. Knowledge of markets, customers, and products is key, as are skills for planning, working with customers, and advancing opportunities. Characteristics such as persistence, curiosity, and empathy remain essential for building customer relationships, but at the same time, success in the digital world hinges on five new competencies.

This chapter explores these five competencies, including how to hire for them, ways to develop them in your team, and the supporting resources your salespeople will need. Finally, the chapter provides insights about how the competencies are relevant for sales leaders too.

The five competencies for salespeople

The factors that are increasingly important for success in the digital world and are becoming more salient in job postings at leading companies are:*

- Anticipating the customer's tomorrow

- Collaborating inside and out

- Leveraging virtual channels and digital tools

- Getting power from data and analytics

- Adapting to constant change

Anticipating the customer's tomorrow

Customer and market knowledge has always been table stakes for success, especially with complex solution sales. But in the digital landscape, customers want salespeople to bring new and deeper business insights.

According to a job posting at pharmaceutical company Merck, virology sales representatives must "stay ahead of market trends, assess impact of dynamics on the current business state and make proactive recommendations to meet the future needs of the business." Salespeople who can

---

*Job postings shared in this chapter were pulled from corporate websites and other online sources during 2022. Some postings are no longer active.

make "proactive recommendations to meet the future needs of the business" are more likely to get access to key decision-makers.

At Microsoft, account executives for digital native customers need "an ability to understand how startup businesses grow and mature their commercial models," along with an "understanding of the partner ecosystem required to support enterprise startup/unicorn customers" and how such customers successfully implement cloud infrastructure solutions. Account executives who harness the breadth of Microsoft's experience—which includes helping dozens of other startups tackle challenges similar to those a particular account faces—can bring a perspective that gets them an agenda-setting front seat at the buyer's table.

At W.W. Grainger, account managers for manufacturing customers "understand customer goals and remain alert and responsive to changing customer needs," and need "knowledge of market data and access to resources to quickly respond to new developments in the customer's business." This knowledge helps salespeople enrich regular business reviews with customers, elevating the buyer's view of Grainger from vendor to partner.

Across industries, the nuanced task of anticipating customer needs is a key source of salespeople's power.

Collaborating inside and out

Consistently, we see the classic idea of salespeople as resourceful and self-sufficient individualists giving way to a new view of them: team players who function as part of a collective.

Thinking of sales as a team sport is a tectonic shift for some industries. The decades-old pharmaceutical sales model consisted of a seller sharing information with physicians. As the health-care environment became more complex, pharma companies added specialized sales and nonsales roles, including community liaisons, patient support professionals, medical reimbursement specialists, and more. All these roles must collaborate to help providers meet a broader range of patient needs.

One wealth management firm has moved from a one-to-one approach to a many-to-one, team-based strategy with their high-net-worth clients.

Instead of working with a single adviser, they now have access to a group of people, including investment product managers and specialists in estate planning. Most clients find this leads to better service and less risk. For the firm, it is less likely that advisers will leave and take clients with them to a new employer.

Many sales teams in service businesses have teamwork in their DNA already. Take the example of our consulting firm, ZS. Many of our customers are large enterprises with many divisions and functions with multifaceted needs. We offer an array of strategy and advisory services, including in areas such as AI and analytics, digital and technology solutions, and more. A single ZS account manager, no matter how skilled or hardworking, can't possibly understand all the detailed needs of a large global customer, plus the intricacies of all the products and services we can offer. Successful account managers leverage the expertise of ZS solution specialists, and sometimes external experts. Further, ZS customers often have complex buying decision processes, so account managers must facilitate collaboration among many decision-makers.

Other sales organizations are similarly team-focused. At Microsoft, a posting for a sales specialist for modern work applications says the role involves "collaborating across different groups inside the customer environment to successfully enable customers to drive transition to digital transformation." A posting for a solution area specialist for Azure Data and AI uses the word "collaborate" nine times and references several teams within Microsoft, including the extended sales team, technical sales professionals, partners, service, global black belts, and marketing. At Merck, virology sales representatives "collaborate and model teamwork with extended members of the Virology Account Team (Community Liaisons, Managed Care, Marketing)." At Bank of America, private client managers "work in close partnership with Private Bank Associates and other specialists to ensure there is a coordinated approach to the clients' day-to-day needs" and "liaise with specialists, service officers, and other resources to ensure the integrated delivery of investment, fiduciary, credit, and banking solutions."

Sales success increasingly depends on collaboration and teamwork, with diverse roles working together to meet complex customer needs.

Leveraging virtual channels and digital tools

Sales organizations in almost every industry have embraced hybrid sales models, engaging customers through a judicious blend of digital, virtual, and in-person interactions. To keep up, salespeople need proficiency with collaboration tools such as Zoom, Webex, Teams, Slack, and SharePoint. These tools facilitate communication not only with decision-makers in the customer's organization, but also with members of the sales team and other internal stakeholders.

In pharmaceuticals, a hybrid approach has become the norm for customer connection. At Pfizer, health and science professional sales candidates "effectively build rapport and relationships with customers across virtual and face-to-face environments" while "utilizing current digital tools effectively (e.g., Veeva Engage, Zoom, Webex, Microsoft Office) and adapting quickly to new/beta tools (e.g., digital triage app) for successful customer engagement." As in-person sales reps' access to health-care providers has declined, providers are opening more pharma company emails, pulling more pharma-created content from websites, and meeting with salespeople virtually.

The tech industry has also adopted hybrid sales models. Sales representatives at MarcoPolo Learning, a provider of early childhood technology, engage with targeted schools and childcare programs "through telemarketing, in-person meetings, conferences, and digital marketing campaigns." At software company Outreach, sales development representatives who cover small and medium-size businesses are required to "leverage sales tools such as LinkedIn Navigator to network with potential customers." Most technology account executives blend communication methods with their customers, such as using in-person meetings to understand the buyer's needs and build a relationship and then virtual methods for follow-up and online product demos, especially when connecting with geographically dispersed buying and selling teams. The power of face-to-face is enhanced when combined with the reach, efficiency, and frequency of virtual.

Asset management companies are also finding that as customers become more open to (and sometimes prefer) virtual connection, hybrid engagement models produce better outcomes. At J.P. Morgan, a hybrid model allows salespeople to have longer and more-meaningful engagements with customers, tailored to specific preferences. At BlackRock, the shifting of many in-person visits to virtual has allowed the company to better tailor efforts to each stage of the buying cycle and to offer on-demand scheduling and service. At American Funds, hybrid selling has created a more adaptable sales organization as salespeople pivot more quickly among topics, activities, services, and modes of engagement.

LinkedIn and other social media sites have become essential tools for helping sellers stay abreast of customer and industry insights, find (or be found by) prospective customers, and build a network of connections, including colleagues, customers, and industry thought leaders. Still, virtual and digital can't replace the power of in-person sales in all situations. (See chapter 14 for more about how social media helps salespeople, as well as when to use digital, virtual, and in-person communication to engage with customers.)

Getting power from data and analytics

As computer power, the volume of data, and the sophistication of analytics grow, an increasing source of salespeople's value is their ability to bring data-based business insights to customers.

At biopharma company UCB, neurology sales representatives are expected to "analyze business and sales data to inform a strategic and tactical approach to maximizing growth." Analytics helps sales reps dynamically target the right doctors with the right message at the right time. Reps work with algorithmic outputs that share next-best-action recommendations, receiving insights about patient disease progression, local health environments, a provider's likelihood of switching therapies, and other factors. These insights allow them to connect with receptive providers and tailor communications to patient needs.

Microsoft's sales executives are using similar types of skills to get value from a tool called Daily Recommender. The tool uses data, such as a customer's consumption level, licenses, and digital interactions with marketing material, to make AI-based suggestions about renewals and product recommendation. Sales executives who use Daily Recommender are spending less time gathering data and more time engaging in meaningful, personalized conversations with buyers. Measures of time in front of customers and leads converted to opportunities are up by as much as 40 percent. Plus, customers are happier because their conversations with sales executives are more relevant. (Read more about Daily Recommender in chapter 16.)

At multinational conglomerate 3M, national key account managers for home improvement need "highly developed Excel skills and competency in handling complex data analytics." These account managers use analytics to show retailers the business impact of in-store programs, category management strategies, inventory planning, and more. This helps 3M prove the ongoing value its solutions bring, strengthening partnerships with major retailers. Although the job posting stretches the boundaries of what most salespeople do (they rarely need to be true analysts), key account salespeople are generally more effective when they can use analytics to give customers deeper insights about their business.

Adapting to constant change

Adaptability has always been important for salespeople. Yet it used to mean selecting the right approach from the finite set of options spelled out in a playbook. Now playbooks, and even sales roles themselves, take on novel dimensions frequently.

At Pfizer, health and science professional sales reps are "change agile and able to adapt quickly to workplace changes" and must "demonstrate ability to quickly learn and embrace new ways of working in a rapidly changing environment."

Apple's enterprise channel account executives are expected to "adapt to change and find the right path without necessarily having all of the pieces to the puzzle" and "shift gears and thrive when asked to explore new ground." For AEs, the speed of industry innovation increases exponentially as existing technologies enable new generations of even better technologies. At the same time, constant advancements are happening within Apple itself. For the iPhone alone, Apple launched twenty new models between 2018 and 2022. AEs must also keep up with ongoing changes to each customer's network, voice, and video environment to ensure that Apple devices integrate effectively.

Across industries, accelerating innovation increases the frequency with which sales roles evolve, new channels emerge, channel partners come on board, and changes to systems disrupt the daily cadence of sales. There can be more-frequent change within the customer's business and the buying organization as well, including who is involved and when and how decision-makers choose to engage. A decision-maker may want to meet in person at first and later may prefer to use digital and virtual channels for repeat purchases and advice about execution. Salespeople who can't respond to this fluidity will routinely miss opportunities and lose out to nimbler competitors.

Hiring, developing, and supporting the five competencies

How do you make sure your sales organization is equipped with these five competencies? Hiring for them is certainly an option. To a large extent, they can also be developed and nurtured through training, coaching, and work-based learning.

Hiring for the competencies

Two items on the list—collaborating and adapting to change—are likely to be mostly in the *hire for* category. In our experience, these are largely inherent traits that people are slow to build.

Some trainable competencies make the *hire for* list too, such as the ability to anticipate the customer's tomorrow. When Google Cloud tripled the size of its sales organization in 2019, it targeted experienced candidates who had demonstrated success at SAP, Oracle, Microsoft, and AWS. Google wanted salespeople who already had industry knowledge and relationships and could hit the ground running.

Other companies screen for digital and virtual sales competencies when they hire. When reflecting on the capabilities of his current people, one sales manager said, "They never signed up to be virtual reps . . . they want to be out in the field." When hiring salespeople now, the company assesses candidates' ability to learn new technologies and willingness to communicate using the channels customers prefer, whether digital, virtual, or in person. Other companies are screening candidates for their willingness to follow AI-based suggestions and share customer insights to help train AI models, a skill that comes naturally to inside salespeople. One organization looks to hire "diggers" who enjoy figuring out what the customer needs and knows, as well as (at least a little bit) "wizards" who are clever at using data to show customers the path to value. Interview questions include: What digital tools do you use to gather information, monitor, and engage? What are all the ways you use LinkedIn to enhance your sales process? How do you network and build your personal/professional brand?

Developing the competencies

As one sales manager told us, "One-third of my people just don't get it; they don't have the digital skills and interest." This presents a significant challenge, yet the flip side of the manager's observation is encouraging: for the two-thirds of people who do "get it," the right development programs can go a long way toward boosting the capabilities they need.

The pandemic-induced shift to virtual work proved that most of the digitally deficient and defiant can climb the learning curve. And digital natives (those born since 1980) will make up over 80 percent of the workforce by 2030. Most employees are already facile with Zoom and LinkedIn by the time they enter the workforce. And CRM tools are easy to learn. A posting by Aflac for a benefits adviser position shows the company believes technology proficiency can be developed, indicating that candidates must "become tech savvy, as it relates to a CRM system, enrollment platforms, etc."

Still, building some competencies requires more than training and coaching. Consider the AEs at Microsoft who sell to digital native startups. They need to understand the evolving technology needs of startups beyond what they can glean from a report. Such a capability is honed over time through experience and apprenticeship in other roles that touch the startup ecosystem.

At one cloud-based software company, new salespeople are connected early on to curated collaboration opportunities. The sales team also leverages technology to encourage collaboration across teams and departments. And at one of our global health-care clients, leaders insist that people consistently back up their reasoning with data at meetings. It is now an ingrained habit.

Supporting the team

While sales organizations hire for and develop the five competencies, companies can provide support resources that help the team with tasks that require these skills. Some companies have a centralized or regional digital concierge, a dedicated person or team that supports salespeople in using digital resources and analytics. The concierge can provide immediate answers to common questions, offer training and help, and ensure that the team has access to up-to-date tools, content, and resources. In some cases, the concierge responds to individual requests for analyses that address specific questions or concerns. Another company has a centralized center of excellence (COE) that feeds on-demand industry and customer research to key account salespeople. *Anticipating the customer's tomorrow* becomes a responsibility of headquarters, in addition to one of salespeople. This also helps keep salespeople focused on customers.

How the five competencies apply to sales leaders

These skills are not important just for salespeople; they are also critical for you as a sales leader in the digital age.

The first and last competencies—*anticipating the customer's tomorrow* and *adapting to constant change*—are closely linked. The ability to foresee and adapt to change has always been vital for a sales leader's sustained success. Its salience is heightened as you face constant digital disruption to your markets and the competitive landscape, as well as rapid evolution in business models (the swift and drastic shift to remote work is one example). You must anticipate change and respond quickly to ensure your sales team stays effective and competitive.

Although *collaborating inside and out* has similarly always been key, this competency now needs even more emphasis. Customers demand a seamless experience, so sales, marketing, and customer service must coalesce around them more than ever before. The support functions of IT and HR are pitching in too to increase the impact and velocity of sales decisions and processes. Collaboration is in; silos are out. The need for external collaboration grows as well. More and more companies rely on partnerships both to meet customer needs and to design and operate internal processes. An example is value-added resellers (VARs) who add features or services (for example, integration, training, ongoing support) to a company's products, giving customers more complete and valuable solutions.

The role of digital in engaging customers and optimizing sales processes continues to grow, and your success increasingly requires you to *leverage virtual channels and digital tools.* You must understand and help select, deploy, and use digital resources for your team. Further, there are numerous ways that digital tools help you save time and perform your own duties more effectively. For example, using Zoom and Teams, sales leaders can conduct virtual meetings, collaborate in real time, and connect with partners and employees regardless of location. To take another example, generative AI can analyze meeting recordings and extract key insights.

Finally, *getting power from data and analytics* is a vital competency for sales leaders in the digital world. As explored in chapter 11, analytics and AI can inform almost every sales decision, from customer strategy to organization design to talent management.

———————

Sales leaders require a multipronged strategy for mastering these essential competencies while transforming the role and mindset of the salespeople on their teams. One thing is clear: for any sales role, an enhanced "digital quotient" is a key ingredient in the recipe for future success. Digital capabilities help sellers and leaders anticipate customer needs and collaborate to meet them. Digital also helps sellers and leaders use new communication channels and leverage data and analytics to drive value. And digital skills are essential for sellers and leaders to keep up with the environment's shifts. One big adjustment is learning how to combine the use of in-person, virtual, and digital sales channels—the topic of the next chapter.

14.

Synchronizing Sales Channels for Maximum Impact

Sales channels are the routes companies use to connect with their customers and prospects. The sales force is one key channel, and the focus of this book. Salespeople communicate with customers in three main ways: in person, virtually such as live video and telephone, and digitally through social media, email, and messaging. At the same time, one type of salesperson, such as an account executive, may work together with other salespeople (product specialists, customer success managers, inside sales) and with digital channels (websites, banner ads) and perhaps with channel partners (agents, distributors, retailers).

It's enticing to imagine the power, precision, and personalization that five, ten, and perhaps even fifteen channels and communication methods all working in concert could bring to customer engagement. It's also easy to see how, as that number grows, it becomes more challenging to synchronize the channels and optimize them together.

A key part of a sales manager's job is to help their people use the various methods effectively while also ensuring their efforts align with those of other channels that share the same customers. With these goals in mind, this chapter covers the following topics:

- Optimizing the use of digital, virtual, and in-person communication methods

- Enabling channel collaboration so that the efforts of your sales team align with those of other channels

- Using a digital enablement concierge to support the sales team's use of digital for customer outreach and channel collaboration

- Adapting communication methods and channels continuously as customer needs, knowledge, and preferences evolve

Optimizing digital, virtual, and in-person communication

We estimate that most field salespeople interact with customers remotely the majority of the time. Some remote connections happen through digital methods such as email and social media. Others occur virtually, either over the telephone or, increasingly, over video calls. Many of these digital and virtual contacts follow up on or lead to in-person conversations. But some involve more-complex interactions, such as when salespeople do software demos over live video rather than at the customer's site. As people's comfort with digital and virtual tools grows, along with the sophistication of the technologies, remote connections become more common in both simple and complex selling situations.

Field salespeople can boost their customer interaction time and productivity by 20 percent or more if, instead of meeting only in person, they judiciously mix in virtual and digital connections. Yet too much reliance on digital and virtual creates risk. By finding the right balance of communication methods and honing their social media skills, salespeople can enhance the overall customer experience and contribute to better business outcomes.

Finding the right balance of engagement

Each connection method has some unique benefits:

- **Digital engagement,** using methods such as email, messaging, and social media, is efficient, convenient, and cost-effective for reaching a broad audience.

- **Virtual engagement,** such as through videoconferencing, balances efficiency and effectiveness. Compared to in-person connections, virtual enables greater reach, allows more-frequent conversations, and makes it possible to cost-effectively bring together stakeholders from multiple locations. Virtual technology also provides an ability to record meetings, summarize discussions using AI, quickly look up information to share, and guide discussions through digital prompts. And augmented/virtual reality applications allow immersive product demonstrations.

- **In-person engagement** fosters the personal connections that bridge knowledge and trust gaps; this is especially important when acquiring new customers. In-person meetings are also helpful when crafting complex solutions.

Choosing the right method starts with understanding the customer's situation and tailoring your approach. (See table 14-1.)

Customer preference is an important consideration, one that can vary over time and with the situation. New buyers may prefer to interact virtually when vetting a supplier; later, they may favor face-to-face interactions for designing solutions, assessing supplier intentions, and building trust. A longtime customer, though, may appreciate the convenience and efficiency of virtual engagements. Using a blended approach allows your team to adapt quickly to what the buyer wants.

Although digital and virtual interactions are efficient, employing too little in-person connection creates risk. A key account manager succinctly

TABLE 14-1

How should a salesperson connect with a customer?

Method	Conditions that favor each method
Digital	• Customer is digitally savvy and knowledgeable about the offering. • Subject of communication is straightforward (e.g., sharing information) or digitally friendly (e.g., product configuration, software demos).
Virtual (remote live)	• Customer-salesperson relationship is one of mutual trust. • Offering is differentiated from competitive offerings. • Buyer is motivated (has urgent need). • Buyer and seller are geographically dispersed. • Buyer and seller want to efficiently assess each other's credibility and suitability early on.
In person	• Buyer does not recognize own latent needs. • Seller does not understand buyer's needs. • Buyer and seller are mutually seeking to discover new opportunities. • Seller does not understand buyer's decision-making and authority. • Seller needs to demonstrate differentiated value. • Seller needs to win buyer's trust. • There are sensitive or confidential issues to be discussed.

summarized why meeting in person with customers has value: "Half my opportunities come from informal customer discussions. And off-the-record conversations never happen over video." Another salesperson shared, "I sense what customers are feeling when I am with them."

When things are running smoothly with a customer, it can be easy to slide too far into digital and virtual engagement. This complacency can lead to being blindsided if your competitors are emphasizing in-person engagement to get close to your customers. The reverse is true as well: if your competitor is relying mostly on virtual, doubling down on face-to-face connection can earn you a beachhead.

Using social media effectively

Social media platforms such as LinkedIn, Facebook, X (formerly Twitter), and Instagram help sales teams enhance customer engagement, build relationships, and boost their company's visibility. Your industry may have its own platforms as well.

While your company uses social media to reinforce its brand, it can also help salespeople establish their own personal brands. There are four primary goals here:

1. Gain insight about and stay abreast of what's happening in the industry and with customers.

2. Be found by prospective customers who increasingly use digital sources to self-educate on issues, solutions, and suppliers. Posting on social media frequently and participating in online communities helps raise a company's and a salesperson's visibility.

3. Find prospects and discover who within each account can help advance the business relationship.

4. Connect meaningfully with (and stay connected to) customers, leads, prospects, colleagues, industry thought leaders, influencers, and others who can help drive sales growth. Using social media, salespeople can initiate conversations, share insights, establish credibility, and cultivate relationships. Connections, such as on LinkedIn, create opportunities for warm introductions to the people a salesperson wants to reach. And people are more open to engaging with others who share a mutual connection.

Table 14-2 lists some social media activities that salespeople, with support from the company, can use to achieve each of the four goals.

Effective and judicious use of digital and virtual outreach and social media is best done with centralized expertise and support. (We explore this later in this chapter.)

Enabling channel collaboration

Salespeople are just one of many channels that customers use when purchasing. The more sales channels a customer uses, the greater the possibility of cross-channel friction. Here are some examples: A buyer types information about their needs into a web form only to have to repeat it for an inside salesperson. Or a buyer gets a quote from a salesperson and a few days later receives an unsolicited email from the company's marketing team offering a better deal. Or an account executive is pursuing a technology upgrade with a customer, while a customer success manager is working with

TABLE 14-2

How salespeople get value from social media

Activities executed by salespeople (with company support)	Get insight	Be found	Find prospects	Connect
Maintain complete, professional social media profiles (e.g., LinkedIn).		✓		
Join industry and customer groups and communities. Follow discussions about markets and trends.	✓	✓	✓	
Monitor customer posts, comments, shares, and interactions with you and competitors.	✓			
Follow competitors. Learn about their latest products, promotions, and strategies.	✓			
Monitor and respond professionally and promptly to mentions of your brand, both positive and negative.				✓
Identify, follow, and collaborate with influencers. Use their endorsements or critiques to capture trends.	✓		✓	
Use and track hashtags linked to events, customer conversations, and trending topics.	✓	✓	✓	
Share insights, industry news, resources, and customer success stories.		✓		✓
Leverage referrals.			✓	✓
Engage in conversations with comments, likes, and shares.		✓		✓

the buyer to escalate the use of the existing technology. These types of redundancies and inconsistencies confuse and frustrate customers, wasting time and resources.

When channel collaboration is successful, buyers switch between channels without encountering inconsistencies or disruptions. Buying is convenient, personalized, and unified across all touchpoints. A streamlined experience leads to better results: cross-channel collaboration has proven to triple revenue gains, as compared with gains made by optimizing channels independently. Plus, collaboration reduces selling costs.

What makes channel collaboration challenging?

The difficulty of collaboration escalates when there are several independently managed channels or sales roles that work simultaneously with the same customers, and each channel or role is important for creating value in the sales process. Yet collaboration often brings the most benefits in this situation. Consider the case of a business software solutions firm that reached its customers using separately managed teams of account executives (AEs), customer success managers (CSMs), and new product specialists, along with inside sales and digital marketing. Here are five primary sources of challenges the firm faced and some examples:

- **Different priorities and strategies across roles that share customers.** Imagine that an AE wants to expand the set of products the account buys, while a CSM emphasizes satisfaction and the value of existing products. Or a new product specialist wants to drive entry and growth while an AM pushes back: "The technology is too new. I can't risk this with my customer right now."

- **Role ambiguity.** The AE and CSM both believe that they should take the lead in pursuing an existing product expansion opportunity.

- **A need to coordinate with different internal groups for different customers.** For example, for a prospect in the early stage of buying, an AE deals with marketing to decide on which product benefits to emphasize. For a customer who is ready to buy, the AE collaborates with finance to structure a deal. And for a customer in the intermediate buying stages, the AE engages a product or solutions team to design the offering. All these may need to happen in the same day.

- **Data gaps and organizational silos.** Data capture can be challenging. For example, social media platforms do not typically share data that identifies individual customers. This makes insight generation difficult. Additionally, data on customer interactions sits in unlinked databases that are managed by different functions. For example, some customer data is in the CRM system that supports the AEs, CSMs, and new product specialists. Other data is in a marketing platform used by digital marketing and inside sales.

- **The complexity of insight generation.** With numerous channels and massive amounts of data, it's not easy to figure out what to do and when.

Two levels of channel collaboration

Collaboration can happen in two ways, both of which rely on capturing records of customer interactions and making the history visible to those that work with the customer:

1. **Coordination** keeps the various channels informed about customer interactions while each channel decides its own course of action.

2. **Orchestration** provides—through either a person or a digital system—a centralized point of optimization and control of what to do when.

Many organizations start to build their collaboration capabilities with a coordination approach. Some then advance to an orchestration approach. Coordination can bring immense benefits but is difficult to do. Orchestration can be even more powerful yet is even more challenging.

Level 1: Coordinating the channels

Coordination is easier when selling involves steps that are sequential, but it's also possible when the steps are not.

With a sequential process, coordination might work as follows. Marketing generates leads through advertising, content creation, and digital campaigns. Inside sales follows up by vetting and qualifying these leads. Then qualified leads are turned over to account executives, who close deals. In this case, the roles have well-defined, sequential responsibilities. Since each role has access to the same data about customers and their past interactions with the company, the customer experience is streamlined and likely to result in a positive outcome.

When the sales process is not sequential, many organizations implement channel coordination with a "trigger" marketing and sales approach. The organization watches for events (such as a webinar registration or a significant milestone) that signify the possible interest or evolving needs of a customer. The trigger sets off a synchronized response across marketing and sales channels. For example, when a customer downloads a white paper, an automated email with additional information is sent to them, and the sales team receives a message recommending a personal outreach. In other situations, it's the salesperson who triggers outreach from a sales specialist, inside sales, or digital channels.

Level 2: Orchestrating the channels

The highest-impact and highest-difficulty approach to collaboration is to centralize the orchestration of the channels. This involves selecting, sequencing, and choosing the right message and content for each channel at each interaction. Either a person or a digital system decides what the company should offer a customer, along with the best message timing and delivery channel (e.g., digital message, phone call, personal visit) for driving engagement and moving the customer toward a purchase.

Orchestration is especially beneficial for recurring revenue businesses in which multiple types of specialists work simultaneously with large customers to ensure the ongoing creation of value. Often, such businesses will use a coordination model to find new customers, then will shift to orchestration once the opportunity is identified, qualified, and passed along to an account executive. In some cases, there is *orchestration* within marketing channels and sales channels, but *coordination* between marketing and sales.

A key question with orchestration is: Who should call the shots? When personal selling is the most important channel (as is typical with key accounts), sales is usually the orchestrator. When there are many small and medium-size customers, the orchestrator can be marketing or a digital system. Let's look at each option.

SALES-LED ORCHESTRATION. The key account team model is a prime example of this approach, since key accounts expect orchestration. A key account manager leads the team and is unambiguously accountable for the customer. It's clear who makes decisions about who should reach out and when.

Some pharmaceutical companies use sales-led orchestration when sharing information about prescription drugs with health-care providers. (Others use marketing-led orchestration or a coordination model.) One top-ten firm has more than a dozen sales and marketing roles supporting just one therapeutic area. There are account managers, five types of specialty sales reps, and numerous marketing roles for managing the content shared via personal and digital channels (e.g., emails, websites, social media). Historically, all these roles and channels reached out independently to health-care providers. Once the sales organization began orchestrating the messages communicated by sales reps and digital marketing, providers began receiving consistent and relevant information.

MARKETING-LED ORCHESTRATION. This approach is common at companies that target a wide range of small and medium-size customers. Take the case of an enterprise SaaS company that targets small and medium businesses for its project management software. Marketing orchestrates outreach to customers across several specialized teams and digital systems. These include content marketing (blog posts, ebooks, videos), social media marketing, lead generation and nurturing, qualified lead follow-up (inside sales), product demos and webinars, and self-service sign-up for smaller accounts.

A cloud services provider used marketing-led orchestration to reduce customer churn. Marketing tracked customers' digital interactions to identify those at risk of defecting, looking for signals such as changes in usage patterns, declining engagement, and unopened emails from the provider. By sharing these insights with the sales team and asking reps to reach out (while authorizing them to offer discounts to at-risk customers), churn went down significantly.

DIGITAL-LED ORCHESTRATION. Companies such as Microsoft and Intuit have centralized their orchestration capabilities for reaching small and medium-size businesses in digital customer hubs. (See chapter 15 for more on DCHs.) This makes orchestration largely an automated process—from identifying early customer buying signals, to qualifying leads, to orchestrating digital and in-person outreach, to closing a sale and onboarding the customer.

How digital is strengthening collaboration

Effective channel collaboration is only feasible with digital enablement. Digital helps address two of the challenges discussed earlier—data silos and complexity. First, a digital platform links data that resides in separate organizational silos (more about this in chapter 15). Second, with linked data, analytics and AI can crunch the numbers to produce insights about what to do. Imagine the task of optimizing customer response and outreach in real time when there are three or more sales roles and five or more digital channels. Fortunately, advancements in marketing and sales tools and platforms make it possible to suggest steps and actions to sellers, or to execute the steps digitally. This is something we could not do a few years ago. Such platforms deliver real-time, analytically derived, and (usually) AI-powered suggestions for orchestrating the message, timing, and delivery channel for each customer. In industries as varied as high tech, pharmaceuticals, and manufacturing, AI is enabling orchestration and the results are invariably stellar. (For more about this, see chapter 16.)

Sales managers' role in strengthening collaboration

Sales managers play a key role in enabling channel collaboration, particularly when it comes to dealing with the challenges of different priorities, role ambiguity, and organizational silos. Sales managers can strengthen the channel collaboration skills and habits of their salespeople, and they also provide help to facilitate teamwork with groups and channels they do not control.

Helping salespeople be effective collaborators

Managers can observe, ask questions, and coach salespeople to be attentive to signals and insights generated from other customer-facing roles, and from digital channels such as social media, website traffic, and email engagement. And just as salespeople rely on signals from other channels, other channels rely on signals from salespeople. You must expect salespeople to record summaries of meetings, phone calls, emails, and any other form of communication. They should also be proactive in getting help from others. For example, if they notice a prospect has been consistently engaging with email content but hasn't responded to direct emails, they might try reaching out via social media to increase the chance of a response.

Working across organizational boundaries

Sales (and marketing) managers play a vital role in making channels work together. At one company, one week every year is designated "customer week," during which all marketing personnel accompany salespeople on customer visits. Aside from such a culture-reinforcing step, role clarity and regular meetings are essential for enabling collaboration across organizational boundaries.

- **Align roles and goals.** Define the responsibilities of each sales or marketing team member at different steps of the customer engagement process. Clarify who leads on what, each team's expected contribution, and how the teams support one another. Establish common planning frameworks, goals, and terminology. Create feedback loops and make sure everyone gets access to the same data and insights.

- **Have regular review meetings.** Include key stakeholders, such as sales managers, marketing leaders, and executives. Focus on aligning around the overall business goals and defining priorities and resource needs. Have regular huddles that allow participants to share insights, feedback, and best practices. Encourage joint planning sessions and cross-functional projects to build a sense of unity.

- **Celebrate success.** Recognize collective achievements to boost morale and strengthen partnerships.

Supporting sales teams with a digital enablement concierge

Competency with digital tools is developed and sustained through a mixture of training, coaching, and work-based learning. A digital enablement concierge can be highly effective in providing sales team members with on-demand assistance in all things digital.

The concierge's job goes beyond tech support. The mission is to increase the usage and impact of digital tools and platforms for salespeople. The digital enablement concierge is a boundary spanner who understands sales and is well versed in a range of digital tools and platforms. They provide strategic guidance on how to integrate digital tools into the sales process, and they help with execution as well. This could involve assisting with using social media to reach a prospect, optimizing email campaigns, conducting virtual meetings and presentations, or leveraging data-driven insights about customer interactions and engagement. A concierge is particularly useful during periods of major digital change, when "hypercare" is needed to ensure people learn quickly and adopt tools effectively. The concierge also works closely with the sales manager, marketing managers, sales operations, and IT to connect the organization's digital strategy to execution.

One concierge typically supports twenty to thirty salespeople across two to five sales regions. This ratio gives each concierge a manageable span of influence and allows sales team members to receive personalized support. The ratio can be adjusted based on the complexity and evolution speed of the digital tools, the ongoing demand for assistance, and the value generated. Aligning each concierge with specific regions provides continuity, while centrally managing the team allows for scaling flexibility.

Because a single concierge supports many salespeople, the role needs to have a regularly scheduled cadence of meetings with the team, as well as the capacity to handle on-demand requests. The regular cadence can include monthly group meetings (aligned with monthly sales meetings), along with weekly or biweekly check-ins with each salesperson. The on-demand component provides the flexibility to respond to the dynamic needs of the team.

Adapting communication methods and channels continuously

Agility is critical for the success of any communication and channel strategy. The needs, knowledge, and digital proficiency of each customer, and of individual decision-makers within a customer's buying organization, change over time. Here are some examples.

CHANGING NEEDS. When John Deere, the farm equipment manufacturer, introduces its soil sensor technology to a farm, the buyer is wondering if the added investment will pay off: "Will this make me money?" After a few growing seasons of demonstrated value, the buyer's focus shifts to "How can I leverage the technology to boost output or reduce inputs?" John Deere must shift from a sales focus to a customer-success focus, often by bringing in a different sales role or a dealer partner.

EVOLVING KNOWLEDGE. When a business customer moves its information systems to the cloud, it relies on the expertise of the cloud provider's account executives and solution specialists. Over time, the customer is increasingly able to address basic technical challenges on their own. Buyers and users troubleshoot issues, perform software updates, and configure systems independently by accessing the self-service documentation, online forums, and knowledge bases on the provider's website.

GROWING PROFICIENCY WITH VIRTUAL COMMUNICATION METHODS. As people's proficiency with virtual communication continues to grow, the use of tools such as Teams and Zoom has become routine. Now, augmented reality and virtual reality are gaining traction. There are numerous examples of their application in sales. An architecture firm uses these technologies to help customers visualize different designs for a new building. A technology company has an immersive VR product catalog that enables buyers to "walk around" and engage with products, as if they were at a trade show. In industries as varied as manufacturing, health care, and travel and transportation, companies are using AR/VR to share complex and customized visual representations of products and services, leading to increased sales and customer satisfaction. Sellers everywhere must be prepared to meet customers on the platforms they prefer.

PRODUCT INNOVATION. The power of using virtual and digital connection methods grows as customers' digital savvy and knowledge increase and supplier-customer relationships get stronger. Yet product innovation is a countervailing force. As enterprise technology companies launch new products and upgrade existing solutions, customers often want to meet with salespeople in person again to learn, collaborate, and customize solutions.

Thoughtful use of the various communication methods, cross-channel collaboration, and an adaptive channel strategy helps you enhance the customer experience and drive better business outcomes. A key prerequisite to accomplishing this is a digital customer hub that captures and shares insights about customers—a topic that is explored in the next chapter.

15.

Accelerating and Streamlining Selling with a Digital Customer Hub

Salespeople, marketers, and service teams are constantly making decisions about customer outreach and response—including who to contact, what methods to use, and what to offer. The complexity of channel selection, sequencing, and collaboration escalates with the growing number of personal and digital channels. And with buyer needs constantly evolving, real-time insights are needed for making informed decisions. When collaboration and personalization are absent, buyers receive inconsistent handling across channels and poorly targeted sales and marketing outreach, leading to wasted effort by sellers, frustration among buyers, and poor results.

More and more companies are addressing these challenges and opportunities by creating an organizational entity called a digital customer hub (DCH). Some call this setup a demand center or a digital customer platform. We prefer the term "digital customer hub" because the word "hub" reflects the many connections that power a DCH. The foundational elements include technology, data from multiple sources, and decision enablers such as AI and analytics. An intelligence engine links data to insights to recommendations to sales actions, and connects all customer-facing sales and marketing channels to each other. The DCH:

- Builds a comprehensive view of a customer that reflects the profile and the history of engagements and purchases. The view is constantly updated as new interactions and transactions occur.

- Proactively provides real-time insights about customers that enable an understanding of where they are in their buying journey and the drivers and barriers of adoption.

- Triggers outreach through digital channels and informs actions by inside or field sales.

- Connects insights to real-time activation by autonomously performing some basic steps of the sales process for most customers, and all steps of the sales process for some customers.

A DCH can have either its own leadership or leadership that is distributed across sales, marketing, sales operations, and IT.

Many companies have started the journey of bringing together digital assets for customer engagement. They are creating and curating content, connecting disparate channels, and adding intelligence capabilities that link real-time insights to recommendations on what content to share, what channel to use, and what to offer the customer. If your company is doing any of this, you are already on the path to building a DCH, even if you do not use that term.

Setting up and operating a DCH comes with technical and organizational challenges, mostly related to multiple systems residing in departmental silos. But successful implementations bring immense benefits, and fortunately, a DCH can be built in stages. This chapter is organized around four topics:

- The role and components of a DCH

- Architecture choices and strategies

- Building a DCH

- The sales leader's role in a DCH

The role and components of a DCH

Let's examine what a DCH does for Microsoft and its customers before getting into its core components and architecture choices.

Microsoft's Global Demand Center

Microsoft was a pioneer in establishing what it calls a Global Demand Center. This DCH brings together all the company's digital customer engagement efforts in one global engine enabled by people with expertise in sales, marketing, data science, and marketing operations. It is supported by a modern customer engagement platform and data capabilities. It identifies business opportunities through inbound marketing (e.g., personalized customer journeys with tailored content and experiences) and outbound marketing (e.g., paid media, events, webinars, and emails to find customers). The DCH also prioritizes and qualifies leads and orchestrates customer outreach. Sometimes, the response is digital (e.g., an email with personalized content). Other times, the DCH provides guidance and content to help an inside or field salesperson. This approach combines human expertise with digital intelligence and efficiency.

The DCH has reciprocal benefits for Microsoft and its customers. The buying experience is streamlined because communications with Microsoft are synchronized across channels. Each buying decision-maker gets content and offers that are tailored to their needs. For Microsoft, lead conversion rates are higher while costs are lower; sales force capacity is better utilized and balanced with the inflow of leads. Ongoing performance monitoring enables the timely diagnosis of issues and the identification of opportunities to improve. The selling organization is nimbler as customers and markets evolve.

At Microsoft, given the company's scale and vast target customer base, the DCH operates as a separate business unit with its own leadership, bringing together digital sales and data science expertise. Other structures are right for other companies. Let's examine the role and components that various types of implementations share.

A DCH in the buyer journey

A DCH supports the (sometimes nonsequential) elements of the buyer's journey on the continuum from when they first recognize a need to when they become a loyal customer. Although there are many possible journeys and sales models, the hub can help any sales organization in the following ways:

- **Finding and being found by prospects.** A DCH centrally orchestrates communication with prospects. It targets advertising with pay-per-click campaigns on search engines and social media. It connects prospects to relevant digital marketing content (blog posts, articles, white papers) and houses tools on the company's website, including online assessment tools and AI-driven chatbots. It hosts webinars and virtual events. It even provides customized content to salespeople so they can actively participate on LinkedIn, X (formerly Twitter), and industry-specific forums. Further, the DCH tracks prospects' engagement with all these resources and refines tactics in real time.

- **Vetting prospects early on for potential value.** The DCH examines engagement across channels to constantly assess a prospect's buying intent. It uses the latest data to transition an anonymous prospect into a well-understood individual. And it continuously rescores the potential value of the relationship for the company.

- **Assigning leads to the appropriate sales channel.** Based on a customer's size and potential lifetime value, the DCH turns opportunities over to the e-commerce platform (which may reside within the DCH) or passes them on to inside sales or field sales.

- **Sharing insights to help salespeople advance toward a purchase.** While sellers collaborate with buyers to define needs, customize solutions, and reach agreement on a purchase, the DCH feeds data-based insights to salespeople to enhance their power with customers. Further, it tracks interactions and keeps everyone informed in real time about what everyone else is up to, facilitating collaboration across roles and channels.

- **Helping close sales.** The DCH provides salespeople and customers with targeted recommendations and personalized offers while orchestrating outreach across sales channels.

- **Reinforcing value and driving growth.** Post-purchase, the DCH continues to engage customers directly or through salespeople. It provides personalized content, product updates, and special offers, enhancing customer loyalty and encouraging repeat business. In a recurring revenue business, the DCH helps document the value realized, manages subscription billing, and provides renewal reminders.

Components of a DCH

The core elements include a team with the expertise to build or configure and to deliver digital marketing programs, along with the necessary data, technology, analytical tools, and marketing channels and programs.

Team and expertise

When functioning as a distinct entity within the organization, the DCH operates under its own leader, whose title may be head of digital marketing or VP of customer experience, VP of demand generation, chief marketing officer, or VP of global demand center, depending on the organization's structure and focus. The team requires people with a range of skills and backgrounds. Technologists and data scientists build or configure, and constantly enhance, the digital capabilities. Marketers create content and manage the digital channels. Commercial operations personnel connect the digital tools with the users who are part of the DCH (digital marketers) as well as with those who use it but are not part of the same reporting structure, such as inside sales and field sales.

Data, technology, analytical tools, channels, and programs

Data is the foundation of a DCH. First-party data comes from within the company (e.g., customer purchase history, past sales interactions, web activity), whereas other data is generated externally. Second-party data tracks customer interactions with other companies such as social media firms. Third-party data is synthesized by external data providers. Examples include demographic and firmographic data about businesses and contact information for leads. Some of the data is structured (e.g., demographics, purchase history) and some is unstructured (e.g., emails or audio recordings of virtual meetings). Organizations often look to partner with others to access relevant data, for example, by teaming up with social media companies to get insights about how customers engage with their platforms.

Technology includes storage for the growing volume of data, computing resources to process the information, and networking resources to connect data and systems to each other and users. Marketing activation platforms streamline workflows across various marketing channels to enable personalized customer engagement. Additional infrastructure is often needed to connect disparate platforms and structures.

Analytical tools include statistical and optimization algorithms, data visualization tools, and AI and machine learning capabilities. These form the intelligence engine that produces insights from the data. The insights help the selling organization drive adoption and value by finding the right customers and delivering the right content through the right channel at the right time.

Marketing channels and programs are components of the DCH that communicate the insights. Digital marketing channels are part of the hub itself. Inside sales is sometimes part of the organization housing the DCH and other times is a separate function that interfaces with it. Field sales, service, and support teams are usually separate organizations that use the DCH to get data and insights using their own CRM and customer support platforms.

These core capabilities come together in various ways depending on the prominence of sales and marketing in the commercial organization.

Architecture choices and strategies

The form of the DCH depends on whether the business is sales-centered, marketing-centered, or is balanced. (See table 15-1.)

The role that a DCH plays in each type of business is illustrated through examples.

TABLE 15-1

Role of sales, marketing, and DCH in different businesses

	Sales-centered	Balanced	Marketing-centered
Customer base	Modest number of large customers	Moderate number of midsize customers	Large number of small customers
Role of sales	Manage complete buying journey, from prospecting to closing and customer success	Help with all deals in later selling stages (solution design, closing, customer success)	Help with some larger deals in later selling stages (solution design, closing, customer success)
Role of DCH and digital marketing	Provide sales with buyer insight and sales collateral	Manage lead generation; provide sales with buyer insight and sales collateral	Manage entire buyer journey; digital plays a dominant part, assisted by inside sales
Example discussed	Schneider Electric	Pharmaceuticals	Intuit

Sales-centered

Schneider Electric, a provider of energy management solutions, has a centralized technology infrastructure, data repository, and analytical toolbox that operate like a DCH, although Schneider does use the term DCH explicitly. The system leverages Salesforce Sales Cloud and Service Cloud technologies. Schneider's sales and service teams can access a linked, holistic view of each customer. An AI-driven intelligence engine creates insights from customer data (including customer profiles, past sales, and interactions) and IoT data (captured by sensors embedded in Schneider products operating at customer sites). A "digital opportunity factory" identifies system upgrades or replacement needs and routes the lead to the appropriate salesperson. AI tools also predict the probability of converting each opportunity to a sale, thereby helping salespeople spend time more productively and reducing the time to close sales by about 30 percent.

Marketing-centered

Intuit leads the financial software market with consumers and very small businesses (those with fewer than ten employees or with a single buying decision-maker). It uses a revamped DCH to help grow business with larger, midmarket companies.

Intuit's connections with its traditional small business prospects are marketing-centered, with some transactions requiring a one-call close. After purchasing, customers receive digital communications to help them onboard. But midsize businesses are different. They have more-complex needs and multiple people involved in purchasing. Intuit requires a better understanding of how these businesses buy, who is involved in the decisions, and what each decision-maker needs. Further, marketing needs the help of salespeople to close sales.

To start, Intuit leveraged its marketing-centered approach and existing data, systems, and digital marketing assets. The next step was to create a central repository of content and campaigns for each customer persona (e.g., CEO, CFO) and buying stage. In parallel, it began developing the DCH technology backbone and operations prowess to support selling to midsize customers through both direct sales channels and indirect channels (i.e., partners to co-sell, sell with, and sell through).

Balanced sales and marketing

A US pharmaceutical company uses an array of channels to share prescription drug information with about one hundred thousand health-care providers, half of whom will not meet with salespeople. These channels include a direct sales force and numerous digital marketing channels, such as company emails, third-party messaging (from sites such as Medscape and WebMD), closed social networks for health care professionals (such as Doximity), webinars by experts and opinion leaders, and online advertising. Physicians can also call a customer support hotline. In addition, the company uses various channels to deliver product information to insurance companies and reaches potential patients through direct-to-consumer advertising. It also offers patient support programs.

The company uses a DCH to synchronize information and outreach across all these channels. The hub houses a data lake, a centralized repository of data that includes customer profiles, transaction histories, interactions with field sales, information from customer service and digital channels, and signals of customer interest, such as engagement on social media or the company's website. The DCH has advanced analytics and AI-powered tools for understanding the relationship between channel selection, content, and results for each customer or segment. These insights are used for planning and real-time execution.

The DCH ensures that each communication with providers is executed through the most effective medium, whether it's an email, a social media post, or a webinar. This targeted approach not only improves the impact of sales and marketing efforts but also enhances the overall customer experience.

The hub also enables the real-time relevance of communications. The company responds promptly when customers "raise their hand." For example, a health-care provider who shows interest in a webinar is sent follow-up information. A patient who expresses an affordability challenge on social media gets a follow-up contact by a member of the company's patient support team. This immediate response mechanism, facilitated by AI-driven insights, maximizes opportunities for engagement and education.

DCH strategies and roles

In addition to the variety of forms a hub can take, companies use a DCH for a variety of strategies and roles.

Schneider Electric's main strategy and role for the hub is to enhance sales force productivity. At Intuit a DCH helps expand business into the midmarket sector, while at pharmaceutical companies it makes the company more customer-centric and synchronized across direct sales, digital marketing, and patient support channels.

Microsoft's DCH strategy and role vary by market segment. For small customers, it manages the entire buyer journey and provides e-commerce capabilities for self-service purchasing. Occasionally, these customers get help from inside sales or field sales if the deal is large and has advanced to the latter stages of buying. With corporate and medium customers, the DCH plays a key early role in managing leads and a late role in customer support, renewals, and value reinforcement. With large enterprise customers, the hub supports a key account team by providing up-to-date customer information and generating data-based insights about potential sales opportunities.

Consider two more examples of DCH implementations.

A FINANCIAL SERVICES FIRM. The firm, which works with mid-market businesses, uses a DCH to support early parts of the sales funnel and free up sales time. With many potential and current customers to choose from, salespeople were spending too much time with prospects in the early stages of buying, leaving too little time for those closer to making a purchase decision. So, the company built a DCH to identify and nurture leads. Digital tools capture leads (for example, by detecting interactions with the company's website). Qualified leads receive an orchestrated stream of digital communications, including automated emails, social media posts, and display ads. Leads are not connected to the field sales team until there are clear signals of buying intent, such as multiple visits to the website, downloads of content, or attendance at a webinar. Digitally nurturing leads before field sales gets involved means salespeople's time is redirected to customers and prospects that are highly likely to convert.

UNITED AIRLINES®. The company uses a DCH to reach small and medium-size businesses. It created a Small Business Demand Center (SBDC) that targets approximately five million accounts. The SBDC finds, acquires, and nurtures customers in an automated way, rather than taking the high-cost, salesperson-reliant approach used by enterprise accounts. The center intelligently targets both prospects and existing customers with customized digital content tailored to their needs. It features automated deal modeling and contracting, allowing customers to apply for and receive contracts, including discounts, through a web portal, with most transactions handled via self-service. Additionally, the SBDC includes an always-on nurturing system to track customer engagement and discover opportunities for cross-selling or upselling.

Building a DCH

Table 15-2 lays out four levels of integration and intelligence for a DCH with increasing sophistication, complexity, and impact.

Some companies (such as the financial services firm and United Airlines) build their DCH from the ground up and jump straight to level 4. This strategy is much more feasible and practical today due to the six-thousand-plus sales and marketing platforms and solutions that are available. Yet if you already have multiple systems in different parts of the organization, a stepwise approach makes sense. That was the case for the pharmaceutical company. It had disparate systems in place for documenting salespeople's interactions with providers and for tracking emails, third-party messaging,

TABLE 15-2

Path to a linked, dynamic, intelligent digital customer hub

Level	Channel strategy and system structure	Customer engagement and digital tools	Analytics
1: Pre-DCH	• Multiple channels • Customer data captured, leveraged, and managed in silos	• CRM and sales tracking • Email marketing software • Email and phone customer support distinct from CRM	Descriptive analytics not integrated with CRM or marketing tools
2: Partially linked	• Data-driven and streamlined marketing and sales • Digitally linked systems within marketing, sales, and customer support but not across functions	• Integrated sales and marketing for lead tracking and nurturing • Digital marketing platform for campaigns across multiple channels • Integrated help desk software for customers	Advanced descriptive analytics and diagnostic insights about customers to inform actions
3: Linked and centrally led	• Personalization and coordination of marketing and sales with customers controlling engagement across platforms • Linked systems under a DCH leader	• Integrated customer data across CRM, marketing, sales, and service • Use of basic chatbots, AI-driven support systems	Advanced descriptive, diagnostic, and predictive analytics and insights about customers
4: Linked, dynamic, and intelligent	• Orchestration of sales and marketing with embedded analytics supporting customer engagement • Linked systems under a DCH leader with digital experts sitting in the DCH	• AI-powered personalization in real time across all customer touchpoints • Advanced AI chatbots and predictive customer support	Real-time data analysis with predictive modeling for strategic decision-making and prescriptive cross-channel actions

social media, webinars, advertising, and hotline support interactions. It also had separate systems for recording engagements with potential and current patients. As a first step, the company linked the data from the CRM system that salespeople used to data from email and webinars. This produced dividends to start. Then, as social media, third-party messaging, advertising, and customer support data were connected, the value grew.

Each step of linking data provided a more complete and real-time view of each customer, making AI-driven insight generation more powerful and leading to better personalization of channels and content.

With DCHs and other digital implementations, seeking perfection can be the enemy of progress. Rather than waiting until every system is 100 percent integrated, your hub should be built in such a way that benefits can be gained as it is being constructed. As the data, analytics, and other DCH capabilities improve, the value will simply grow.

The sales leader's role in a DCH

Sales leaders can use four key strategies for implementing a hub and assisting the sales organization in boosting impact with it:

- Understand the complexities of a DCH and have realistic expectations

- Advocate for customers and salespeople and leverage their input

- Help embed reshaped roles and processes into the organization

- Champion DCH usage

Understand the complexities

When implementing a hub, sales leaders should be prepared to invest time before seeing results. We often hear them complain, "All our data is already in our CRM system. Why is it taking more than a year to connect this to the website traffic and the marketing customer databases?" For nearly all companies, organizational and technology challenges make connecting these disparate systems difficult.

ORGANIZATIONAL CHALLENGES. The biggest obstacles to establishing a DCH are at the interface of technology and people.

A hub relies on the cooperation of many people who manage a growing plethora of digital and personal channels and resources. As additional digital assets are added over time, it often means onboarding a new organizational silo into the DCH as well. It's not atypical for digital marketing organizations to have separate managers for email marketing, social media, search engine optimization, and webinars. Additional roles handle inbound customer complaints and content development, not to mention the numerous sales roles. Being within the DCH makes the actions of each one visible to others—each specialized function must get used to increased scrutiny and less autonomy.

Organizational silos are not an easy problem to solve. The crux of the answer starts with customer centricity. Use the DCH to align all functions around the customer: keep buyer connections and content synchronized with how buyers work and with the challenges they face. Leadership by the CEO and other top executives is essential for bringing the power to exert influence across organizational boundaries. They can communicate this vision and reinforce it by ensuring all customer-facing functions share goals linked to customer success.

TECHNOLOGY CHALLENGES. Creating the linkages for a hub is never easy, and creating more links leads to more complexity.

Sales and marketing channels often use different vendors whose solutions work on proprietary digital platforms. For example, CRM, email marketing, social media engagement, the e-commerce website, and the customer portal can all work with their own platforms and databases. Each might use different customer identification codes or alternative spellings of names. This makes linking customer data from disparate systems time-consuming and error-prone.

Business customers often have complex organizations. Sellers have relationships with multiple contacts, departments, locations, and subsidiaries. The CRM system is organized around these buying points and influences. Meanwhile, marketing databases are typically built around individual interactions.

The challenges may appear daunting. But by understanding the complexities, having realistic expectations, and supporting the organization in a stepwise approach, sales leaders help energize continued integration across systems and organizational boundaries.

Advocate for customers and sales force members

Whether designing a hub or enhancing it, sales leaders should channel the voice of the customer and the sales force—sharing feedback with the DCH team to ensure attention stays focused on providing value for both.

When Microsoft built its DCH, it leveraged the capabilities to provide salespeople with real-time recommendations about offers and customer actions. The addition of two user-centered features boosted adoption significantly. First, salespeople were given the reason for the recommendation. Here is an example: "Expansion opportunity: Azure sign-up within six months. Rationale: Usage of other Microsoft products and firmographics." Second, salespeople could reject recommendations and provide a reason. Through multiple feedback loops, the relevance of DCH suggestions improved as did their adoption rates.

By sharing feedback from both customers and salespeople with the hub's team, sales leaders can help fuel the continuous improvement of the DCH's capabilities. Customer feedback increases the relevance of content and provides specific suggestions for actions to take. Salespeople's feedback, in addition to providing insight about the quality of AI-generated suggestions, sheds light on issues such as the ease of use of digital tools, how well DCH recommendations fit into the sales workflow, and how responsive the hub is in following up on actions that salespeople trigger.

Help embed reshaped roles and processes

A DCH changes how the sales and marketing teams work together, as well as the roles of sales and marketing personnel. Sales leaders can help both teams adapt to a more customer-centric and digitally enabled approach in several ways.

REDEFINE SUCCESS METRICS. In the typical predigital sales model, marketing controlled the early part of the sales funnel by generating leads, then sales assumed control. Now informed and self-sufficient customers routinely disrupt this sequence. A prospective buyer might go back to view a marketing-led webinar after talking to a salesperson. Sales and marketing must collaborate throughout the buying process, stitching together the channels and resources most likely to drive conversion and loyalty. The history of data and insight that is embedded in the DCH, along with shared success metrics, enables the collaboration. For example, the effectiveness of a marketing campaign was traditionally measured with metrics such as the number of leads generated and the cost per lead. These metrics remain relevant, but it's also important for various roles and channels that touch the customer to focus on shared downstream metrics, such as the revenue generated. This keeps everyone aligned on the same goals and encourages cooperation to maximize effectiveness.

HELP THE SALES TEAM ADOPT A "PLANNING WHILE DOING" RHYTHM. The typical predigital sales cadence involved annual and quarterly sales planning followed by daily execution. A DCH supports a new rhythm in which analytics continuously reprioritizes sales activity based on real-time signals of customer need. This is a big adjustment for many leaders, who are used to managing by a static tactical plan while transferring accountability for quarterly goals from the top down. As managers adapt, they must support their salespeople through the change as well. (You should also recognize that this agility may come naturally to the salespeople who are adept at customizing their tactics to customer needs.)

BUILD A COLLABORATIVE RELATIONSHIP WITH MARKETING. In the traditional model, marketing focused on strategy, segmentation, and planning, while sales concentrated on tactics, individual customer engagement, and execution. A DCH transforms this dynamic from a linear, sequential process to a collaborative partnership. Marketers now work together with data scientists to develop predictive algorithms. Further, marketing's role extends to identifying diverse decision-makers and crafting and delivering personalized content through digital channels and the sales team. This shift has brought marketing and sales into the trenches together, with a DCH serving as the link that unites their efforts.

Champion DCH usage

Sales leaders can champion the hub's usage by promoting the benefits of adopting it. Here are a few methods to try.

MODEL THE RIGHT BEHAVIOR. When making decisions, such as about channel design or structure, use DCH analytics and make your usage visible to salespeople. Before visiting a key account, seek out and become familiar with data from the DCH about the account's history and engagement with other channels.

BE A MULTICHANNEL COACH. Ask salespeople questions about how their customers use other channels and any insights they have gained from the DCH. Encourage salespeople to be willing to consider the hub's suggestions, even though they are not always right. Reiterate that rejecting bad suggestions helps to improve future ones.

PROMOTE CROSS-FUNCTIONAL COLLABORATION. Organize or participate in meetings or other initiatives that involve collaboration across sales, marketing, customer support, and other relevant teams. Use the insights and data in the DCH to align the strategies and efforts of these teams, with a goal of creating a more cohesive customer experience.

ENCOURAGE SALESPEOPLE TO KEEP CUSTOMER DATA CURRENT. While sellers have to be good users of the DCH, they must also contribute to it by keeping their pipeline data up-to-date and routinely logging their interactions to help build valuable customer profiles.

The growth of DCHs is resulting in a streamlined customer experience that offers self-service when needed and involves more personalized, relevant, and synchronized interactions across sales and marketing channels. Although implementing a DCH poses technical and organizational challenges, a successful deployment significantly improves sales productivity and customer value. Building a hub is a journey, and a typical path involves adding linkages and intelligence over time. For salespeople, interactions with a DCH often come in the form of an always-on, AI-enabled personal digital assistant—the topic of the next chapter.

16.

Amplifying the Power of Salespeople with Digital Assistants

While marketing has traditionally thought about products and market segments, sales has always focused on personalization for individual customers. Now, digital capabilities allow marketing and sales together to think about segments of one and, using AI, to further personalize their approach according to a customer's particular moment or step in the buying journey.

Personalization—of content, channels, offerings, and pricing—is made possible at scale by data. This includes data about customers' knowledge, needs, opportunities, purchase history, decision-making processes, past interactions, and channel preferences. Personalization is no longer just a sales skill; it's an organizational capability.

For the salesperson, the ability to personalize can be enhanced by an always-on, AI-enabled personal digital assistant. The assistant mines both quantitative and qualitative data (often brought together in a digital customer hub—see chapter 15). The assistant offers up suggestions, usually through a CRM system, allowing salespeople to boost productivity, save time, and increase their impact. In high tech, pharmaceuticals, financial services, and other industries, the use of digital assistants has proven to lead to measurable results, including an enhanced customer experience, better engagement, higher conversion rates, more sales, and stronger customer retention. And their impact will only grow as the assistants improve and salespeople become better at leveraging them. These tools are not just for early adopters and technology "geeks," and they are not just for large sales forces. Proficiency with using digital assistants is a growing success factor for salespeople and leaders alike in every company.

This chapter is about:

- Empowering salespeople with AI-driven tools

- Adopting and implementing AI assistants

As organizations get better at using AI to share data-based insights and recommendations with salespeople, it's important to recognize that the recommendations are only suggestions. Data is almost always incomplete, and the future is not the same as the past. The power here comes from combining a digital assistant's input with salespeople's own judgment about what actions to take with customers.

Empowering salespeople with AI-driven tools

The salesperson's digital assistant has two personas:

- **An analytical assistant** focuses on analyzing numerical data and creating insights and suggestions to help sales teams make informed decisions.

- **A verbal-visual assistant** focuses on synthesizing mostly nonnumeric data (text, image, video) to create content and enhance communication.

The two personas work collaboratively. For example, the verbal-visual assistant detects the sentiment of the customer and feeds it to the analytical assistant, which identifies an upsell opportunity. Then, the verbal-visual assistant weighs in with words and visuals the salesperson can use to communicate with the customer.

Analytical assistants

An analytical digital assistant supports salespeople in using data to drive impact throughout the sales process, from finding to acquiring to serving to growing customers. Examples of instruments in the analytical toolbox include the following:

- **Lead scoring.** AI helps salespeople find customers by analyzing various characteristics of leads (demographics, behavior, engagement, past conversions) and predicting the likelihood of conversion. Salespeople prioritize those leads with higher probabilities of success.

- **Dynamic offer design and pricing support.** AI helps sellers acquire customers by optimizing offers and pricing in real time. By analyzing customer needs and behaviors, along with market trends, competitor pricing, supply and demand, and other relevant factors, automated models help a seller design and price an offer that's dynamically curated specifically for the customer.

- **Upsell and cross-sell opportunities.** AI helps salespeople grow customers by identifying relevant product combinations or upgrades that are likely to appeal to them. These recommendations are based on the customer's profile, purchase history, and behavior patterns, along with data about what similar buyers have purchased (look-alike modeling).

- **Propensity to churn.** AI helps sellers retain customers by looking at measures that reflect the health of a customer's relationship with the business and assessing the likelihood that the customer will discontinue their relationship. The models also suggest targeted retention strategies or interventions that can prevent churn.

- **Next-best-action suggestions.** AI helps salespeople personalize their approach with customers by predicting and recommending the next best action to take at a given moment. Suggestions include individualized product recommendations, tailored offers, and specific communication strategies, based on individual customer preferences and business objectives.

Verbal-visual assistants

A verbal-visual digital assistant uses generative AI to help salespeople save time and boost their impact when language-based or visually oriented tasks are required. It also supports their competency development and more. Let's look at some of these benefits.

SAVING TIME TO INCREASE FOCUS ON SELLING. About a quarter of salespeople's time is dedicated to generating customer-specific materials to help with sales. Using a gen AI–powered verbal-visual assistant cuts that time drastically, leaving more time for value-adding activities.

- **Content summarization.** Gen AI summarizes reports, articles, or documents into concise, digestible summaries. It can also transcribe and summarize recorded audio or video conversations and sales calls. This helps salespeople reduce the time they spend doing background research about customers and the market. Gen AI can also tease out customer sentiment from recordings of support calls and online reviews.

- **Content generation.** It also automates the creation of sales and marketing content, including personalized emails, product descriptions, social media posts, and videos. Content is tailored to customer

UCB climbs the digital slope with an analytical assistant

At global biopharmaceutical company UCB, the commercial organization supported product launches with data-based insights. By integrating data and applying advanced analytics, UCB produced some nonintuitive insights. For example, it was commonly believed that the poor patient adoption of one new product was due to the sales force communicating ineffectively with health-care providers. However, analytics showed this intuition was wrong. Providers were in fact prescribing the product, but many patients were not starting the treatment because of affordability concerns. With this data-based insight, UCB shifted focus to improving the copay support program, instead of debating about who in the sales force was to blame. Performance improved significantly.

As UCB's confidence in the power of analytics grew, so did the scope of leveraging data and algorithms to inform decisions throughout the sales and marketing organization, and in the executive suite. The company was ready to take analytics to the point of action between sales reps and health-care providers. It launched an analytical assistant tool to give reps just-in-time insights derived from data about patient disease progression, local health environment dynamics, a provider's likelihood of switching therapies, and other factors. These analytics helped sales reps dynamically target the providers.

preferences, interests, engagement, and purchasing patterns. The delivery of timely and targeted marketing messages enhances the customer experience and increases the likelihood of purchase.

- **Personalized proposals.** Gen AI assists salespeople with creating personalized sales proposals or presentations. This saves sellers time while also increasing the odds of success because materials highlight specific customer needs, benefits, and solutions.

BOOSTING THE IMPACT OF CUSTOMER ENGAGEMENT. Gen AI helps sales teams engage with customers more efficiently and effectively through more personalized interactions.

- **Chatbots and virtual sales assistants.** Gen AI powers chatbots and virtual sales assistants that engage with customers, answer their questions, and assist in the sales process.

- **Email campaigns.** It also assists in crafting email marketing campaigns by creating subject lines, body content, and calls to action that are tailored to each recipient.

IMPROVING COMPETENCIES THROUGH PERSONALIZED UPSKILLING. Gen AI enhances sales learning and development programs by providing personalized, engaging, and efficient learning experiences.

- **Personalized training content.** The tool assesses people's unique learning preferences and requirements, tailoring training programs and self-learning content to each salesperson. Often these capabilities are delivered through a learning experience platform that links learners to relevant content from both inside and outside the organization. (See chapter 17 for more on learning experience platforms.)

- **Coaching.** Gen AI simulates realistic scenarios with customers and offers immediate feedback to salespeople, fostering their growth and development. It also gleans insights from recorded conversations.

Microsoft puts it all together with AI assistants

At Microsoft, where sales account executives interact with millions of software buyers each year, customers' expectations of the sales team have skyrocketed. There was a time when it was cumbersome and sometimes impossible for AEs to get a true picture of each buyer's needs. They had to manually assemble and synthesize data that was scattered across Microsoft's business units. Time and effort were wasted, and interactions with clients suffered.

Daily Recommender: The analytical assistant

In 2018 Microsoft launched tools to equip salespeople with insights and suggestions about actions that would benefit customers. Armed with this information, sales teams spent less time gathering data and more time engaging in personalized conversations with buyers. Productivity, measured by time in front of customers and the effectiveness of the interactions, rose by as much as 40 percent. An internally developed tool called Daily Recommender delivered the insights and suggestions to salespeople. For example, algorithms detected that one customer company had spent a significant sum for on-premises software licenses and that twenty-seven of its employees had recently interacted thirty-four times with Microsoft marketing materials. Daily Recommender advised the account rep to contact the customer about purchasing more Microsoft 365 subscriptions—and to reach out quickly, because third-party data indicated that the customer had started trials with a competitor. By following up on the suggestion, the rep was able to deliver a solution that was well matched to the customer's needs while simultaneously bringing in additional revenue.

Daily Recommender was not a one-way communication tool. With every suggestion came the question of whether the salesperson thought it made sense. The employee could flag a recommendation as "Great suggestion—in progress" or "Nice try—I know the customer is not interested" or "Sorry—I don't think this is a good idea." The feedback loop helped improve the algorithms, which improved recommendation adoption rates.

Viva Sales: The verbal-visual assistant

In 2023 Microsoft launched Viva Sales, an application with embedded gen AI technology. The application helped salespeople and sales managers draft tailored customer emails, get insights about customers and prospects, and generate recommendations and reminders. Both Viva Sales and Daily Recommender capabilities were integrated into Microsoft's own CRM (and ERP) platform, Microsoft Dynamics 365, which the company also licensed to its customers. (Viva Sales could be integrated with other

CRM systems too.) This gave salespeople access to both analytical and verbal-visual AI capabilities through a single system.

In addition to Microsoft, Salesforce has integrated Einstein GPT into its CRM to provide salespeople with analytical and verbal-visual assistance. Companies such as SAP, Oracle, Adobe, HubSpot, and Zoho have similarly incorporated such capabilities. In addition, hundreds of companies offer gen AI tools that can be integrated with CRM systems.

The result is that these technologies have been democratized—they are available to companies large and small. In fact, smaller companies have an edge in adopting AI assistants because implementation is less complex when there are narrower product portfolios, fewer organizational and data silos, and a smaller number of people involved in decision-making.

Adopting and implementing AI assistants

Integrating AI (including gen AI) into a CRM system is a valuable step, but it's not enough to fully realize the potential. Sales leaders must work with and through technical teams—such as commercial operations, data science, and IT—to prepare the sales organization, drive adoption of the tools, and ensure their sustained usage and value.

Three issues are important for sales leaders:

- Facilitating the tools' adoption and usage by the sales team

- Managing AI's risks by working with technical and legal teams

- Learning to use AI themselves while adding value to the sales team

The change management ideas in chapter 20, especially the checklist for digitalization, are a valuable guide for addressing relevant challenges. In addition, here are some success strategies to consider.

Facilitating adoption and usage

For sales force members, the change from following old ways of working to using a digital assistant is significant. The transition is easier for some than others, depending on factors such as familiarity with technology and individual work style. You can help enhance the usability and adoption of AI assistants in the following ways.

- **Embed AI assistants in salespeople's natural workflows.** The best AI assistants increase impact and efficiency simultaneously. Partner with the technical team to ensure the technology works seamlessly with the tools and platforms salespeople already use daily, such as CRM systems, email software, and other communication apps. For example, you can enhance the current CRM system with AI features to save time (e.g., automated data entry) and increase impact (e.g., smart customer insights and recommended sales actions). When the new features have a straightforward learning curve and don't disrupt salespeople's routines, adopting them becomes natural and intuitive.

- **Fine-tune generative AI so it understands your business.** Gen AI models work best when they are trained on the specific context and needs of the sales environment, including your data, industry, products, and customer base. For instance, if your business is banking, a gen AI model is much more effective if it understands banking-specific jargon, language, and frameworks. Although the technical team is responsible for training the algorithms, the sales team has a role too. The tools get better as salespeople use them and validate or correct their recommendations. Encourage users to provide feedback so that the models learn and provide increasingly accurate and contextually relevant summaries, suggestions, and insights.

- **Build a community.** At regular meetings with your team, discuss how people are using AI digital assistants. Work with your company to set up digital collaboration spaces that allow users to share best practices, challenges, success stories, and tips—this significantly enhances adoption and effectiveness. Online communities can also serve as a support network for troubleshooting and as a source of ideas for ways to evolve the tools and better use AI.

Managing AI's risks

AI technology is evolving rapidly, and it comes with risks. Although technical and legal teams play the primary role in addressing these issues, you can help to guide the team through these challenges in the following ways.

- **Adapt to and communicate about AI's evolution.** By staying informed about ongoing developments in technology (even though the details are handled by the technical team), you can regularly apprise your sales team of new capabilities, changes in tools, and the potential impact on their work. The ongoing communication encourages flexibility and readiness for change, helping the team adapt more easily to the landscape while maintaining their confidence and competence.

- **Manage AI's biases and other undesired consequences.** AI systems do make wrong or biased inferences from data. Your technical and legal teams can assist you with the ongoing monitoring of your systems and the training of your people. You'll want to be aware of policies around data privacy, security, and usage (especially when handling sensitive customer information), as well as audits and compliance checks to make sure ethical guidelines and regulatory requirements are followed. Further, you'll want to stay informed about contingency plans that the technical and legal teams have for potential AI failures or inaccuracies. Human oversight and intervention help mitigate the risks and maintain people's trust in AI-assisted sales processes.

Learning to use AI yourself

Integrating sales assistants can have a steep learning curve for sales managers too. Because you have a broad range of responsibilities, you typically have less direct daily interaction with AI-driven tools. Often, tech-savvy members of the sales team are more adept at using these tools than others on the team (perhaps including you). Leveraging the team's diverse strengths can help. Here are two approaches to consider.

- **Use reverse mentoring.** Identify the team members who are proficient in AI tools and willing to share their knowledge. Often, these are not the most experienced members of your team, but rather less experienced sellers who understand technology. Learn from these tech-savvy mentors. They can help you enhance your own skills as well as the skills of the entire team, such as by demonstrating features or sharing practical tips at meetings. Recognize the contributions of these mentors to encourage this practice.

- **Link strategy and goals to AI-assisted execution.** As a manager, you do not need to know every technical detail. Instead, focus on understanding how to use AI technologies to link strategies and goals to execution. To drive immediate impact, keep an eye on how these tools help streamline work, improve customer engagement, and drive sales outcomes. For longer-term impact, consider too how AI can optimize processes, enhance customer relationships, and contribute to initiatives focused on sustainable growth and success. Your ability to bridge the gap between strategy and technology can be a powerful asset in maximizing the benefits of AI in sales.

AI digital assistants provide salespeople with a huge opportunity to amplify their productivity and effectiveness. By harnessing AI, sales teams are automating repetitive tasks, gaining valuable customer insights, and receiving recommendations about how to bring personalized value to customers. Effectively using a digital assistant allows a salesperson to spend more time fostering meaningful customer relationships, leading to improved sales outcomes. With the right training, coaching, support, and encouragement, your team will harness increasing benefits from AI and digital assistants over time, driving ongoing growth in value for customers and the company.

17.

Boosting Talent Management with Digital

Companies launch new products and adapt their sales strategies, structures, and roles frequently. Accounting for turnover (both voluntary and involuntary), reassignments, and promotions, some sales forces find themselves having to replace as many as half of their salespeople every year. Hiring, onboarding, coaching, and training are constantly in high gear. Sales leaders are at the center of this frenzy, and digital tools can help. As the old, steady, and repeatable processes for managing talent give way to a more market-sensing and agile approach, digital is a key ingredient in boosting impact, speed, and efficiency.

Managing sales talent has many parallels to managing customers. You must find, develop, and retain salespeople while growing their value. Further, similar challenges emerge when digitalizing both talent management and customer management processes. Digital talent management efforts are often siloed. Learnings from one context are not easily shared with others. The adoption of digital systems is erratic. With personalization as the goal, just as it is in customer management, talent management has more impact when it blends in-person, virtual, and digital connection, and when it leverages data and analytics at each step of the process.

A variety of systems are used to support talent decisions and processes, from hiring the best people, to launching their careers, to sustaining their success. These digital platforms and tools play complementary roles in sales talent management. (See table 17-1.) Although CRM systems are used primarily to manage customer relationships, we include them here because some of their functionalities and data inform talent management (for example, performance tracking and goal setting).

Talent management has moved beyond manual résumé screening, classroom-only training, and static monthly reports for tracking sales goal achievement. The vast majority of organizations now use digital capabilities to make better decisions and to streamline their processes. Many of these capabilities were mentioned in section 2 of this book. Examples include

TABLE 17-1

Typical digital platforms and tools for supporting talent management

System	Purpose	Owner	Users
Recruiting platform	Find and connect with job candidates	HR–hiring manager	Hiring managers, sales managers
Learning management system	Organize, deliver, and track training and assessment materials	HR–training and development manager	Salespeople, sales managers, HR
Sales performance management system	Manage account assignments, sales reporting, goals, objectives, KPIs, and incentives	Sales operations, IT	Sales managers, salespeople
Human capital management systems	Manage employee records, payroll, and benefits	HR–payroll and benefits manager	HR
Customer relationship management system	Manage customer information, interactions, and sales pipeline; provide customer insights	Sales operations, IT	Salespeople, sales managers, marketing, customer support

social media for sourcing talent, online microlearning modules for training, and digital nudges that use real-time data to motivate people.

This chapter expands on the growing number of ways that companies are using digital capabilities to strengthen talent management. The first part shares insights about how these capabilities are improving decisions and processes in three areas of talent management: recruiting, learning and development, and incentive programs.

The second part of the chapter tackles the overarching challenge that talent management systems are not linked or are only partially linked. Sales leaders must bring together insights from disparate systems to make good talent decisions. By linking systems through an always-on support platform—what we call a digital sales talent hub—organizations can greatly speed up their processes and enable rapid strategic and tactical change in response to a dynamic marketplace.

Digital recruiting

Digitalization helps sales organizations manage all aspects of the talent acquisition funnel. Having digital capabilities leads to better candidates getting hired and onboarded in less time.

Managing and tracking the recruiting process

Most companies that hire more than a handful of salespeople each year use a digital recruiting platform (RP) to streamline the hiring processes. The functions of an RP include posting openings on job boards and the company's website, sourcing candidates through various channels, scoring and tracking résumés and applications, scheduling interviews, and keeping candidates informed about their status. Such systems also track key metrics (time to fill, acceptance rates, recruitment funnel status) that provide insights about ways to improve recruiting. By combining RP metrics with performance data, sales organizations can do even more to diagnose what's working and discover improvement opportunities—often in real time. (See table 17-2.)

TABLE 17-2

Metrics for evaluating and improving sales force recruiting

Metric	Helps with decisions about
Number of applicants and hires from each source, and investment in each source	• Which candidate sources to use • How much to investment in each source
Candidate conversion rate at each step of the process and reasons for attrition	• How to improve each step of the process
Time to fill and time to hire	• Which steps need attention to accelerate the process
Feedback on candidate experience	• How to make the process rigorous and mutually rewarding
Quality of hires (performance in year one, two, and five)	• Which candidate sources to use • What profile of candidates to look for
Strength and variety of candidate pool and hires	• How to eliminate biases in process
Retention (year two, year five)	• Which candidate sources to use • What profile of candidates to look for • How to improve onboarding

Sourcing talent

Almost every employer uses online channels (company websites, job boards, social media platforms, professional network platforms) to post job openings and reach a large pool of candidates, including passive talent. Many companies use analytics to improve the effectiveness of online candidate sourcing. Companies mine data on sites such as LinkedIn to characterize and identify potential candidates for sales roles. Machine learning provides insights about how likely people are to join if made an offer and to succeed if they join. These assessments involve comparing candidates with current and past employees who share a similar profile. Those who score high on both dimensions receive a "warm outreach" from a direct or a one-step LinkedIn connection.

Some companies who recruit hundreds or thousands of salespeople each year are training models to identify job candidates who could have a lasting impact on organizational success. For example, analytical tools can take candidate scoring algorithms to the next level by suggesting candidates who will stay with the company long term, who can adapt as needs change, who are likely to bring others with them when they join, or who are well suited to advance in the organization. These tools are allowing recruiters to reach a broader and higher-quality applicant pool, including nontraditional candidates.

Attracting prospective employees requires a focus on not just finding them but also being found by them. Prospective employees have access to a plethora of digital information about employers, such as through Glassdoor and LinkedIn. It's easier to attract sales talent when your company has a strong digital presence with social media and website content that resonates with prospective employees. Strategies include continually analyzing and improving content and boosting its visibility through search engine optimization and by posting consistently on social media.

Selecting talent

When there is a large number of candidates for a job, many companies use automated résumé screening to whittle down the applicant pool. But there is a growing complication: as candidates tailor their applications to the keywords and qualifications that the automated screens look for, companies must continually improve their selection criteria and algorithms to screen for authenticity and stay one step ahead. Beyond résumé screening, digital capabilities support early applicant screening methods such as online sales aptitude tests and simulations that score candidates on their ability to complete specific job-related tasks.

Interviewing is still at the heart of candidate selection for most sales jobs, and technology can make the process more efficient. Most companies use both virtual (video) and in-person interviews, with the right blend depending on the sales role, the number and location of candidates, and the stage of the hiring process.

Automated video interviews (AVIs) make virtual interviews even more convenient and efficient, especially when there are many candidates in the early screening stages. AVIs can take different forms. At a basic level, a candidate's answers to prerecorded questions are captured; a human evaluator watches the video and determines whether the person will advance. At the next level of automation, AI-assisted interviewing tools evaluate candidates based on facial expressions, tone of voice, use of keywords, and other criteria. Then the AI model shares a hiring recommendation with a human evaluator, who makes an advancement decision. At an even more automated level, the interview is AI-led, with the model making the decision on its own without human involvement. AVIs in any of these forms are best used to precede or supplement a live (virtual or in-person) interview.

With live interviews, AI tools can support the interviewer. By analyzing the competency model, the job description, and the candidate's résumé, these tools can suggest insightful interview questions. When interviews are conducted virtually, the tools can prompt the interviewer in real time—for example, suggesting a follow-up question that creates a more holistic view of the candidate or reminding the interviewer about competencies that have not yet been discussed.

Ultimately, the choice of interview format depends on the situation. A hybrid approach almost always makes sense: you might start with an automated interview to screen candidates, follow up with live video interviews, and conduct final-round in-person interviews for the top candidates.

Digital learning and development

Digital capabilities are enabling a more personalized, self-directed, and peer-influenced approach to learning and development—an approach that judiciously blends in-person, virtual, and e-learning methods. Because many e-learning methods are available on demand, salespeople can access information at the moment it's needed, reinforcing a culture of continuous learning.

Learning management systems and learning experience platforms

Most companies that have a larger sales organization use a learning management system (LMS) to plan, implement, and assess the learning process. The LMS serves as a centralized platform for delivering educational content and for administering, tracking, and reporting on people's development plans and progress. This enables more structured and consistent learning programs, making it easier to identify skill gaps and areas for improvement.

A newer technology, a learning experience platform (LXP), is a system that provides a personalized, social, online experience. LXPs focus more on the user's experience and are designed to encourage exploration and discovery of content. An LXP indexes and tags content from knowledge bases, documents, expert blogs, social networking sites, and more, including sources both inside and outside the organization. Predictive logic helps determine which content is likely to be most relevant based on an individual's role, skill level, and professional development goals, along with data about what learners in similar situations are studying. An LXP allows users to set their own goals, use self-assessments to explore strengths and opportunities for improvement, and track their development plans.

Both LMSs and LXPs use a variety of metrics that provide insights about ways to improve learning and development programs. An LMS maintains metrics about training, such as course enrollment and completion rates, user satisfaction, knowledge retention, and compliance. An LXP can also track user experience with a broader range of resources, including engagement with user-generated forums, preferences for different formats of content, and participation in online peer learning groups. Metrics can also provide insights about the impact of learning programs over time—from employees' attitudes and knowledge at the completion of a program, to the impact on their behavior over the next few months, to their results a year or more later.

Emerging capabilities in e-learning

Companies are providing more and more of their sales training through e-learning. Popular ways to deliver content include virtual instructor-led training, microlearning modules, and mobile access to training materials.

Generative AI, virtual reality, and augmented reality technologies are making digitally enabled learning even more interactive, immersive, and memorable. VR/AR can simulate real-life sales scenarios, such as asking the learner to respond to typical customer questions and objections or testing for product expertise. This allows learners to engage in role-playing exercises in a risk-free virtual environment. Salespeople receive instant AI-driven feedback and guidance for improvement, while the technology adapts content to individuals' needs. As these technologies become more immersive and accessible, a digital-first mindset for sales force learning is sure to prevail.

The role of digital in self-discovery and coaching

Technology can arm sales managers and their people with information to help them improve. Digital makes it easier for them to gather and analyze data from the CRM, sales performance management (SPM), and other sources. This data helps both the manager/coach and salesperson glean insights about performance and identify areas for improvement. Assisted by AI, the salesperson might learn, for example, that they aren't using the most effective tools and content. Or the manager might observe that the salesperson has a set pattern of product offers and sequences that can be improved upon. The data enables a more productive coaching discussion around these insights. Further, AI tools help the coach improve, for example, by analyzing coaching notes to find gaps in what was discussed or to discover new opportunities to explore with a salesperson.

Virtual communication technologies allow managers and their people to connect in immersive ways without being physically together. This approach can work in situations when there is already trust between the sales manager and the salesperson. However, most coaching doesn't translate well to a virtual environment. One salesperson told us, "I don't mind occasionally taking my manager with me to meet customers in person, but having him sit in on my Zoom calls is awkward and embarrassing."

AI-based tools can supplement in-person coaching, especially in the inside sales world, where calls are routinely recorded with the customer's permission. The tools provide coaching feedback by analyzing content, language, tone, inflection, and other elements of communication. Some companies are finding that this works best with core performers (not with high or low performers) and that a combination of AI-based and human coaching has synergistic effects.

Digitally boosting incentive plan traction

An incentive plan is motivating only if salespeople understand it and know their progress toward achieving their objectives. Dashboards and digital tools, when designed well, increase the motivational power of sales incentives. The best ones give salespeople real-time access to action-oriented and customized information.

Digital self-service tools for salespeople are increasing in usage and power. Sales reports capture up-to-the-minute transaction information. The best reports suggest actions that the salesperson should take. For example, instead of just reporting sales, the dashboard shows sales relative to opportunities, highlights underdeveloped accounts, and makes a recommendation about what to do to create a win-win for both the customer and the seller.

Incentive tracking and forecasting features add another layer of direction. What are salespeople on track to earn? If they close a deal that is currently in progress, what is the impact on their incentive pay? These types of what-if capabilities can boost the impact of incentives on goal achievement.

Infrequent but targeted and personalized messages also help drive salespeople to their highest levels of performance. AI-based (or rule-based) systems can use real-time data and analytics to deliver important messages and provide salespeople with insights. For example, an insurance company offered an "early success" bonus for sales agents who achieved a milestone sales level within their first month. Initially, new agents could track their progress toward the milestone by pulling down sales information from the company's intranet. But that process was cumbersome; many agents didn't bother and didn't know where they stood, so the motivational power of the bonus was unrealized. When the company began pushing emails out to report on agents' real-time progress, along with encouraging messages customized to each person's situation, the company markedly increased the number of agents achieving the success milestone.

Some companies use gamification elements in their incentive approach, such as friendly competitions, challenges, or rewards for achieving specific objectives. For example, telecommunications company Yota implemented a *Star Wars*–inspired game with its point-of-sale team. For two months, sales employees were on the "light side," while the sales plans were on the "dark side." To win, sales team members had to build up "military" potential to charge their ship's battery and shoot a laser. They did this by achieving sales plans (for example, selling more modems than the norm) and completing training. Those who performed best in the game got bonuses and prizes.

Linking digital talent platforms

In many sales organizations, the systems for talent management come from different vendors—what the organization considers best-in-class solutions. Typically, the systems are not linked, so it takes managers a great deal of time to assemble the integrated view needed to make talent decisions. If systems are linked, it becomes possible to glean insights from the data— insights that enable faster talent processes and better decisions.

Sales organizations can make talent management more responsive to market changes by connecting these systems through an always-on support platform—what we call a digital sales talent hub. (See figure 17-1.) The hub brings together digital assets (data, technology, algorithms, and an intelligence engine) that deliver data-based insights across talent management decisions and processes.

The DSTH aids managers with a range of job responsibilities. It helps leaders develop talent strategy and work with HR to design sales success profiles. It supports key talent processes, such as those for acquiring, developing, and retaining talent, and for coaching and managing performance. The goal is to seamlessly connect all the systems while providing appropriate privacy safeguards, governance, and controls.

Several examples show how integration, whether done by a digital system or a manager, enables more agile and effective decision-making.

Developing a talent strategy and implementing change

Talent strategy refers to linking business goals to a forward-looking, high-level view of recruitment, onboarding, professional development,

FIGURE 17-1

Linking systems through a digital sales talent hub

performance management, succession planning, and employee engagement. An integrated view of talent data can be especially helpful for developing a talent strategy and accelerating change. The time required to design and implement complex transitions, such as a change in sales force size or structure, can be cut by as much as 50 percent. Here are two examples.

Shifting sales strategy and deploying new sales structures and roles

A company is restructuring its field sales force by moving more selling steps to inside salespeople, adding a key account role for a few named accounts, and adding a new product launch task force. The overall headcount for field sales is expected to grow modestly.

With a DSTH to link sales and HR data, the cycle time from defining roles to having people working in them can shorten from a year to months. Analyzing sales performance data can immediately identify the initial cut at the skills and competencies of successful people, providing insights for then developing the forward-looking role definitions and hiring profiles. Desired profiles can seamlessly feed into recruiting platforms to find matched internal and external candidates. By the time new salespeople are either reassigned or hired, the LMS is already prepared to begin their onboarding.

Assisting with downsizing

When sales organizations decide to downsize, leaders must make talent decisions objectively while minimizing the disruption to customers and the business. Linked talent systems provide quick access to the data needed to match salespeople to available jobs, including information about tenure, job location, customer relationships, performance ratings, and competency assessments. Managers can work with HR to ensure these criteria are applied consistently. By integrating all the data, the DSTH helps bring speed and fairness to what is always a painful process. Linkages also help with making transition plans for salespeople (those staying and leaving) and for disrupted customers.

Efficiently managing performance by linking results, activities, and competencies

With a DSTH implemented, you can quickly collate insights from multiple sources. Imagine that the sales performance management system indicates a salesperson is falling short of the new customer acquisition goal. The CRM system reveals a bottleneck: although there are many prospects at the early stage of the pipeline, few are converting into customers. Further, the human capital management system adds context: the salesperson is an experienced hire from an account management role and has had minimal experience in customer acquisition.

Together, these insights help you identify ways to help the seller. You can enlist the assistance of a solution specialist, coach the salesperson on joint visits with prospects, or help the salesperson make inroads with a prospect. You could assemble these insights from the independent systems; however, if the systems are connected, you save time. In fact, with a fully connected hub, many insights can be automated. The hub detects a performance issue, identifies potential solutions, and sends a digital message to the seller and the manager, suggesting potential remedies. This can also help salespeople be more accountable for their own success.

Coordinating digital nudges across talent systems

Talent systems can supplement manager coaching with automated nudges that increase sales teams' focus on key priorities. Consider an example from an enterprise software sales team. A CRM system uses AI to share the following insights with a salesperson: "Renewal at customer is due in three days with potential of $271,000, and there is an expansion opportunity for a platform product sign-up within six months." Separately, the learning management system sends a reminder to the same salesperson: "Sign up for the Winning by Using LinkedIn workshop scheduled for 2 p.m. Friday." A third system, one that monitors sales performance, issues an unrelated rule-based nudge to the salesperson: "Congratulations on the $170,000 win. Two more and you will be over your quarterly goal!"

On their own, each one of these timely prompts can be highly effective. But when disconnected systems send too many nudges simultaneously, the salesperson is likely to act on only the most urgent one. Or worse, they may ignore them all. The key to maximizing the impact lies in integration. Logically sequenced and appropriately spaced nudges enable the salesperson to effectively balance immediate tasks with long-term developmental goals. With linked systems, managers spend less time looking up and integrating data and more time coaching and helping with customers.

Implementing a hub

Creating a DSTH is not easy. The technical challenges are amplified when systems are managed in separate organizational silos. CRM and SPM systems are more likely to be linked because they are often managed by the same team, such as sales operations. Connecting only these two systems would create considerable value, but as more systems are connected, the value multiplies. Recruiting and learning management are often housed elsewhere, by separate groups within HR. To bring together systems that are managed in separate organizational silos, the CEO and executive team usually need to make it a priority.

From a technology perspective, connecting systems from multiple vendors is a major challenge. Yet doing so can have a measurable impact.

Technology company Oracle has its own integrated platform, which it used to bring all its talent data together in a single source of truth. The result was a more connected experience for employees (including sales team members)—from recruiting and onboarding to performance management, career development, and learning.

The capabilities and impact of a DSTH grow over time. Early successes often focus on reducing the time and cost of key talent management steps, and on improving the quality of talent decisions through enhanced visibility into people and performance. Those who take digital talent capabilities to the next level—by integrating talent systems—are creating competitive advantage by boosting their responsiveness to market shifts and personnel changes while better aligning their talent decisions with business strategy.

18.

Managing a Recurring Revenue Business

Every company dreams of keeping a customer forever. The first requirement to achieving this is to continuously provide value to that customer. Digital subscription and consumption businesses have continuous value realization built into their offerings. Salesforce is an exemplar of this type of business. Starting as a software-as-a-service provider of CRM, Salesforce became a behemoth in *many things as a service* (software, platform, infrastructure) with applications for sales, service, and marketing, along with various development platforms, messaging and collaboration applications, and more.

In the digital-first world, companies with physical products are increasingly creating recurring revenue business models as well, which affects what salespeople do and how you manage them. Industrial supplier W.W. Grainger has a KeepStock program that allows large customers to outsource their inventory management to streamline procurement processes.

Kaeser, a manufacturer of industrial air compressor stations, gives customers the option to buy a station outright or to contract for compressed air as a service with its Sigma Air Utility. A custom system is installed at the customer's site, sensors monitor usage, and the customer pays for the compressed air they consume.

Recurring revenue businesses like these are not new. In consumer products, manufacturing, and chemicals, for example, revenues are realized steadily over time. Cargill provides cocoa and grains to Nestlé, International Paper supplies packaging to Amazon, Toray Industries delivers synthetic fibers to Adidas—these are all examples of recurring revenue businesses. In the technology industry, IBM introduced computer time-sharing in the 1960s. By 1974 LexisNexis was selling its massive database of legal and business content as a service. What *is* new about this approach is that cloud technology, embedded sensors, and other digital capabilities allow products once sold as one-off purchases to be enhanced or replaced by services that generate recurring revenue streams. Sensors and digital tracking let the seller track usage metrics and quantify the value that customers realize.

If you are not already managing a recurring revenue business, chances are that this opportunity will reach you sooner rather than later. This chapter covers what recurring revenue means for the sales organization. Three topics are discussed:

- Strategy, process, and metrics for recurring revenue sales

- Driving the performance of recurring revenue businesses

- Supporting customers and salespeople with the transition to a recurring revenue model

Strategy, process, and metrics

When a recurring revenue buyer makes their first purchase from a seller, it's only the start of the value exchange between the two. Most of the value—on both sides—accrues over time. As customers benefit from a purchase, they return and buy more. The business partnership gains traction and momentum.

Sales strategy and process

In recurring revenue businesses, the sales strategy is finely balanced between two pivotal goals: keeping and growing current customers and acquiring new ones. The revenue stream from existing customers provides a foundation of stability, while the acquisition of new customers contributes to a growing future. Clearly, there needs to be continual value on both sides to make a long-term partnership work.

For sellers, the benefits start with predictable revenue streams. A strong focus on customers leads to ever-deeper customer insights that can drive retention, growth in usage, and opportunities to upsell and cross-sell new products and services. If switching costs are high, it's hard for competitors to enter. And the insights gained through regular customer interactions allow for more targeted and effective product innovation and sales strategies.

For buyers, the benefits start with stable access to products or services that receive regular updates and enhancements. The scalability of services creates flexibility for buyers to adjust their usage based on changing needs. The ongoing relationship with the seller leads to better, more-personalized customer service and support and the potential for solutions that are customized to specific needs. Typically, there are lower up-front costs than in traditional purchase models; this can make a solution financially accessible for a broader range of customers. But buyers do worry about high switching costs and potentially escalating prices, which are tensions that you need to be prepared to manage.

Should a company with physical products build a recurring revenue business?

For such companies, transitioning to or adding a recurring revenue business is valuable when the benefits are significant and sustainable for the company and for some or all buyers. And there is a risk to not making the shift if the competition does. There are several potential sources of company and customer benefits.

- **Digital tracking of product utilization and health.** Fueled by the growth of IoT, embedded sensors in physical products can report on their usage and performance. GE Aviation offers a usage-based sales model that provides customers with jet engine monitoring and diagnostics that enable predictive maintenance. Kaeser has a similar model that uses sensors in its air compressors. John Deere's combines can come with subscription-based soil sensor data and insights, allowing growers to microtarget water and fertilizer use.

- **Frequent updates and upgrades.** This benefit is especially pertinent for products with embedded software. Siemens and GE offer subscriptions for specialized software and services to help customers operate and maintain complex industrial equipment. The software gets smarter over time.

- **Specialized operational skills.** When solutions require advanced operational competencies, a seller who has experience with hundreds of installations will be more proficient than a buyer who knows only a few. Orica, a provider of explosives and blasting systems for the mining industry, offers Rock-on-Ground service that brings customers the skills and resources needed for managing blasting operations: designing a blast, supplying explosives, loading the pattern, and firing the shots. Companies that sell complex products, such as Siemens, GE, and Xerox, have for years offered maintenance contracts that create recurring revenue streams. PPG's auto painting business is another example. The company offers auto manufacturers an "INSITE" turnkey coatings systems and management program.

- **Community or ecosystem.** Caterpillar and John Deere have built ecosystems around their products, including online platforms where businesses can share insights. A strong user community often leads to the creation of self-service support resources, such as forums, Q&A threads, tutorials, and wikis. A robust ecosystem can extend into marketplaces for accessories, third-party apps, and consulting services. DJI Enterprise has a lineup of commercial drones. The company partners with third-party developers to offer apps and integrations that extend the drones' capabilities for specific industry needs, such as precision agriculture mapping and construction site monitoring. Siemens' MindSphere and Rockwell Automation's FactoryTalk enable similar ecosystems.

There are also naturally subscription-suited products, such as consumables. Grainger's KeepStock is one example. Another is Xerox, which offers managed print services where businesses subscribe for supplies and maintenance.

The success of any sales organization depends on finding, acquiring, serving, and ultimately growing business with customers. Recurring revenue businesses place disproportionate emphasis on the last two steps. And there is an added twist to these steps: a healthy dose of *helping the buyers realize value*, often using customer success managers who have this very mission.

Metrics

In addition to metrics that are relevant to most businesses (such as revenues, gross profits, and win rates), there are some pipeline, customer health, and result measures that are specific to recurring revenue businesses. (See figure 18-1.) These help you assess performance around three key goals:

- Optimize customer acquisition costs (by keeping them in line with the value generated)

- Maximize customer lifetime value

- Drive recurring revenue growth

Optimize customer acquisition cost

Customer acquisition cost (CAC) is the total cost associated with finding and acquiring a new customer, including efforts in marketing promotions, sales, discounts, and more. A common benchmark is that the number of months needed to recover the CAC should be less than twelve.

FIGURE 18-1

Metrics specific to recurring revenue businesses

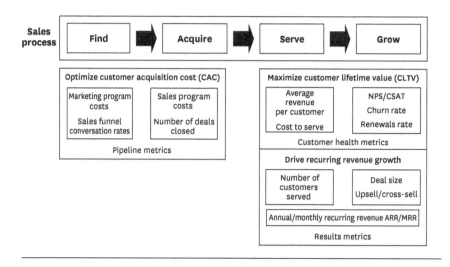

Pipeline metrics provide insights about CAC by measuring the efficiency and effectiveness of various steps of the sales funnel and predicting future revenue potential and sales costs. A strong pipeline generates a high volume of leads at low cost and optimizes conversion rates. Metrics for tracking pipeline strength include the following:

- **Marketing program costs:** focuses on the *find* step, in which marketing has a lead role

- **Sales program costs:** focuses on the *acquire* step, in which sales has a lead role

- **Pipeline advance rates:** tracks the number of leads that go into each step of the sales process (for example, qualify, develop, communicate value, close), the conversion rate at each step, and the overall conversion rate (ratio of initial leads to closed customers)

- **Deals closed:** looks at the number of new customers acquired as well as the average size of the deals signed

Maximize customer lifetime value

Customer lifetime value (CLTV) is the expected total value a buyer can bring over the entire relationship with the business, considering revenue generated from all sources (e.g., subscriptions, upsells, renewals) less the cost to serve and grow the customer. A common benchmark is that CLTV must be more than three times CAC. Customer health metrics are leading indicators of CLTV.

Metrics for tracking customer health include:

- **Number of products and services purchased.** This measures engagement with key programs and offerings.

- **Average revenue per customer.** This can be tracked monthly and is even more meaningful when it is compared to the cost to serve the customer.

- **Measures of customer satisfaction.** These include **Net Promoter Score,** which measures the likelihood that a customer will recommend a business or product to others, and **customer satisfaction score,** which measures a buyer's satisfaction, typically on a one-to-five scale.

- **Measures of customer retention. Customer churn rate** measures the percentage of buyers that cancel or unsubscribe within a specific period. A high or growing churn rate could indicate that you're spending too little time on customer retention. **Renewals rate** is the flip side of customer churn.

Drive recurring revenue growth

The overall performance of the business is usually measured on two time frames:

- **Monthly recurring revenue** is the monthly rate at which revenue is generated.

- **Annual recurring revenue** provides a longer-term perspective on revenue and its stability.

Other results metrics that track dynamics affecting these two include:

- Number of customers served

- Upsell/cross-sell and deal size, reflecting growth realized with current customers

- Customer revenue retention and growth, measuring the business's ability to keep customers and to grow business with them through upgrades and expansions

The combination of pipeline, customer health, and results metrics provides insights about how to manage and drive performance of a recurring revenue business—as we will explore next.

Driving performance

The success of a recurring revenue business demands focus on customer acquisition, as well as on retention and growth. Success depends on a continuous cycle of customer acquisition, integration into the ecosystem, and ongoing efforts to optimize customer success and mutual long-term value.

Customer acquisition

To attract and engage new customers, recurring revenue businesses follow either a product-led or a sales-led approach to communicating value.

Product-led versus sales-led growth

With a product-led growth model, the business offers free trials or freemium versions of its product. These models are common at SaaS companies, such as Zoom, Atlassian, and Tableau. Potential customers get to experience the value of the product firsthand before committing to a subscription. The product needs to prove its worth quickly through an intuitive user experience and clear demonstration of value. By tracking user engagement, the company identifies prospects most likely to benefit from upgrades to premium versions and concentrates sales efforts there. Freemium offerings allow companies to scale the business more efficiently with lower sales expenses, broader product outreach, and higher customer retention rates.

A sales-led growth model, on the other hand, relies on a traditional marketing and sales approach to acquire customers. The business uses a mix of digital methods, including content marketing, social media outreach, and search engine optimization, to find prospects. Then, sales steps in to follow up on qualified leads. This model also encompasses the sales of complex products or services, where the focus is on understanding customer pain points and presenting a tailored offering. For example, Kaeser targets enterprise clients who require customized solutions, extensive support, and a clear understanding of ROI before making a commitment. Companies that offer physical products with recurring revenue rely on a sales-led, rather than a product-led, growth model when acquiring customers.

Communicating the value

The value proposition for recurring revenue businesses highlights not just the immediate benefits but also the long-term value of committing to the service. This can include:

- **Continuous improvement:** access to ongoing product updates and new feature releases, and the promise to adapt to customer feedback

- **Support and community:** availability of customer support, resources for learning, and connections to a community of other users

- **Cost-effectiveness over time:** demonstrating how the flexibility to scale, efficiency gains, and incremental revenue generated justify the cost over time

Prospective customers look for evidence that a product or service will solve their problems and is worth the investment. In recurring revenue models, this evidence can come in several forms:

- **Customer testimonials and case studies:** success stories from similar customers or industries

- **Data and benchmarks:** performance metrics or ROI calculations that provide concrete evidence of what customers can expect

- **Third-party reviews and awards:** recognition from industry analysts, press, or awards that lend credibility and attract attention

Customer retention and growth

Many recurring revenue businesses assign the responsibility for customer retention and growth to a specialized role: a customer success manager. Here, we discuss the role of the CSM in consumption-based businesses and whether the same person can balance both customer acquisition and customer success.

In high-tech sectors, more and more sales (such as cloud services) are consumption-based, meaning buyers pay for what they use or consume. Not surprisingly, such companies pioneered the use of CSMs. But the role is becoming more common in other industries too. Medical technology company Intuitive Surgical has a CSM-like role called clinical sales associate. These people work on-site with surgical teams to support their usage of the company's robotic surgical system and to continuously expand the user base. Cargill and International Paper have customer success–focused roles as well.

CSMs straddle the gap between service and sales, between company interest and customer interest, and between product expertise and customer insight.

The CSM role

An IT buyer at our consulting company who deals with numerous suppliers astutely positioned the CSM role:

> *Although Alice has the CSM title, she tries to knock down my door every time she smells an expansion opportunity. She is just a pushy salesperson. But Susan is different. She is a CSM who truly*

epitomizes the role. She brings ideas about how we can use her products better. She advocates for us in her company's product enhancement road map. She keeps us informed about what's coming. Every month, she spends a full day on-site with us. Every quarter, we review our spending and look at other issues that are important to us. These include cost reduction, speed of handling critical problems, security, and the path forward.

A CSM's responsibilities depend on the complexity of solutions and the size of customers. For simpler solutions and smaller customers, one CSM may handle fifty accounts remotely. At the other end of the spectrum, for key accounts with complex needs, there may be a dedicated, mostly on-site CSM. This individual acts as the coach of the customer relationship, bringing in technical experts, trainers, and others as needed.

Many CSM jobs are hybrid roles in which the employee interacts with customers virtually over live video and occasionally in person. Consider the example of John Deere. Growers who purchase large farming equipment, such as a combine, can add on a paid subscription service that helps make farming operations more profitable and sustainable. The service uses data from embedded sensors to help growers optimize their plant separation and microtarget their water and fertilizer. Deere has CSMs who onboard, train, and support its independent dealers on the technology and who can assist with renewal and targeted expansion opportunities. Most of the training interactions between the CSMs and the dealers are virtual. Additionally, some dealers have precision agriculture teams to assist growers with using the service. These teams often tap into a digital display on a grower's equipment remotely, providing help even when it's not convenient to interact in person.

The CSM job title reflects a change in the mindset of sellers. Instead of "win the customer," the focus has shifted to "show the customer the path to value." This is not always easy, especially at companies with hard-driving, results-oriented sales cultures. Unless leaders purposefully act to change attitudes and behaviors, CSMs will be viewed by customers as accomplices in making the company's quarterly sales goals, not as true trusted advisers.

This is why CSM teams are usually managed separately from sales. Although the two teams collaborate, CSMs have their own management structure, hiring profile, success metrics, and incentive plan that reinforce the right mission and culture.

CSM profile, success metrics, and incentives

The success profile for this role is more like one in consulting than one in sales. As advisers, CSMs must leverage their knowledge of company offerings and the customer's business, as well as their skills in structured and creative problem-solving. They are often hired with specific experience in the buyer's industry or context.

Excessive emphasis on short-term, revenue-focused performance metrics and incentives can divert their attention away from customer success and toward closing sales. This diminishes the business relationship and reduces the CSM's impact. At the same time, without some revenue accountability, these employees may spend too much time addressing urgent support needs for friendly customers while ignoring growth opportunities. Their performance metrics can include customer usage (e.g., retention, renewals, consumption) and satisfaction (e.g., NPS and other customer feedback). Results metrics over longer time frames and lower incentive pay are also better suited to the role. Many CSM incentive plans have team-based components. In the high-tech industry, a typical salary-to-incentive ratio is 75:25, while the average pay mix for traditional account executives is 55:45.

Balancing customer acquisition and customer success

Some organizations have a single role that handles both the acquisition and the ongoing success of customers. Getting the right balance can be challenging when the same person does both, but it is not impossible, especially in smaller organizations or startups where roles tend to be more fluid.

Having a single point of contact can provide a seamless experience for the customer, from the initial sale to ongoing support and success. Buyers appreciate continuity in the people they interact with. But there are complications.

Sales and customer success require different skill sets. Sales focuses on solution design, persuasion, negotiation, and closing deals, whereas customer success is about nurturing, supporting, and solving problems. A person focused on both areas might prioritize one over the other for several reasons. For example, the salesperson might gravitate toward what's easier to do or what they are good at. Further, customer demands, or a push to meet short-term sales targets, might cause a seller to spend too much time on one activity while neglecting the other.

Combining customer acquisition and customer success into a single role thus requires clear prioritization, with effective time management to handle the distinct demands of each. The incentives must align, and performance management systems have to encourage the right relative emphasis.

As the business scales, it becomes necessary to separate these functions to ensure both effective customer acquisition and sales growth in existing customers.

It also generally makes sense to split the roles when a business has both onetime purchases and recurring revenue offerings. John Deere is a great example: An infrequent purchase of a $500,000 combine is accompanied by an added paid subscription service. For a salesperson or a dealer used to the large equipment sale, the relatively modest-value service sale can be a time-consuming distraction. The challenge of keeping the two roles together is even more severe. Thus a separation of roles is called for.

Managing the transition to recurring revenue

While recurring revenue business models are highly desirable for companies (and their investors), transitioning to such a model is often not easy for customers or salespeople. The sales organization must adapt to selling a different offering, often to a different set of customers. As a manager, you are at the center of helping both salespeople and customers manage the transition.

Selling a new offering to different customers

As products are enhanced or replaced by digitally infused services, the revised offering can target a narrower or expanded pool of customers.

A narrowing pool of potential customers

When potential buyers narrow to only larger ones, deals become more complex and sales cycles grow longer. Orica's Rock-on-Ground service for the mining industry relies on sensor-provided data for analyzing rock mass, detecting where rock has moved post-blast, and transporting it to the right destination. Customers commit to a multiyear contract, and Orica gets paid per million tons of rock delivered. The service appeals to a subset of its current customer base—those with large operations that can benefit from a long-term, outcomes-based contract. This brings more issues to iron out: outcome promises, metrics, responsibilities, conflict resolution mechanisms, escalation, and termination scenarios, to name a few. There are more senior buying decision-makers involved, including representatives from a broader range of functional areas. Outside consultants are typically involved as well. The increased cycle length and deal complexity calls for a sales team of strategic account managers with new capabilities.

An expanding pool of potential customers

In other cases, the shift to a recurring revenue business broadens the customer base to include smaller buyers. In 2013 Adobe shifted from selling onetime perpetual licenses for boxed publishing and design software to selling monthly SaaS subscriptions for Creative Cloud. Before this, its customers paid a larger up-front license fee plus a modest annual maintenance fee; now customers would have to renew their subscriptions every year. Although the entry cost for customers was lower, the long-term cost would rise.

The smaller initial cost allowed Adobe to broaden its market reach. Potential users, especially small businesses and freelancers, could access professional tools with less up-front investment. Further, they could subscribe to specific applications rather than having to buy the entire suite of Adobe products. The subscription model, complemented by cloud capabilities, allowed the company to offer free or low-cost trials of its applications. These factors led to more than a doubling of its customer base within ten years of Creative Cloud's release. Further, Adobe could sell Creative Cloud to small customers directly, allowing it to end relationships with partners and resellers and eliminate the sales team supporting them. With large corporate customers, Adobe's own salespeople would play a key role in the transition to the new SaaS model, as we explore next.

Getting salespeople and customers on board

Sales organizations can face numerous challenges when transitioning to a recurring revenue business. In Adobe's case, many large corporate customers were initially unhappy about the shift to Creative Cloud, as the cost of buying subscriptions for a large number of users escalated over time. In addition, some small businesses and freelancers felt they were being robbed of their perpetual licenses. Thirty thousand customers even signed a change .org petition asking Adobe to abandon the SaaS transition.

Its salespeople were on the front lines of working with customers, many of whom were upset and skeptical that the SaaS model was a better value. Adobe launched new education and support programs to bring salespeople out of their comfort zones and help them see the benefits for customers. It began compensating the sales force differently by adjusting the timing for revenue recognition. To ease the transition for customers, the company gave existing buyers a 40 percent discount in the first year and provided a steady stream of product upgrades to overwhelm customers with added value.

Despite the initial pushback, the new model gained strength quickly. Adobe was able to get product innovations to customers faster and revenues grew consistently. Salespeople and managers played a key role in helping customers embrace the new business model.

Salespeople's role in addressing customer pain points

Salespeople are well positioned to help customers address several pain points that may be associated with the transition to a recurring revenue business. For Adobe, those pain points were financial. Other times, the challenges involve disruptions to processes, systems, and people.

When the transition requires the revamping of customer processes and systems, sales teams can work with customers to define the right strategy and pace for implementing change. Consider SAP, which faced technical challenges as it evolved its Business Technology Platform from a proprietary tool to a cloud-based infrastructure that customers could use with the cloud provider of their choice. Although the new offering enhanced flexibility, reliability, and agility for buyers, the transition was challenging for some; many used SAP in multiple locations and for business-critical capabilities, like logistics and payroll. Migrating all these systems to the cloud without disrupting operations was complex and costly. The sales team helped guide customers in using online migration guides and tools to enable a successful transition.

Sometimes the shift to recurring revenue eliminates customer jobs and roles. In 2018 Philips Lighting was renamed Signify, signaling a shift in the company's primary business model—from selling light fixtures to selling lighting as a service to large commercial and public sector customers. Initially, some prospective buyers were reluctant to give up control and commit to a long-term outsourcing arrangement. Building owners and managers often had a staff of people who installed and maintained lighting systems. Retraining them was rarely practical given the complex, digitally connected systems, and many would lose their jobs. Signify developed customer use cases to demonstrate the potential for energy and cost savings. Salespeople and managers relied on these use cases to help prospects get over the hurdles. IBM used a different strategy when it began providing data center outsourcing services: it hired many of its customers' displaced employees to join the IBM team supporting its buyers.

———————

As you face the challenges of managing in a recurring revenue environment, you will play a key role in helping your sales team adapt and ensuring that customers see the path to value. The focus of the next section is how to be successful in bringing constant improvement and change to your sales team.

.

Driving Improvement and Implementing Change

19.

Continuously Improving Your Business

Rapid, ongoing change—in buyers and markets, company strategies, product and service offerings, and digital technologies—creates the imperative for sales leaders at all levels to adapt and improve their organizations constantly.

The book has already shared many ideas for boosting performance with your customers and your team, especially with the help of digital. This chapter covers essential processes of *how* to put the best of these ideas into practice. It will explore:

- Discovering improvement opportunities

- Prioritizing what to do and when

- Addressing opportunities through multidimensional solutions, which cut across content from several chapters

We begin with how pharmaceutical giant Novartis used a structured approach to improve its sales organization.

The sales productivity hunt at Novartis

The proactive annual hunt dates back to 2000, when Novartis tapped one of its top global sales and marketing executives to lead an initiative aimed at boosting the performance of over fifteen thousand salespeople across more than forty countries. Sales and marketing leaders from select countries came together in Chicago for a three-day workshop. The meeting started with a primer on sales effectiveness, followed by brainstorming ways to improve. The group coalesced around initiatives for addressing common challenges while allowing each country to adapt them to its own context. It was decided to direct attention to one major initiative per year.

In the first year, the focus of the improvement efforts was *focus*. Workshop participants agreed that there was an opportunity for salespeople to better prioritize which health-care providers to spend time with. In the United States, data analysis confirmed that sales force time was scattered across too many physicians. The marketing team provided new data and tools to help sellers direct their efforts to approximately 35 percent of the physicians whose patients could benefit most from the company's products. The new focus strategy and its benefits were reinforced through training, coaching, and tracking, leading to a significant improvement in productivity.

In the second year, attention turned to making sales interactions more effective. Sellers were observed on calls to identify the behaviors that set top performers apart. Then Novartis launched a new training program called Performance Frontier—The Next Generation in Sales Excellence, which centered on the differentiating behaviors. Managers reinforced them in regular coaching sessions. In a 2003 survey asking physicians to identify their most valuable interactions with pharmaceutical representatives, respondents chose Novartis sellers 46 percent of the time when the salesperson had completed the training. The percentage dropped to 22 percent when the salesperson had not yet been trained. In addition, trained sellers who had previously been rated as average realized twice the sales growth rate compared with those who were not yet trained.

The productivity hunts are not just one-and-done initiatives. Instead, these efforts are compounded and built upon each other year after year. The program to help salespeople focus on the right physicians has evolved into an AI-driven avatar that uses the CRM system to continuously give salespeople up-to-the-minute insights about physicians' needs. And Novartis has used the performance frontier concept for more than two decades to shape hiring profiles and training programs for sales roles across the globe.

Discovering opportunities

Change at Novartis was driven by the company's desire for continuous productivity improvement. In other situations, adjustments to the sales force may be driven by a plan to implement a well-defined business strategy or to achieve a specific objective. (Later in this chapter, we will explore how Google adapted its sales strategy and organization as it sought to expand its presence in the cloud services market.) To identify areas where your organization can seek improvements, begin by looking comprehensively at the sales system.

Identifying opportunities

The sales system can be viewed as a chain that links company strategy to sales decisions, processes, and resources that produce outcomes for salespeople, customers, and the company. Improvement opportunities can be found in any of the links of this chain. (See figure 19-1.)

No matter where the opportunities are, solutions are in the "sales decisions, processes, and resources" link—the part that sales leaders control to drive the outcomes. Consider the two initiatives at Novartis:

- With the first year's focus initiative, the opportunity was rooted in *salespeople's activities and behaviors*—they could do better by spending time with a smaller set of physicians. The solution

FIGURE 19-1

Where to find improvement opportunities in the sales system

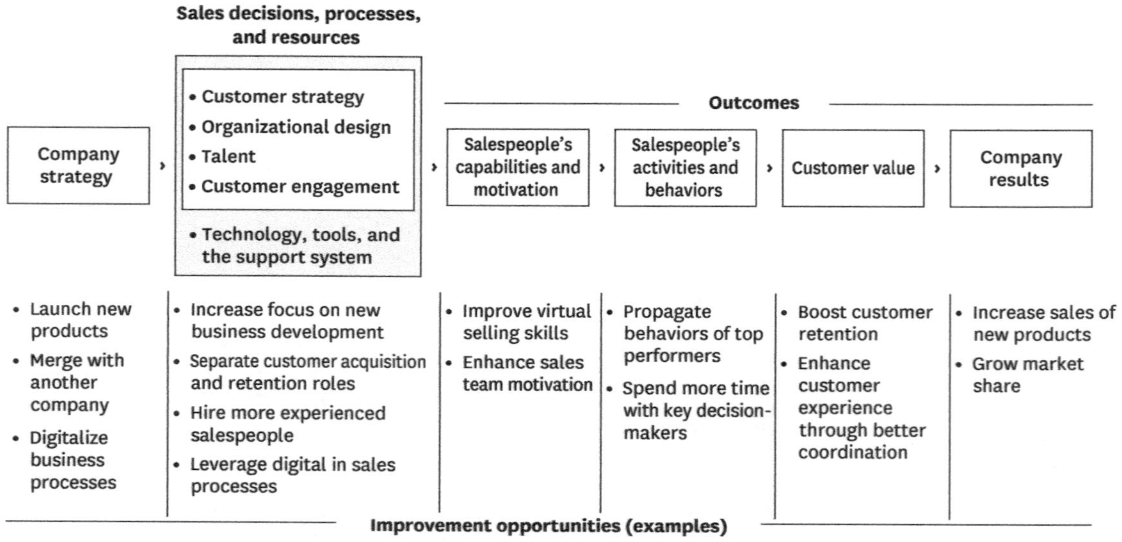

Sales decisions, processes, and resources

Company strategy	Sales decisions, processes, and resources		Outcomes			
			Salespeople's capabilities and motivation	Salespeople's activities and behaviors	Customer value	Company results

Sales decisions, processes, and resources:
- Customer strategy
- Organizational design
- Talent
- Customer engagement
- Technology, tools, and the support system

Improvement opportunities (examples)

Company strategy	Sales decisions, processes, and resources	Salespeople's capabilities and motivation	Salespeople's activities and behaviors	Customer value	Company results
• Launch new products • Merge with another company • Digitalize business processes	• Increase focus on new business development • Separate customer acquisition and retention roles • Hire more experienced salespeople • Leverage digital in sales processes	• Improve virtual selling skills • Enhance sales team motivation	• Propagate behaviors of top performers • Spend more time with key decision-makers	• Boost customer retention • Enhance customer experience through better coordination	• Increase sales of new products • Grow market share

involved *customer engagement* decisions and processes (improved data and tools), while reinforcing focus through *talent* processes such as training, coaching, and performance tracking.

- With the second year's performance frontier effort, the opportunity was discovered by studying *salespeople's capabilities and motivation* and the *activities and behaviors* that differentiated top performers. The solutions focused on *talent* decisions and processes—a training program supported by manager coaching.

A holistic review of the sales system helps you and your team look beyond your usual viewpoints and beliefs. The review is even more valuable when you bring in stakeholders with different perspectives. For example, marketing people have insights about product and customer performance. Sales and HR managers have ideas about the talent dimension. Salespeople bring understanding of the sales process and customer receptivity. Sales operations will gravitate to metrics that highlight opportunities. These metrics and KPIs, along with the variety of perspectives, can help everyone strengthen their insights.

Gaining insights from metrics and KPIs

It is easy to forget that the reason for tracking performance metrics and KPIs is to pinpoint how to get better. They can help you find ways to improve current processes, understand the causes of high and low performance, and identify opportunities for sales team members to spend time more productively.

Tracking metrics within current processes

A good place to start is to examine productivity metrics and KPIs for each sales system component. Each can be a target improvement area. Some metrics measure the quality of sales decisions, processes, and resources directly. Examples include:

- **Customer strategy:** customer retention rates, customer lifetime value across target products and segments, pipeline health metrics such as customer acquisition cost, sales pipeline velocity, and conversion rates. These metrics also measure customer engagement—the quality of customer strategy execution. (See below.)

- **Organizational design:** coverage of target segments and the number of sales territories with too much or too little account workload or potential

- **Talent:** hiring (e.g., time to fill vacancies, candidate success by recruiting channel), training (e.g., participation and completion rates, knowledge retained), incentives (plan engagement, cost versus budget), and talent retention (e.g., turnover of high performers)

- **Customer engagement:** the same metrics used to measure customer strategy (see above) reveal insights about customer engagement—the quality of execution of the strategy

- **Technology, tools, and support team:** next-best-action adoption rate and impact, proposal turnaround time with Gen AI tools, user satisfaction with tools and support

Other metrics focus on the downstream outcomes of sales decisions, processes, and resources. Examples include:

- **Salesperson outcomes:** capabilities and motivation (competency assessments, job satisfaction assessments, quantity of effort) and activities and behaviors (allocation of effort across markets and products, social media usage and impact, quantity and quality of virtual engagement)

- **Customer outcomes:** new account wins, Net Promoter Score, customer satisfaction, customer churn rate

- **Company results:** sales goal achievement, sales force costs/cost of sales, market share gain or loss

To complement the tracking of internal sales system metrics, an outside-in perspective from market research and market scans can help you uncover changing customer preferences, market trends, and competitive dynamics.

Examining performance differences

Differences in outcome metrics such as sales revenue or growth, market share, or customer satisfaction scores can provide valuable insights. Are there certain regions, customer segments, or sales teams that are performing well above or below the norm?

Sometimes, differences highlight sales actions that drive performance. For example:

- A manufacturing company discovered that judicious and effective users of virtual customer outreach were markedly outperforming their peers who were relying exclusively on in-person contacts.

- A telecom company found "data doubles" for low-performing, high-potential customers—that is, other customers who had a similar demographic profile (for example, the same industry and scale) but who were buying much more. Sales strategies and actions that had worked with the more successful accounts were then used to boost sales at low-performing accounts.

- A medical supply company had several products in its portfolio, and the amount of sales time devoted to each product varied by the seller. By analyzing differences in time allocation and results by product across salespeople, the company identified opportunities to improve how salespeople spent their time.

Other times, performance differences reveal something about the sales manager or territory. For example:

- A manufacturing company tracked the performance of salespeople over their first twenty months on the job. New employees reporting to top-performing managers did much better than those assigned to average-performing managers.

- A business services outsourcing company compared the performance of its fifty metro sales territories with that of its fifty nonmetro territories. Average sales per territory were the same for both groups, yet the nonmetro territories had 79 percent more prospects and 49 percent more unrealized market potential than the metro territories. Salespeople in metro territories visited prospects on average four times a year; in nonmetro territories, the average was fewer than three visits. There was a coverage problem.

Comparisons on performance are a great way to find improvement opportunities.

Looking for role pollution

This occurs frequently in sales organizations at all levels. Salespeople, managers, and leaders are drawn into tasks that deviate significantly from their core responsibilities. Usually, these are tasks that others in the company should be doing—logistics or customer service and support, for example. Often, role pollution stems from people naturally wanting to be helpful but reacting to urgent requests that divert their effort from important priorities. Excessive company-mandated administrative requirements can be value-draining as well.

To diagnose role pollution, look at how the sales team spends its time. Are there processes that can be made more efficient? Can some low-value tasks be eliminated, simplified, automated, delegated to cheaper resources, or outsourced? Are internal meetings adding value?

Incorporating longer-term thinking

A natural source to find improvement opportunities is your team, those who are on the front lines and have insights about what's working and what's not. For salespeople and leaders, the pressure to meet immediate targets often means that the focus is squarely on the short term. However,

TABLE 19-1

Questions to encourage future-oriented thinking

	Time horizon	Examples of future-oriented questions
External changes	One to four years	How are market dynamics evolving? Are customer needs changing? What competitive launches are happening? Are regulatory or economic changes expected?
Internal changes	One to four years	Are there company changes—such as new products, new markets, mergers, or rightsizing—on the horizon?
Incentives	One year	Does the incentive structure align with our future strategy and salesperson profile?
Hiring profile	One to two years	Can current sales team members acquire the skills and competencies needed for the future?
Digital tools	One to two years	Are there opportunities to leverage data and digital tools? Are competitors moving ahead of us in this area?
Organizational design	Two to four years	Are there significant gaps or stresses in the organizational structure? Do we need more specialized customer or product expertise? Are we experiencing serious coordination challenges?

efforts to drive improvement are more likely to have a lasting impact when short-term thinking is balanced with long-term thinking. The customer engagement activities of today also drive results in the future. Building lasting customer relationships is a long-term pursuit, especially with new customers. Building the sales team's strength is no different. It may take months before a manager's coaching leads to competency improvements that show up in a salesperson's results. It may take a year for new hires to become fully productive. And, after a sales restructure, it may take two years for the new model to prove fruitful.

Table 19-1 shows the types of questions you can ask to encourage team members to think about improvement opportunities that have a long-term impact on success.

The questions in table 19-1 stay away from the daily activities of customer engagement and sales performance management. The answers are the starting point for launching focused initiatives that could be vital for sustained success.

Rationalizing and prioritizing opportunities

Comprehensive efforts to discover improvement opportunities across the sales system often lead to a long list of possibilities. The next steps are to rationalize and then prioritize the ideas.

Rationalizing the possibilities

This task can reduce long lists of opportunities to a manageable number. Use a small cross-functional team to:

1. **Categorize ideas.** Create buckets and combine what's similar. Figure 19-1 provides a useful way to group ideas. Some buckets will be for sales decisions, processes, and resources (customer strategy; organizational design; talent; customer engagement; technology tools and support team). Other buckets will focus on outcomes (salespeople's capabilities and motivation; salespeople's activities and behaviors; customer value; company results).

2. **Form idea clusters or chains.** Some clusters can be specific— improve the retention of new hires or improve the quality of leads. Others can be more general—reduce sales force costs, enhance new product uptake, or grow existing customers. Chains are formed by linking causes to effects. For example, an idea to increase upselling and cross-selling (an outcome) is connected to spending too much time on customer support and service (a behavior), which is connected to considering a new customer success role (structure) and using a data-driven approach to map customer potential (digital enablement).

3. **Drop infeasible and low-impact ideas.** Decisiveness helps make this process efficient and leaves more time for opportunities that have the greatest chance for impact.

4. **Identify ideas that are duplicated or are closely aligned with in-progress initiatives or processes.** Pass these ideas along to the relevant leader.

5. **Flag "just do it" ideas.** These are practical, straightforward, nondisruptive opportunities that can be implemented easily by an individual or team, though they must be assigned to the right one. Here are some examples: have the CRM system automatically flag when a customer advocate or key contact changes companies; send an alert to targeted salespeople when a seller's social media post gets high traction so others emulate the approach; initiate a daily huddle during the competitive launch period to quickly identify and disseminate effective strategies and responses.

Although we present the steps as sequential, the process can be iterative. The goal is to get the number of significant ideas down to a single digit for prioritization.

Prioritizing by impact and ease of implementation

Once you have a manageable list of possibilities, look at two dimensions to identify the highest priorities to pursue:

- What is the potential impact of implementing a solution?

- How easy will the solution be to implement?

Assessing the impact

To assess the potential impact of an idea, consider its strategic significance. Will it address critical pain points or capitalize on significant opportunities in your market? Will it create competitive advantage? Does it align with your organization's long-term goals? Then define clear, measurable goals and KPIs for measuring progress toward them. These can reflect results (increase in revenue or market share), customer satisfaction (improvement in Net Promoter Score or customer retention), or sales process productivity (higher conversion rates or reduced sales cycle length). Initiatives that focus on a specific decision area, such as hiring, can have more-targeted goals and KPIs, such as shortened time to fill vacancies, higher offer acceptance rates, or improved quality of hires. By quantifying the expected results, you can evaluate the initiative's potential to deliver meaningful improvements to your sales process and performance.

Assessing the ease of implementation

Ease here is about feasibility, resource requirements, and potential challenges associated with execution. Begin by breaking down an initiative into action steps and tasks, then assess the following:

- **Resources.** What human, financial, and technological resources will you need? Do you have the necessary skills and expertise, or is external assistance required from the sales organization or from the company?

- **Timeline.** What are the possible dependencies, bottlenecks, and downstream ramifications? Quick wins may be prioritized if you're looking to make a rapid impact.

- **Readiness for change.** How easily can your team adapt to new processes, tools, or strategies? Is there potential resistance or cultural barriers to overcome within the sales organization or from other stakeholders?

- **Risk.** What hazards and challenges could hinder the initiative's success? What mitigation plans can address these risks?

- **Technology and tools.** Can existing technology and tools support the initiative? If new investments are necessary, will there be implementation or integration challenges?

Choosing the right initiative

By looking at both impact and ease of implementation, organizations can create a matrix or scoring system to rank and prioritize improvement initiatives. (See table 19-2.) Initiatives with high impact and relatively low implementation complexity are easily the top priorities. However, it's important to strike a balance between quick wins and longer-term strategic initiatives to drive sustainable growth.

TABLE 19-2

Improvement opportunities (example)

Opportunity/challenge	Impact (5=highest)	Ease of implementation (5=easiest)
Balance account acquisition and business expansion focus (uneven right now across salespeople)*	5	3
Redeploy the sales force for better customer coverage (has not been looked at systematically for over two years)	3	3
Hire people with industry experience (solutions now are more complex than our team is accustomed to)	4	2
Reduce turnover among new hires and top performers	4	1
Address the lack of intensity in the sales team members who are living on their past success	3	1
Implement field-based digital concierges to support the sales team with all things digital*	5	4

*Selected initiatives

Addressing initiative overload

Rationalization and prioritization are essential to combat a common challenge in sales forces: initiative overload. When sales teams are bombarded with too many projects, it will detrimentally affect productivity, morale, and performance.

Overload happens when the rationalization and prioritization process gets shortchanged because leaders feel pressure to bring continuous improvement to their team. It plays out across different organizational functions and levels, creating scenarios such as the following: The C-suite mandates a 20 percent cut in sales force costs. Concurrently, a product team seeks more sales support for a launch, while marketing develops a central content repository for digital outreach. Sales attempts to streamline customer engagement, HR revamps talent management systems, and IT integrates technological systems across functions. These initiatives are layered on top of existing ones.

A lack of prioritization exacerbates the situation. Each initiative is treated as equally critical, leading to a logjam. Sometimes separate initiatives conflict with one another. Often, they compete for scarce resources, making it tough for any single initiative to gain momentum. There can be clashes between departments as well as duplications of effort. In one large organization, two separate digital initiatives were launched by different departments, both focusing on customer analytics—one through AI and the other through a new CRM system. It was only when the chief digital officer intervened that they were merged into a single, more coherent effort, thus avoiding duplication and ensuring data consistency.

For sales teams, initiative overload is compounded when high-performing leaders and salespeople are drawn into various task forces, diverting their attention from core responsibilities. The sales force has the capacity to help out with many initiatives as long as the workload is spread across team members. But if the same people are consistently tapped to participate, the result is not just inefficiency but also burnout among the most capable team members.

The solution lies in the formation of a small, central, senior-level team, operating like an air traffic control tower. The team ensures that each initiative aligns with the company's strategic direction and protects the sales force from being overwhelmed. It offers oversight, guidance, and coordination to help streamline efforts, prioritize, and reduce the risk of conflicting or redundant initiatives.

From opportunities to solutions

Effective solutions for addressing high-priority opportunities almost always come with uncertainties. Further, they usually involve changing more than one part of the sales system: a combination of customer strategy, organizational design, talent, and customer engagement. Usually, digital enhancements to the supporting technology and tools are also required. The changes can affect both immediate and longer-term performance.

Proof of concept with pilots and experiments

Often, solutions for improvement come with many unknowns. For example, a new sales force technology promises to deliver many benefits, but the investment is significant, and the best way to design and implement a solution is not clear at the start. A proof of concept is a structured and practical test to verify the feasibility and impact of a new idea before full-scale implementation. For example, it can be a pilot or an experiment.

Pilots

This approach involves a small-scale trial for working through uncertainties and testing an idea prior to its broader rollout. Sometimes pilots are used to inform a go/no-go decision. A business services firm piloted a specialized account management team to target small to midsize high-potential accounts. The success led to a new business unit focused on "emerging giants." Oracle ran a pilot by giving a few of its account managers an inside sales assistant in India. When this led to improved sales velocity, it expanded the program to the entire US sales team. Other times, pilots help shape the design of the solution or the implementation process. For example, before launching a next-best-action suggestion tool, a company ran a pilot with a small group of users. They tried out an early version of the tool and provided feedback to shape its design and the implementation process. Later, members of the pilot group acted as advocates for usage of the tool by others on the sales team.

Experiments

Experiments involve trying at least two approaches to doing something in a controlled way, and then measuring and comparing the impact. The approach that produces the better outcome is scaled more broadly. Experiments are usually easy to do with digital outreach, and in this context they are often called A/B tests. One company tested different LinkedIn messages to attract candidates to sales job postings. By experimenting with different message content and tracking and comparing outcomes, the company discovered ways to match the message to the targeted candidate, thus tripling response rates. A similar approach can be used with emails to prospects.

There are also natural experiments, situations in which customers, markets, salespeople, or territories have different conditions and different outcomes. Consider two examples:

- An apparel company noticed that territories with fewer retail stores had better customer retention and prospect conversion rates. It rebalanced salespeople's account assignments for improved coverage and impact.

- At a professional services firm, one account manager had success with a new biotechnology client by connecting the prospect to a referral from a well-known company in the computer technology industry. Now out-of-industry referrals are used frequently by the firm's account managers. Another account manager secured a challenging new client by bringing in experts on video sales calls with the prospect. That tactic too has become common practice across the firm.

Implementing multifaceted solutions

Addressing high-impact opportunities almost always requires changing multiple decisions, processes, and resources. Here's an example. A sales leader observed, "My people are slipping into 'easy work'—spending most of their time with loyal, familiar customers and waiting for orders. They are avoiding the 'hard work' of acquiring new customers." Many hypotheses about the problem and solutions emerged. (See table 19-3.)

Some of the solutions would be easier to pull off, while others would be more disruptive. Since the leadership team was not ready for a major change, the easier solutions were implemented, including remedies in the following areas:

1. **Learning and development.** Regional workshops shared new business development strategies and showcased local successes to encourage a can-do mindset among salespeople.

2. **Goals and incentives.** Sellers received new business goals while a revised incentive plan shifted focus to growth rather than volume.

3. **Company resources.** The organization provided salespeople with "co-investment" funds they could tap into to help a new customer reduce the cost of transitioning to a new supplier.

TABLE 19-3

Lack of new business development: Possible causes and solutions

Possible cause	Likely solution	Disruption
Salespeople are managed to boost revenue; new business is not separately tracked and prioritized	Performance management	Less
Salespeople do not know where the opportunities are; information about account potential is lacking	Customer prioritization and digital support	
Salespeople lack the resources they need, such as prospecting help and co-investment budgets	Company and manager support	
Digital marketing and sales efforts are not aligned	Orchestration	
Salespeople do not have needed competencies	Learning and development	
Salespeople are satisfied with their books of business and are not motivated to go after new opportunities	Incentives and recognition	
Salespeople have too much on their plates; they do not have the time to pursue new business	Team structure and size	
Wrong sales profile for the job	Hiring	
New customers do not value the offering	Value enhancement	More

4. **Digital marketing support.** Sellers could ask marketing to reach out to specific prospects in their territory with targeted blog posts, white papers, and LinkedIn advertising and outreach.

This suite of evolutionary changes did lead to increased short-term turnover among salespeople but also successfully put focus on driving more new business and better company results.

Balancing solutions that impact the now, near, and far

Less disruptive and quicker-to-results solutions often make sense. But you want to keep an eye on the longer term too. An opportunity such as increasing new business development involves solutions that deliver results over an extended time horizon. If the manager provides support and encouragement to help a salesperson bring in a new customer, this could produce a quick win. The impact of other solutions (such as adding a customer acquisition role and hiring more proven "hunters") shows up further in the future. These longer-term solutions often have a bigger impact but are harder to pull off.

TABLE 19-4

Driving performance in the short, medium, and long term (examples)

Goal	To see results this quarter	To see results this year	To see results in future years
Develop and retain talent	Manager recognizes and appreciates people	Manager trains and coaches on key competencies	Leaders hire the right people, and the company creates opportunities to build rewarding careers
Motivate peak performance	Manager provides feedback on goal attainment	Company provides attractive incentives and recognition programs	Leaders create and sustain a winning sales culture
Help people maximize productivity	Leaders communicate priorities	Company provides support to reduce role pollution (e.g., sales time spent on service requests)	Company provides enablers (e.g., data, systems, and tools)
Align sales effort with opportunity	Company shares data to help salespeople target the right accounts	Manager redistributes work among salespeople to improve customer coverage	Leaders create specialty sales teams to bring expertise to key products and markets

Consider several examples of managerial actions that help achieve goals across different time frames. (See table 19-4.)

The best mix of solutions creates impact *now* to pay the bills, in the *near* to shape tomorrow, and in the *far* to pave a path to the future.

Anticipating long-term consequences of actions today

Balancing focus on the now, near, and far also requires anticipating the future consequences of today's decisions. Some actions that boost immediate results can actually hurt performance down the road. See table 19-5 for several examples.

Capturing market opportunity at Google Cloud Platform

Putting all these concepts together, let's take a look at Google, which made a sweeping set of sales force changes with long-term impact in the cloud services market.

TABLE 19-5

Potential negative consequences of short-term focus (examples)

Organization level	Decision area	Action for maximizing short-term performance	Potential negative long-term consequence
Sales force	Sales team structure	Redesign a sales region to accommodate a longtime manager who wants to move to a location that is not ideal for the business	The gerrymandered region fails to perform. Worse, the poor design of the region outlasts the tenure of the manager it was created for.
Sales force	Sales compensation	Attract motivated salespeople and grow sales by paying large short-term individual incentives in the form of commissions	Salespeople build a book of business and live off easy sales to loyal customers. Sellers stop driving growth as hungry competitors move in.
Sales manager	Hiring	Hire quickly to fill a key account manager role	It takes more than a year to recover from the "warm body" hire, jeopardizing the customer relationship.
Sales manager	Pricing	Agree to a request for a deep price discount to make a sale	The product or service is devalued in the eyes of customers and profit margins erode. Customers come to expect these discounts.
Sales manager	Promotion	Delay the promotion or transfer of a good performer to keep current-period sales going	The company loses the person to a competitor.

In 2018 Google Cloud Platform had a market share of 6 percent, a distant third behind Amazon Web Services and Microsoft Azure. Seeking to seize the opportunity to accelerate revenue and grow share, GCP hired Thomas Kurian from Oracle to be its CEO—the first signal of a shift to a more sales-driven key account playbook. When Kurian joined, the GCP sales team was less than one-tenth the size of the teams at Amazon and Microsoft. The rush was on to build an enterprise-savvy sales organization to jump-start faster growth.

Solutions for transforming the GCP sales organization affected every decision area.

CUSTOMER STRATEGY. GCP's past success had come from bringing cloud solutions mostly to small and medium enterprises, consumers, and students.

Now, focus shifted to the larger enterprise side, leveraging the company's advantages in machine learning, artificial intelligence, and search. GCP pursued customers in five industry segments: retail, health care, financial services, media and entertainment, and industrial and manufacturing, targeting C-suite decision-makers.

In the following three decision areas, GCP emulated the playbook of its competitors, such as Oracle, Salesforce, SAP, AWS, and Microsoft.

ORGANIZATIONAL DESIGN. GCP revamped its channels and roles. It more than tripled its direct sales coverage from 2018 to 2019, established industry-specialized direct sales teams, and expanded its indirect distribution while increasing the number of people supporting channel partners. It also increased headcount for teams focused on solution delivery, customer service, and enterprise support.

TALENT. The company went on a hiring spree, acquiring technology industry veterans from its cloud technology competitors. It expanded its channel partner network and boosted partner training, support, and incentives. To attract and motivate talent, GCP mirrored the sales compensation plans of its competitors, shifting some base salary into a larger bonus opportunity. In 2022 it tripled the size of its support teams in Argentina, Poland, and India, led by another experienced hire, Sunil Rao from Accenture.

CUSTOMER ENGAGEMENT. Processes for channel and customer engagement were adapted to the new solution-driven, value-focused sales process. Changes were made to numerous customer-focused business processes, including the handling of customer support requests, forecasting and order entry, and systems for helping channel partners drive deals. The flexibility of customer engagement processes was critical as the enterprise cloud computing market grew and evolved.

By 2023 GCP's market share had increased to 10 percent. This growth would not have been possible without the multidimensional approach to expanding the sales team and aligning the sales model with the business strategy.

Success in today's complex and ever-evolving sales environment requires an ongoing effort to discover, prioritize, and find solutions for addressing improvement opportunities. This leads to continuous change for the sales organization. Helping your team embrace ongoing change is part of everything you do to create impact as a sales leader. And that is the topic of the final chapter of this book.

20.

Navigating Sales Force Change

Supporting your team through change is key to your job and career success as a sales leader. When your company launches new products, changes the roles of salespeople, or deploys a new digital platform, you help make it happen. While change is hard, especially when it is significant and multifaceted, there are time-tested playbooks that lead to success.

This final chapter lays out a seven-step process to help an organization prepare for, implement, and sustain successful change, including how to navigate the most difficult changes. Throughout, we'll consider sales force changes at several sales organizations, including Microsoft and Deacero.

Microsoft: Digitalizing the sales force

There was a time when Microsoft sales executives found it cumbersome and sometimes impossible to get a true picture of their customers' needs. Sellers had to manually assemble and synthesize data that was scattered across business units and systems. In 2016 the company's leaders launched a major effort to use technology, data, analytics, and AI to integrate and provide the information salespeople needed. New tools were deployed, including a system called Daily Recommender, which delivered data-based suggestions to sales executives and partner sellers about the next best action to take with each customer.

Deacero: From taking orders to selling value

A global steel and wire manufacturer, Deacero has a vast product portfolio and long-standing customer relationships. To achieve aggressive growth targets, the company wanted to move from an "inside-out" sales process, in which its teams focused on getting orders for what was in inventory, to an "outside-in" strategy that relied on anticipating market trends and proactively prioritizing accounts and products. Deacero launched Win the Week, a program of sales sprints that gradually introduced new capabilities and activities to transform how sellers worked.

Big change is not easy

Attention to change management helped both Microsoft and Deacero avoid three types of failure that are common with large-scale organizational change initiatives:

- They become overwhelming in their complexity and never really get going. As one leader complained, "We're eighteen months in and still at the PowerPoint stage."

- They progress to a working solution, but broad adoption throughout the organization is poor. Those affected may not trust the solution, may see too little value in using it, or may view it as burdensome and therefore not worth the effort.

- They are successful at first but fail to evolve and sustain usage and value. This route takes longer to unfold and can happen when solutions or skills fail to keep up with changing needs.

The initiatives at Microsoft and Deacero involved significant changes to how salespeople were accustomed to working. Both companies paid keen attention to change management in designing and rolling out their new sales playbooks.

Seven steps to successful change

A disciplined approach can help ensure that an organizational change is well-designed, adopted, and sustained over time. Seven steps can guide it. (See figure 20-1.)

Step 1. Select strong leadership and assemble the right team

Preparing the organization for change starts with putting together a strong team, including senior leaders who support the project, the right project leader, and cross-functional teams.

Senior leaders

These executives inspire others around a vision. They find the right project head, marshal needed resources, and break through organizational road-blocks. With major change initiatives, there are almost always role changes and power shifts among managers and functions such as sales, IT, marketing, and sales operations. Senior leaders can help build and sustain consensus across organizational silos and resolve inevitable conflicts. By providing visible and sustained support throughout the change process, they demonstrate that they value change. This helps maintain commitment among people across the organization.

Project leader

One of the best predictors of success with a complex change initiative is the profile of the person heading the effort.

At Microsoft, the digitalization initiative was led by a boundary spanner, a person who spoke the languages of, and was respected by, both the business and the IT communities. This individual had empathy for the commercial mindset ("Get it done, produce results") as well as the technology mindset ("Design for the long term, control risk"). This fostered collaboration while bringing discipline to ensure deadlines were met.

FIGURE 20-1

A seven-step process for implementing change

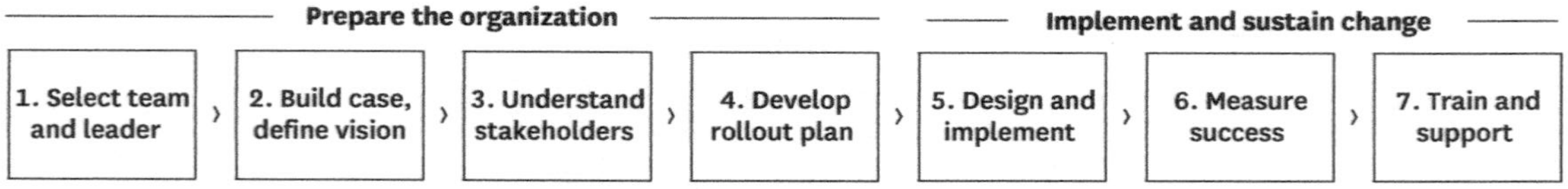

——— Prepare the organization ———   ——— Implement and sustain change ———

| 1. Select team and leader | > | 2. Build case, define vision | > | 3. Understand stakeholders | > | 4. Develop rollout plan | > | 5. Design and implement | > | 6. Measure success | > | 7. Train and support |

Deacero's initiative was led by a different kind of boundary spanner. The leader understood sales and digital but also knew the intricacies of producing steel and wire products—which was critical so that selling could be synchronized with production.

When change initiatives have a hefty digital component, a boundary spanner with sales and digital credentials is key to success. Sales stakeholders have certain priorities: identifying new opportunities, winning over customers, and getting results. IT has equally important priorities that potentially conflict with sales': controlling costs and risks, developing enterprise capabilities, and ensuring longer-term sustainability. Boundary spanners can dream with the business stakeholders in the vision phase, but when it is time to select technology platforms and tools, they can help business stakeholders align with realistic priorities and the IT mindset. They can also keep their eyes on the value and fit for users when designing and deploying solutions.

Cross-functional teams

The boundary spanner at Microsoft led a cross-functional project team that included dozens of people from IT, sales, and marketing.

A typical team structure for a complex sales transformation initiative looks like the following:

- A steering committee provides oversight and resources and keeps stakeholders aligned. It includes the project leader and executives from many functions, such as sales, marketing, IT, finance, and operations.

- The project leader harnesses a program management team that oversees and coordinates work throughout the change journey. Members typically include representatives from sales and other functions affected by the change, as well as orchestrators such as project managers and change management experts. If the project involves technology, technical experts including data scientists, user experience experts, and software architects are part of the team.

- Additional cross-functional teams participate for periods of time as their skills are needed. The number and composition of these supplementary teams depends on the scope and scale of the effort.

Diverse teams, when leveraged well, ensure value for all stakeholders. Teams that lack functional diversity are invariably strong on some dimensions but fatally weak on others, leading to challenges in adoption or sustainability.

Step 2. Build the case and define the vision

Building a business case for change, and defining the vision of what it will look like, often starts by bringing stakeholders together to share ideas and articulate opportunities and pain points. Take the example of a company that wanted to leverage technology and AI capabilities to improve customer insight and responsiveness. Workshops aimed at building the business case and defining the vision included salespeople, sales managers, marketing representatives, IT and data science professionals, and more. Discussions focused on identifying ways to overcome barriers faced by sellers in serving customers. As stakeholders converged on the "what" of the change, a "destination postcard" was developed, representing the desired outcome and showcasing a future state. (See figure 20-2.)

The people most affected by the change, especially salespeople and sales managers, had their fingerprints all over the new way of working. These people shared insights, experiences, and perspectives that led to more effective, relevant, and accepted solutions. When planning any kind of organizational transformation, it's more powerful to do the change *with* the people, not *to* the people.

Step 3. Understand the stakeholders

For significant changes, recognize early on which stakeholders are affected and how.

Take the case of an industrial manufacturer that needed to revitalize growth. The company set out to revamp its customer engagement process. Rolling out a new sales playbook would be a significant change, not only

FIGURE 20-2

Case and vision for change (example)

<table>
<tr>
<td>

Case for change
(opportunities and pain points)

- Fast-growing market, but order-taking culture
  - Too little sales effort in large opportunities
  - Lack of focus on customer success and growth
- Silos with poor coordination across sales roles and between sales and marketing
  - Long sales cycles because resources and people are often unavailable when needed
  - Opportunity to inform salespeople about digital signals of customer interest (e.g., marketing knows when a prospect views the website, but sales does not)
- Missed opportunity to leverage digital
  - Disconnected digital systems
  - Not taking advantage of AI
- Customer information lost if salespeople depart

</td>
<td>

Destination postcard
(the vision)

- Streamlined customer engagement process with resources deployed to the right opportunities at the right time
  - Coordinated customer outreach across all sales and marketing channels
  - AI-based recommendations for salespeople about offerings and sales steps
- Revamped CRM system
  - Improved institutional memory
  - Delivery of AI-derived insights to salespeople

</td>
</tr>
</table>

for salespeople but also for customers. Numerous other stakeholders at the company would be affected as well.

The company developed a stakeholder map (see table 20-1) that captured who was affected by the change and how. The map defined connections between groups (who influenced who), each group's current needs, and the roles that groups would play in the transformation.

Each stakeholder group had concerns about the change ("red thoughts") but also saw some positive aspects to change ("green thoughts"). Red and green thoughts are triggered by one of three underlying forces: understanding, competence, and commitment. Table 20-2 shows examples for one key stakeholder group—salespeople.

Anticipating the red and green thoughts laid the foundation of the rollout plan for helping each stakeholder group embrace change.

TABLE 20-1

A stakeholder map

	Who influences them?	What are their needs?	What is their role in transformation?
Customers	Salespeople, sales managers	Better seller coordination	See value in new approach
Salespeople	Sales managers, marketing managers, HR/ learning and development	Help with making goals	Adopt process, excel in execution
Sales managers	Sales heads, sales excellence, marketing, CXOs	Keep customers and salespeople happy, make goals	Help and coach salespeople to adopt new playbook
Marketing managers	Sales leaders, CXOs	Brand growth, make the numbers	Support with new value proposition and collateral
HR/learning and development	Sales leaders, CXOs	Employee engagement	Align competency model, develop training
Sales excellence	CXOs, consultants	Make and show impact	Create and disseminate new playbook, ensure adoption
Chief experience officers (CXOs)	Analysts, media, consultants	Sustain growth, differentiate, improve operations	Sponsor, set "North Star," show and sustain support

TABLE 20-2

Salespeople's red and green thoughts about a new sales playbook

	Red thoughts	Green thoughts
Understanding: What is the change, why is it important, what is my role?	• "All my customers are different. This 'process' stuff is too theoretical." • "It's too complex and will not work." • "Sounds like a lot of work." • "Things are working fine now. Why change?"	• "I will become more valuable to my customers." • "This gives me great ideas." • "I have tools to predict and manage success. I will waste less time."
Competence: Do I have the knowledge and skills to work in the new way?	• "Will I be able to learn and work with all these tools?"	• "I will grow and expand my skills." • "This keeps me up-to-date and increases my value."
Commitment: Do I have the motivation and passion to change?	• "Are they trying to micromanage us? Don't they trust us?" • "Will the manager use the data to breathe down my neck?" • "Will this digital stuff replace me?"	• "I can see how this will help me coordinate what I do with the marketing people."

Step 4. Develop the rollout plan

To create a positive experience, the emotional and behavioral aspects of change must be managed just as rigorously as the analytical, technical, and organizational aspects. The importance of understanding and addressing the red thoughts and reinforcing the green thoughts of each stakeholder group (not just sales) cannot be overstated. Many well-understood and rational change initiatives have failed because the change team did not acknowledge and create a plan for navigating stakeholder emotions and perceptions. By focusing on understanding, competence, and commitment, it is possible to win the hearts and minds of all involved, especially salespeople. Only then is it possible to win their hands and make change permanent. Early success creates a virtuous cycle of adopting new methods and seeing benefits that lead to sustained and amplified change.

Deacero proactively designed its change experience to acknowledge the concerns of stakeholders. Many salespeople had reservations about the need for a formalized customer engagement process. Further, the company had tried to launch a similar initiative a few years back and the project had failed. Bad memories lingered. The implementation process had to guard against words and phrases that might evoke these fears. (See table 20-3.)

TABLE 20-3

Avoiding language that reinforces sales force concerns

Sales force concerns	Examples of language to avoid
"A one-size-fits-all approach can't work for my customers. There is an art to selling."	"If you follow the process described in the manual, anyone can be successful."
"My manager wants to control what I do."	"This provides you with guidance and standards and helps us monitor and assess performance."
"What I'm doing now works fine."	"This will eliminate lack of discipline, inconsistencies, and capability gaps."
"This new playbook is really complex."	"We will provide you with a comprehensive manual, numerous templates, and many hours of training."
"This sounds just like the last initiative that failed."	Any words or phrases that might inadvertently bring up memories of the past initiative.

While the change design and experience avoided triggering red thoughts, it was also carefully crafted to draw out salespeople's green thoughts. This started with a compelling and credible answer to "What's in it for me?" for field salespeople, communicated through a simple and engaging destination postcard. Language suggested that the new playbook allowed sellers to make their own choices so that they drove the process, rather than the process driving them. The idea was reinforced by drawing an analogy to a tool that was commonly used and valuable to salespeople—"it's like a GPS for navigating complex customer relationships." Managers got practical coaching guides with which they could embed the new process into coaching sessions.

Step 5. Design and implement the solution

Companies use two main approaches—waterfall and agile—when designing and implementing organizational change. Each approach is suited to specific circumstances. With waterfall, a sequential way of working, the change (for example, a CRM system upgrade) is mostly designed before implementation begins. Agile is more fluid and incremental, with design and implementation (for instance, a new digital system) progressing in tandem.

Waterfall

With this approach, progress flows in one direction with minimal feedback loops between phases. One company used waterfall when it implemented a CRM upgrade. The requirements and solution for the upgrade were well defined, relatively stable, and unlikely to change significantly. Waterfall involves the following sequential steps:

1. Gathering and documenting project requirements

2. Designing and developing the solution to meet the requirements

3. Implementing the solution

4. Providing ongoing support after the solution is deployed

Agile

Agile is an iterative approach that focuses on collaboration, adaptability, and continuous improvement. It embraces uncertainty and delivers value incrementally, making it well suited to most complex sales digitalization initiatives, where requirements evolve. Agile also involves weeks-long sprints of designing, building, deploying, learning, and then iterating pieces of the solution.

Microsoft used agile when it built Daily Recommender. The development team adhered to a 10/10/10 rule for each sprint: 10 hours to define a business problem, 10 days to design a model to address the problem, and 10 weeks to pilot the solution. The team focused on creating a good user experience and a simple interface, which paid off. Salespeople could master the tool simply by using it. Users could accept or reject each next-best-action suggestion, and their choices and feedback trained and improved the algorithms.

An agile approach was also key to the success of a 2020 digitalization initiative at biopharmaceutical company UCB. The project involved building and rolling out an AI-enabled tool for field sales reps. The tool made recommendations about which customers reps should visit, what message to deliver, and how to ensure communications were timed according to patient needs. The project involved three phases:

1. **Proof of concept.** A predictive algorithm was developed and simulated using historical data to demonstrate that the approach was feasible and could lead to a better result.

2. **Minimum viable product.** A usable solution was created quickly and deployed with an Early Experience Team (EET) who represented the larger sales team, not just top or technology-savvy members. The EET provided feedback throughout the journey and actively shaped the eventual solution.

3. **Ongoing evolution.** The project team worked in two-week sprints to make modifications and launch new releases. When EET members

saw how quickly their feedback was incorporated, they owned the solution. This was instrumental in bringing the larger field force on board.

Successful change requires a thoughtful decision about which approach is best. If agile is used when waterfall is called for, there will be repetitive review meetings and wasted effort. On the other hand, if waterfall is used when agile makes sense, solutions will have poor adoption or impact. However you design and implement a change initiative, the next step is to monitor post-implementation performance and adjust as needed.

Step 6. Seek early value and measure success

Quick wins and ongoing measurement help ensure the success and sustainability of change efforts. These initiatives can be lengthy processes. Tangible and visible successes, even if they are only small victories, demonstrate progress and generate momentum. This is especially important during the initial stages of a change effort, since quick wins boost morale, build confidence, overcome resistance, and engender support.

At Deacero, the implementation team collected and disseminated success stories from salespeople about the impact of change on customer experience and perceptions, while managers praised and supported successes within their teams. At Microsoft, the development team gauged success by tracking usage, including the percentage of data-based suggestions that salespeople accepted. This allowed them to quickly identify the adjustments needed to keep suggestions helpful, relevant, and constantly improving over time.

Continuous monitoring and evaluation of a change initiative's progress, impact, and effectiveness can enable learning, course-corrections, and accountability. Regular measurement makes it possible to identify issues or deviations early on, when timely adjustments can prevent failures or inefficiencies that could derail the initiative.

Step 7. Train and support those affected by the change

In times of transition, training and support smooth the path forward.

Training

This has an important role in bringing about a successful change. When it involves new technology, the best training programs focus more on the business process and skill set needed, and less on specific features. One company deployed a new digital coaching system whose training program was called "A Visit to Your Salespeople." Managers worked in pairs and practiced using data and analytics to prepare and conduct coaching sessions. Answers to "How do I use the tool?" questions were provided in short videos.

Support

Training by itself is not enough. During times of major change, added support is needed to help those affected understand the value, develop the competence, and build the confidence to embed change. An effective approach is to provide "hypercare" or intense support during the initial phases of a significant change implementation, such as the introduction of new technology or processes. A support structure can have several components.

- **Hotline and digital-enablement concierges.** This dedicated live phone or video line allows sales teams to quickly get answers to urgent questions, resolve issues, and receive guidance. The hotline provides troubleshooting, explanations, and reassurance during the transition period. Some companies who face rapid constant digital change go a step further by deploying digital-enablement concierges. These are specialists who offer on-demand, personalized support. Concierges are especially effective when they go beyond tech support and focus on helping sales teams boost impact with the use of digital tools.

- **Chatbots and video bots.** These AI-driven tools have emerged as a powerful way to provide immediate, round-the-clock support. They answer common questions about issues encountered during a change. The AI models can improve over time by learning from the data collected as the issues come in to the hotline and to the chatbot itself.

- **Peer-support networks.** These networks provide a mechanism and environment where sales teams can share insights, challenges, and solutions fosters a sense of community and collective learning. Such networks can operate on a digital platform and are supplemented by peer learning sessions during monthly sales team meetings, for example.

Manager as an agent of change

The sales manager is pivotal in guiding the sales team through changes. Managers act as the bridge between the company's strategic vision and the sales force executing that vision.

At Deacero, salespeople had to reprioritize their customers while learning new techniques for selling solutions and managing key accounts. They also had to get comfortable selling the company's full suite of products. Deacero used sales sprints (discussed in chapter 3) to help salespeople build confidence and master the new capabilities needed to execute the transformed process. Sprints broke down these unfamiliar strategies and goals into small, manageable tasks linked to specific customer advances. Managers and salespeople met one-on-one to discuss each week's progress and learnings, set goals for the following week, and discover what the organization and manager could do to support employees' efforts. Within the first six months, sales reps exceeded goals that were previously thought unachievable, resulting in a 16 percent revenue increase.

Managers provide clarity, motivation, and reinforcement of the training and support systems. Moreover, as happened at Deacero, managers offer personalized support, helping team members understand how to make the changes work in the trenches. Through regular individual and team check-ins, feedback, and idea-sharing sessions, managers help their teams adapt and thrive.

Feedback loop

Once a new solution is deployed, people are more likely to sustain and increase their engagement with it when they can share feedback about how well it is working and what can make it better. Not only does this feed-back improve the solution, it also gives people a sense of ownership that motivates their continued usage and trust. When Microsoft first rolled out Daily Recommender, the underlying data was far from perfect. Salespeople could share on-the-ground insights that were used to improve the data and the recommendations. Because sellers could accept or dismiss any suggestion, they were less likely to view the system as "Big Brother" and more likely to view it as helpful.

Sustaining change

Deacero, Microsoft, and numerous others have successfully brought trans-formative change to how their salespeople work. A key factor in driving a positive outcome with such initiatives is a disciplined approach to prepar-ing for and implementing the change—while also taking proactive steps to sustain its success. At Microsoft, the development team approached the implementation of Daily Recommender with an "always ready, but never done" mindset. This perspective is important with any major change ini-tiative. In fact, steps five, six, and seven of the seven-step process are best viewed as a continuous loop. Momentum can be sustained through the ongoing tracking of feedback and results, the continuous reinforcement of value, and the evolution of solutions as new opportunities arise and cus-tomer and company situations change.

By adapting the seven-step process described above to your situation, you can successfully bring change to your sales team—even in the most difficult of circumstances, as we describe next.

Managing difficult changes

The efforts described in this chapter, including those at Microsoft and Deacero, were complex yet successful. The complexity of change efforts falls on a spectrum.

Many of the shifts managers face daily are relatively easy to implement. Companies routinely launch new products, adopt new marketing materials, or tweak a sales enablement tool. Salespeople expect these changes and are used to them.

But success eludes many of the more complicated initiatives. Digital transformations and restructurings of sales roles are examples of hard changes, ones that markedly alter people's responsibilities and affect their daily work cadences. Further, such initiatives may cut across pockets of organizational authority—sales, marketing, and finance, for example. More stakeholders being involved means even more complications. And if new and unproven technologies are involved, complexity further escalates, as does the care needed to avoid slow progress, poor adoption, and lack of sustained impact.

The most difficult changes

The most difficult initiatives are those that have only bad news for stakeholders—whether salespeople, customers, or both. For salespeople, this might mean pay cuts, diminished opportunities (reduced territories, products taken away), or reduced autonomy. For customers, difficult changes include those that increase cost, disrupt relationships with trusted salespeople, or shift customer responsibilities to selling partners or digital channels, signaling a downgrading of the buyer's importance.

In some cases, a change has a negative impact on both customers and salespeople. For example, a wealth management firm decided to serve customers with less than $5 million in assets through an online portal rather than through personal advisers. With the shift, the firm reduced the commissions that advisers earned for these accounts.

When these difficult situations arise, managers are immersed in the dual challenges of taking care of the emotional needs of those affected and maintaining the flow of business.

Protecting key customer relationships

Customers often become anxious when they hear that major change at a supplier is imminent. Will the new salesperson know about their needs? Will a new channel create transition and service problems? Will the new pricing plan cost more over the long run? Opportunistic competitors can take advantage of this uncertainty. Even loyal customers may reason that because things are changing, the time is right to consider other offerings.

Effective transitions use a combination of communication, incentives, and support. Here are some examples.

COMMUNICATION. When an industrial supplier restructured its sales force, many account relationships were disrupted. Before implementing the change, a sales manager and the salesperson taking over an account (along with old sales team member, when possible) met with each key account buyer to assure them of their importance and to promise continued attention and support. After the change, managers regularly followed up with those buyers until a rhythm with the new salespeople was established. At one wealth management firm, when a financial adviser departs, managers are expected to reach out to all key accounts within twenty-four hours and to try to meet with those accounts within a week.

INCENTIVES. Adobe switched to a recurring revenue model in 2013. Instead of paying up front for the license to its software plus a small annual maintenance fee, customers now paid for subscriptions that had to be renewed annually. Although the first-year cost was less, the cost over time was much more. Many customers were unhappy—especially small businesses and freelancers, who felt they were being robbed. Adobe gave existing customers a 40 percent discount in the first year and provided a steady stream of product upgrades to overwhelm customers with added value.

SUPPORT. As Microsoft gradually ended support for physical servers, an "Azure Migrate learning path" gave customers online educational resources with a step-by-step process to understand, assess, set up, and migrate their virtual and physical servers, desktops, databases, and applications from on-premises to the Azure infrastructure. Incentives and personal support smoothed the transitions.

Retaining top-performing salespeople

The uncertainty of change also affects the sales team. Salespeople may wonder: Can I be successful in this new way? Will it increase my workload or reduce my earning potential? Competitors could take advantage by attempting to hire away your top people. Sales force recruiters often target employees at companies that are going through transitions.

As with customers, effective transitions for salespeople use some combination of communication, incentives, and support.

COMMUNICATION. In the most difficult change situations, companies must be forthright about the business reasons for what's happening. People appreciate honesty, even if the news is bad. At the same time, managers should show empathy. During conversations, you can validate people's emotions, listen to concerns without interrupting or dismissing them, and respond with compassion. Role-playing difficult conversations helps, especially when you're facing many difficult discussions, such as when several team members are losing their jobs or must relocate. For those the company is keeping, more-frequent communication from leaders and managers, both before and after the change, encourages retention.

INCENTIVES. To foster growth, a medical device company reassigned some underpenetrated accounts to salespeople who had more time to develop the opportunities. This reduced the short-term earning potential of some top performers. So, to encourage a positive attitude about the change, for six months salespeople who lost accounts still received a portion of the bonuses these accounts generated. The company also offered sellers who gained reassigned accounts an extra 25 percent incentive (on top of the regular bonus), spurring them to embrace the opportunity.

In another example, to align with market realities, a company downsized its sales force and made the incentive plan less lucrative. To take the edge off salespeople's pain, in the first quarter after introducing the new pay plan, incentive payouts were calculated using both the old plan and the new one. Sellers received whichever amount was higher, giving them time to adjust.

SUPPORT. Managers can work with the company to get support and temporary offsets for those affected adversely by change. Resources available may include severance packages for those who lose jobs or reimbursements and relocation services for employees who are transferred. Other forms of support help salespeople adjust to new responsibilities. For example, people who survive a downsizing often have to take on redefined and expanded roles. Managers can provide guidance and coaching on how to reprioritize the increased workload, while the company provides training and information support (e.g., account histories, new target lists).

A checklist for implementing complex sales digitalization

Most challenging changes in the digital world involve adopting technology. This type of change has its own nuances and challenges. Individuals are more likely to embrace new technologies that they believe are both useful and easy to use. Remember that it's the ease of use and the usefulness *as perceived by users*, not by the leader or the implementation team, that makes or breaks adoption.

To ensure progress, adoption, and sustained impact, sales organizations that realize the most value from digitalization efforts adhere to five practices:

- Choosing the right leaders

- Incorporating accountability measures

- Deploying cross-functional teams

- Adopting an agile approach

- Enabling organizational change

A checklist (see table 20-4) highlights the key items to pay attention to at each stage of the implementation journey.

TABLE 20-4

Checklist for sales force digitalization success

	Preparing the organization	Implementing the solution	Sustaining success
Leadership	• Have an executive sponsor accountable for success. • Head up the team with a boundary-spanning leader (one who relates to both sales and IT). • Maintain commitments on budgets and resources.		
Accountability	• Articulate the business case. • Define key performance indicators. • Identify overlap and linkages with other initiatives. • Create a governance framework for the initiative.	• Review the business case. • Measure key performance indicators. • Implement the governance framework.	
Team	• Form a cross-functional core team including some users. • Understand and specifically address stakeholder perceptions and emotions	• Deploy the core team and smaller cross-functional teams. • Deploy an EET (Early Experience Team)	
Agile approach	• Conduct agile training.	• Create a minimal viable product. • Get feedback from EET. • Conduct sprints.	• Monitor usage and feedback. • Prioritize new features.
Change	• Identify needed process changes and mindset changes.	• Get buy-in from frontline managers. • Use peer influencers to boost engagement. • Conduct case-based user training. • Provide hypercare early.	• Provide ongoing user training and support. • Seek and act on feedback. • Align incentives and other programs.

Sales leaders have a pivotal dual role in enabling successful sales force change. First, you are an implementer of change. As your people look to you for guidance and direction, your words and actions have a large impact on whether the team embraces the change successfully. Second, you are a designer of change, called on to share an on-the-ground perspective about customer and sales force needs. Your input ensures that what looks good on paper will also work in practice. One thing is certain—if sales leaders at all levels don't buy into change, there is no chance that the frontline sellers will.

Conclusion

At the outset of this book, we identified three crucial forces that are reshaping sales management today: informed and assertive customers, the digital transformation of sales, and constant, rapid change in business and society. These forces impact how sales leaders manage talent, leverage digital technologies, drive improvement and change, and create mutual value for customers and the company. In each of these areas, the book shared lots of ideas, including frameworks for structuring your thinking, insights from real-world examples, and checklists to remind you of frequently overlooked dos and don'ts.

Five key takeaways

With so many topics covered in the book, you will likely have trouble keeping them all in your head at once when you want to apply them in your work. Whenever you are facing a challenge or an opportunity as a sales leader, keep the following five takeaways in mind. They can help ground and guide you as you navigate this complex and changing environment.

1. The sales organization is part of a sales system of decisions, processes, and resources that connect company strategy to customers, thus driving results.

These decisions and processes are organized into five categories. *Customer strategy* links business goals to priorities about who to sell to, what value to offer, and how to connect with customers to create mutual value.

Organizational design includes the sales channels, roles, and structures for providing effective and efficient customer coverage. *Talent* is about designing and operating processes to hire, develop, manage, and motivate salespeople and managers. *Customer engagement* involves designing and operating processes and systems for executing sales and support activities with channel partners and customers. And *technology, tools, and support teams* (typically in a sales operations function) enable decisions and processes.

Sales heads set the strategic direction and are accountable for designing and improving the sales system. Managers localize and implement strategies, manage talent, and oversee execution. And salespeople are accountable for realizing mutual company and customer value. Together, sales leaders and salespeople drive company results.

2. Salespeople and sales leaders are custodians of customer relationships and a company's sales.

A sales team is a powerful force for designing customer solutions, building trust, and facilitating productive relationships between buying and selling organizations. Sales leaders have a multifaceted role in connecting salespeople and customers, bridging strategy and tactics, and linking planning and execution.

By working with and through salespeople, a manager—the force behind the sales force—brings value to customers and the company. A winning formula balances the manager's responsibilities around customers, salespeople, the business, and change management.

Sales sprints are a powerful approach for linking planning to execution. Managers and salespeople work together in timeboxed periods of one to two weeks to complete specific actions that advance customers toward a purchase decision. Sprints are bookended by one-on-one reviews and brainstorming meetings between the salesperson and the manager.

3. Successful companies emphasize talent management to boost the sales force's impact and speed.

A company's success hinges on leaders understanding the unique strengths and areas for improvement of each sales team member. Winning involves bringing the right people on board and providing them with a mix of learning and development opportunities to continuously refine their competencies. Leaders strive to keep star and core performers motivated while elevating the skills of those with potential and preventing disengagement across the board. They boost and guide their salespeople's efforts with thoughtfully designed incentive plans and motivating goals. A focus on retaining top talent is key, even as efforts are made to maintain strong customer relationships in the face of inevitable turnover.

4. Digital is transforming every sales decision and process.

Digital forces and the constantly growing knowledge and evolving needs of customers affect how channels are designed and how salespeople succeed. Buyers expect a seamless experience across channels—both personal and digital ones. Digital infrastructure and expertise in a digital customer hub enable channels to be synchronized and provide data-based insights for customer selection and engagement. Further, every talent process is helped by data and digital. By linking talent systems for performance management, learning management, and recruiting, companies can speed up recruiting and onboarding and be more responsive to market changes.

5. In a rapidly changing world, leaders are constantly driving improvement and implementing change.

Your success as a sales leader requires an ability to continually reprioritize, adapt, improve, and innovate, all while you enable your team to design, prepare for, implement, and sustain successful change. A systematic approach to finding and prioritizing opportunities, and to implementing change, is the key to unlocking growth and success.

What's next for you?

Use the book's content as a springboard. Expand on the ideas, integrate your own insights, and adapt them to your circumstances, whether you are entering a new market, dealing with sales team retention, infusing your team's decision-making with AI tools, or tackling another opportunity or challenge.

We encourage you to use this handbook collaboratively with your team. By exploring and discussing the concepts together, you can harness the diverse perspectives and experiences of your people. Navigating the book jointly can also enhance team cohesion and drive collective growth. Together, you and your people can transform the handbook from a reference to a dynamic launchpad for action.

The opportunities and challenges you face will continue to evolve due to shifts in your role and customers' expectations, market dynamics, and digital advancements. While you can immediately leverage the ideas that help you today, the book is a reference you can return to later. It's not one-and-done. Now that you have read the book, go forth, implement change, and come back to discover more.

Index

Acknowledgments

Writing this book has been an enlightening journey, made possible by the contributions and support of many: our academic colleagues and students, our consulting clients, the talented staff at ZS, and the outstanding team at *Harvard Business Review*.

First and foremost, we owe the deepest gratitude to the late Professor Andy Zoltners, our colleague and the "Z" of ZS. Andy's partnership in our numerous collaborative endeavors—consulting, growing a company from two employees to fourteen thousand, and writing articles and books—was both a privilege and a profound part of our professional journeys. Andy has left an indelible mark on the field of sales management. His legacy of excellence, mentorship, and innovation continues to inspire and guide us. His teachings, values, and vision endure through his impactful work, the vibrant community he built, and his contributions to the concepts in this book.

We are grateful to our academic colleagues for providing a fertile environment for our ideas to be born and shaped. Thousands of MBA students and sales executives have participated in our classes, including those at the Kellogg School of Management and the Indian School of Business. These interactions have helped mold our theories and frameworks. Our academic peers have also challenged and vetted our publications for originality and impact.

As consultants, we have worked personally with thousands of executives, sales managers, and salespeople all over the world. ZS consultants have assisted thousands more at companies in many industries. These clients have helped us discover, develop, and refine the concepts explored in the book. Their real-world challenges and success stories have provided a rich tapestry of experiences to draw from and added a depth of practicality and relevance to this book that theory alone could never achieve.

We would like to thank the consultants and technology experts at ZS. They were instrumental in helping us write the book, using their creativity and practical knowledge to share and evaluate ideas. Special contributions to the book's content came from Namratha Agarwal, Chad Albrecht, Torsten Bernewitz, Samir Bhatiani, Jason Brown, Ty Curry, Peter MacLean, Namita Powers, Dharmendra Sahay, Srihari Sarangan, Marshall Solem, and Tony Yeung. Sellers and buyers within ZS have enriched this book by discussing their strategies, negotiations, and approaches to building customer and supplier relationships.

Additionally, we want to thank Dan McGinn, executive editor at *Harvard Business Review*, for his help with dozens of our articles. Dan is always searching for innovative ideas that are relevant to and practical for business leaders.

We were very fortunate to have an outstanding team at Harvard Business Review Press working with us on this project. Our editor, Dave Lievens, guided us through the entire process, going through every chapter in detail multiple times, and never failing to find ways to improve our drafts. Dave was quick to highlight the strengths in our ideas, and if there was an omission or an opportunity for improvement, he was there to provide us with suggestions. Thank you, Dave, for making this a far stronger book than its first draft. We also very much appreciate the work of the four early manuscript reviewers—Scott Edinger, Rich Gravelin, Lisa McLeod, and Kate Rowbotham—who took the time to read the entire book and provide substantive and constructive feedback.

This book is a testament to the collective wisdom, experience, and dedication of all those mentioned above. We are deeply grateful for your contributions and hope that this work does justice to the insights and knowledge you have shared. Thank you for being part of this journey.

About the Authors

The three authors are leaders at ZS, a global management consulting and technology firm. Founded in 1983 by marketing professors Andris Zoltners and Prabhakant Sinha, ZS leverages leading-edge sales and marketing analytics to help clients improve outcomes. With deep roots in data, analytics, technology, and commercial strategy, the firm has delivered solutions and services to clients in a broad range of industries across the globe, helping sales organizations improve their efficiency and effectiveness and drive their long-term growth.

PRABHAKANT (PRABHA) SINHA is a cofounder of ZS and has consulted for firms all over the world. He was an associate professor of marketing at Northwestern University's Kellogg School of Management until 1987 and has led executive education programs at the Kellogg School, London Business School, the Indian School of Business, and other leading institutions. He is a coauthor of dozens of articles for *Harvard Business Review*, several award-winning articles for academic journals, and ten books, including a series on sales force management.

ARUN SHASTRI is a principal at ZS, where he helps clients leverage data science and advanced analytics to drive organizational effectiveness and transform their digital capabilities. He is a contributing writer on AI for *Forbes*, a cohost of the podcast *Reinventing Customer Experience*, and a frequent contributor to *Harvard Business Review*. Arun teaches sales executives in the Maximizing Sales Force Performance program at the Kellogg School of Management.

SALLY LORIMER is a business writer and a principal at ZS, where she has helped numerous clients implement strategies for improving their sales effectiveness and performance. She is a frequent contributor to *Harvard Business Review* and a coauthor of a series of books on sales force management.